The HUNTERS
AND
The HUNTED

The HUNTERS
AND
The HUNTED

GEORGE LAYCOCK

Drawings by Joseph Fornelli

Published by Outdoor Life® Books
Meredith® Press, New York

Copyright © 1990 by George Laycock

Published by
  Outdoor Life ® Books
  Meredith ® Press
  750 Third Avenue
  New York, NY 10017

Distributed by Meredith Corporation, Des Moines, Iowa

  Produced by Gracie Square Publishing Service
  Book design by Jeff Fitschen
  Picture research by Imagefinders, Inc.
  Typography by Trufont Typographers

Library of Congress Cataloging-in-Publication Data

Laycock, George.
    The hunters and the hunted / George Laycock ; drawings by
Joseph Fornelli.
        p.   cm.
    Includes index.
    ISBN 0-696-11005-9
    1. Hunting—United States—History.   2. Game and game-
birds—United States.   I. Title.
SK40.L38   1990
799.2973—dc20   90-061484
                                                                CIP

Printed in the United States of America

10   9   8   7   6   5   4   3   2   1

Contents

Picture Credits

Adirondack Museum
Blue Mountain Lake, New York:
    page 21

American Museum of Natural
    History
New York City: page 8

Amon Carter Museum
Fort Worth Texas: page 15

The Bettmann Archive
New York City: pages 7, 24, 27
    (bottom), 101, 144, 183, 185,
    196, 238, 239

Buffalo Bill Historical Center,
    Whitney Gallery
Cody, Wyoming: pages 186–87

Corcoran Gallery of American
    Art
Washington, D.C.: page 242

Elman Pictorial Archive
Stewartsville, New Jersey: pages
    27, 35, 85, 105, 136, 142, 245,
    246–47, 250, 251

Frederic Remington Art Museum
Ogdensburg, New York: page 105

Harry T. Peters Collection
Museum of the City of New York:
    page 245

Library of Congress
Washington, D.C.: pages 4, 31, 19,
    29, 56, 57, 58, 70, 91, 95, 106,
    110, 112, 113, 121, 125, 132, 134,
    138, 150, 161, 192, 193, 233,
    255, 258, 260

Museum of Fine Arts
Boston, Massachusetts: 131

National Archives
Washington, D.C.: pages 215, 219,
    221

National Gallery of Art
Washington, D.C.: page 54

National Park Service
Washington, D.C.: pages 108–09

New York State Historical
    Association
Cooperstown, New York: page 32

Sid Richardson Collection of
    Western Art
Fort Worth, Texas: pages 80–81

Smithsonian Institution
Washington, D.C.: pages 5, 72

Thomas Gilcrease Institute of
    American Art
Tulsa, Oklahoma: pages 10, 140,
    156–57, 176–77

Walters Art Gallery
Baltimore, Maryland: pages 117,
    152, 199, cover

Woolaroc Museum
Bartlesville, Oklahoma: page 189

Preface

The world is filled with hunters, whether they are covered with fur, feathers, scales, or synthetic fibers. Our primitive ancestors were hunters. How well they fared determined whether or not they survived, so those of us here today come from long lines of successful hunters.

While our ancestors killed animals to survive, today we hunt mainly for sport. Gradually we have acquired knowledge and adopted new ways of looking at the outdoor world. We see that both predator and prey are essential in this world we share.

As people multiplied, the impacts on American wildlife intensified. Hunting pressure was one of these forces. This book is a look at hunting in America and its effect on people and wildlife from prehistoric times to the present. To tell this story, I have chosen grim accounts of early excesses, humorous anecdotes of outlandish hunts, and tales of incredible skill and daring. Together they present a complex drama reaching from the American wilderness to the developed country we share with the wild creatures today.

1

Those First American Hunters

O n that long-ago spring day when the Indians ambushed him, eighteen-year-old James Smith was riding through the western Pennsylvania forest, carrying a message to British General Edward Braddock's wilderness road builders. He and his companion on that dash through the woods knew that theirs was hazardous duty, but in 1775 frontier living was filled with high risk.

The young men were always alert and watchful, but the little screen of green saplings near the trail, and the three warriors crouched behind it, escaped their notice until too late. The Indians shot and killed Smith's companion. Smith was thrown from his panic-stricken horse and captured.

Smith knew, as did every man working on the road, that the Indians had refined their methods of killing captives slowly and that these western Pennsylvania tribes, then in the service of the French, usually put their captives to death. By some quirk, however, instead of being tied to the stake, Smith was adopted into the tribe. This marked the beginning of his remarkable education in the ways of the Mohawks, who lived by their hunting skills.

Indians frequently adopted captives into the tribe, sometimes as replacements for tribal members lost in battle. As with Smith, they expected the adopted one to show the bravery and other admirable qualities of the lost relative. In due time Smith was permitted to go hunting, perhaps with everyone understanding the probability of his unauthorized departure. Smith lived as a Caughnewago, a branch of the Mohawks, for five years before slipping away one day and vanishing into the forest.

During those years he kept a journal, which he later expanded into a book of his adventures. From this volume, and writings of others who lived as Indian captives, we learn much of how native Americans felt toward the wild animals around them and how they hunted and took the wild game on which their lives depended.

Smith wrote that bears were always favorite game, and Indian hunters traveling through the forest constantly scanned the trees for bear sign. Wintering bears sometimes den in large hollow trees, and claw marks on the bark were signs of occupancy that always excited the hunters.

On one bear hunt Smith and an Indian companion located a tree den. Smith cut a sapling to serve as a primitive ladder to the lowest limb of the den tree. His companion equipped himself with a bundle of dry sticks, tied to his belt a piece of rotten wood in which a smoldering coal glowed, and, using a pole with a hook attached to one end, pulled himself up the tree from limb to limb. When he reached the bear's entrance hole, he set fire to the bundle of sticks, then dropped it into the hollow tree. The bear snorted, and the hunter shinnied down to wait for the grumbling, chuffing bear to exit. As the beast came sliding down the tree, the Indian killed it with a single arrow behind the shoulder.

On the same trip the party spent most of another day chopping down a large, "well-scratched" bear tree with tomahawks. From it they took an old bear and her three cubs. The party was off hunting for about two weeks, wrote Smith, "and in this time killed four bears, three deer, several turkeys, and a number of raccoons. We packed up as much meat as we could and returned to our winter cabin." Their hungry people, by then completely out of food, could eat again from the bounty of the forest whose creatures supported them.

In season, these forest Indians tapped the huge maple trees, caught the sap in elm-bark buckets, and boiled it down into maple sugar. This delicacy was eaten right along with their meat. The sugar was mixed into bear fat, making a sauce in which the people dipped pieces of roasted venison.

Smaller animals were often taken with deadfall traps. Raccoons were always welcome. The Indian trapper searched the creekbeds for their tracks, then constructed his trap, and made small brush barriers on either side to guide the raccoon into the trap. When the animal touched the trip string, the log fell and the dead raccoon was waiting when the trapper came for it. Foxes were taken in similar traps, set at the entrance of a den or the end of a hollow log and baited with pieces of venison.

Sometimes Indians simply ran an animal down by staying with it until it could run no more. One Indian told Smith of taking bears, buffalo, and elk in this manner in the prairie openings. The runner claimed that once, when a light snow lay on the ground, he had even run a whitetail deer to earth.

But this swift-footed storyteller met his greatest challenge one day when he and Smith came upon three wild horses. They took the trail of the horses and began running at sunrise. The horses ran all day, with the two men trotting along behind them. By sunset, when they decided to give up the chase, the Indian said that the day had not been a total waste; they had at least made the horses very tired.

We sometimes hear that Indians were the first conservationists, that they took no game they could not use and were never wasteful. But this may grace the image of the native American with a nobility foreign to him. Primitive people were opportunists. They had to be. Hunger was always near, and tomorrow might bring only a broth made from bones picked clean by vultures—or maybe nothing at all. Given the opportunity to kill a deer, duck, raccoon, swan or songbird, or buffalo, the animal was generally taken, and one deer hunt described by James Smith brings this attitude out sharply.

Coming one day to a broad, open prairie in northwestern Ohio, his party of Indians decided that the situation was ideal for a "ring hunt" using fire, instead of shouting hunters, to drive the game. Some of the group stationed themselves in a small, previously burned area, while others ringed a much larger area around them with fire. Soon the startled deer smelled the smoke and began to move toward the center of the ring and the waiting hunters. At the end of the hunt dead deer, numbering more than ten for each

WHITETAIL DEER by John J. Audubon. For the Indians of the eastern forests, the whitetail was the animal most important to their survival. They depended on venison for food, and they used every part of the deer for clothing and tools.

hunter, lay all around them. Unfortunately, the fire burned on, blackening an area fifty miles long and twenty miles wide. Smith also describes a winter of abundant game when they "killed much more than we can use" and, for want of a way to bring it to camp, "left part of it in the woods."

When Smith escaped several years later and returned to his own people, he organized a band of rangers who specialized in defending frontier settlements against the Indians by practicing the Indian-style fighting he had learned.

For the people of the eastern forests the most important species was the whitetail deer. It was the game of choice then, as it remains today, and by the time an Indian family finished with a deer almost every part had been put to use. Archaeologists know this, in part, from studies of Indian villages and campsites. The hides became clothing; a shoulder blade became a scraper for women working the skins; awls and other tools were fashioned from the bones, while any remaining bones went into the soup stock. Sinews became sewing threads, and the partly digested stomach contents provided a highly nutritious concentrate for feeding to the sick. The brains were used in tanning leather, while a section of antler served as a tool for chipping flint into new arrow points for killing more deer.

These early hunters perfected various methods of taking deer. They learned to read the signs left by the animal. They knew where

As portrayed in this fanciful early woodcut, Indians often hunted deer camouflaged as their quarry. Usually they draped themselves in deerskins and held branches to imitate antlers.

deer fed and bedded and the paths they traveled between those areas. They could tell how recently a deer had passed and judge its size and age. They could bleat like a lost fawn to attract the doe, and a hunter might even drape his body in the skin of a deer, hold a forked stick above his head like antlers, and gradually move in upwind among the deer to get a close-up shot. The Indians also set snares along deer trails. It is said that the unsuspecting Pilgrim fathers first learned about these snares when hoisted skyward, feet first, on rebounding saplings.

Long before the arrival of gunpowder, the Indians were highly effective hunters of all kinds of North American game. Their earliest weapons were stones and spears. Next came the throwing stick, or atlatl, which served as an extension of the arm and gave the spear an added boost. Then some ancient genius began experimenting with the bow and arrow. The Indian hunter's training with this weapon started when he was still a small boy, lobbing arrows at buffalo chips. Father, uncle, or grandfather turned this early target practice into games and, once the lad gained proficiency, rolled the buffalo chips along the plains, converting them to moving targets. By the time he was a young man, the gifted Indian bowman could shoot with uncanny accuracy and amazing speed. Carrying half a dozen arrows in his left hand, he could shoot them, one after the other, so fast that all were in the air at the same time.

With or without gunpowder, any method that worked to take bison was good. For many tribes, hunting these large, dangerous animals meant the difference between living and starving. The Indians put the various parts of the buffalo to more than a hundred uses around their camps.

Zenas Leonard, an early beaver trapper in the western moun-

Stones and spears were the Indians earliest hunting weapons. This is an atlatl, a throwing stick with which a hunter could launch a spear with added force.

tains, wrote of the "surrounds" on which he accompanied Indian hunting parties. First, a town crier rode through the camp announcing the time of the approaching hunt, and the whole camp was expected to turn out for the frolic. On the morning of the hunt all the hunters, perhaps several hundred of them, rode off in style, mounted on their finest ponies. They found the buffalo, surrounded them, then began closing in, whooping and shouting to move the beasts into an ever-tightening mass. In this manner, wrote Leonard, "they sometimes caught several hundred buffalo and many other animals at a single surround."

Leonard also described the killing places where whole herds of buffalo were driven over cliffs, killing and crippling more than the hunters could possibly use. Or they sometimes drove the herd into a box canyon, blocked its only escape, then began to "butcher their prisoners at leisure." One chief showed Leonard the skulls of some

Once the bow and arrow was invented, Indians had a superior weapon for hunting and warfare. Trained from childhood, they developed great skill and speed with the long bow.

seven hundred buffalo in such a killing place and told him that they had all been killed during a single hunt four years earlier.

Some tribes specialized in using hunters as buffalo decoys. Draped in a buffalo cape, including head and horns, the hunter moved upwind, working his way gradually closer. He mimicked the movements of the buffalo and was sometimes able to lead them toward a V-shaped trap or other killing place before they sensed the danger.

Before they developed these mass killing methods, or had horses to aid them in the chase, Indian hunters specialized in taking buffalo by still-hunting. Draped in the skins of the wolves that

Before they had horses, Indians hunted buffalo by draping themselves in wolfskins and stalking the animals within range for a shot with the bow and arrow. This early painting (183?) by George Catlin shows an Indian hunter and the artist himself concealed in wolfskins, approaching a herd of buffalo.

tagged along with the herds, the hunters crawled in toward the grazing animals until they were close enough to release arrows aimed at the lungs. In this manner, if all went well and the gods smiled, a hunter might bring down more than a single animal.

Before they had horses, the Indian buffalo hunters often relied on the ancient practice of setting up a *piskin*, two converging lines of rocks and brush to direct game into a confined killing place. The buffalo were herded through a funnel-shaped area into a log enclosure, where they could then be killed as they milled about. The arms of the trap were made of piles of rocks or brush. On the day of the hunt women and children would hide behind the barricades until the buffalo moved past them, then emerge and set up a commotion to keep the animals moving forward. Finally a young hunter draped in a buffalo robe would serve as a Judas figure to lead the herd over a slight rise and down into the waiting corral, or sometimes over a cliff to their death. When all went well, this system worked beautifully and the Indians feasted.

A similar method was used in the Far North to move caribou, the deer of the Arctic, into the killing places. Families of Eskimos or Indians moved to the killing places and stayed for the weeks of the hunt. The rings of stone that secured the edges of their tents, as well as the human effigies they built of stone along the cliff tops, still mark some of these sites.

After the Plains Indians acquired horses, they no longer had to sneak up on foot to shoot buffalo or drive them into a cul-de-sac, or over a cliff, to kill them. They became as skilled as horsemen anywhere in the world. They clung to the sides of their horses at full gallop, rode in close to hard-running buffalo, and, if need be, could shoot beneath the neck of their mount to take the thundering buffalo at close range, sometimes sending an arrow completely through the beast. The advent of the mounted hunter exerted more pressure on the American buffalo populations than they had ever known—or would know—until gunpowder replaced the bow and arrow.

THE BUFFALO HUNT by Charles M. Russell (1900). Once they had horses, Indians became formidable hunters. This painting graphically depicts the skill and daring of the mounted Indian. Armed with his short bow, he could shoot beneath the neck of his mount and drive an arrow right through a buffalo. But he often met his death when a maddened bull gored his horse and trampled him underfoot.

For the mounted hunters of the Plains, the buffalo chase was sport as well as profession. There were few pursuits, except perhaps the running skirmishes with other tribes and the occasional bout with a grizzly, that promised more excitement than did the buffalo chase. The buffalo hunter's bow was short and powerful, and sometimes wrapped with deer sinew to give it added cast. His flint-tipped arrows were aimed at a point behind the short ribs, so they would push forward and penetrate a vital area. This wild-spirited hunter, long hair flying in the wind, clinging to the back of his horse by the pressure of his knees, was in a hazardous business. The angry, panic-stricken buffalo often turned on him, gored his horse, then, if it could, trampled the rider in the dust. Early western artist George Catlin wrote of seeing buffalo chasers abandon their horses to avoid being crushed between the running beasts, sometimes leaping over the backs of the buffalo to get away.

Catlin observed at least one unhorsed hunter being pursued by a huge, maddened bull. At what seemed the last possible moment, the hunter stripped a section of buffalo robe from around his waist, sidestepped smoothly and threw the robe across the bull's eyes and horns, then, in a lightning-fast movement, drove his spear into the side of the beast and brought him down.

Sometimes the Indians hunted animals they did not need for food. Among the more difficult challenges for the Plains Indian brave was the acquisition of golden eagle feathers, tokens of wealth and power needed for dress and ceremony. This task was especially difficult because the high-flying eagle is equipped with the world's finest eyes. To capture an eagle, the hunter dug a pit to hide in, then covered it with a framework camouflaged with grass. Next he tied a rabbit to the frame above the pit. Finally, after performing various religious rites invoking the aid of the great spirit, the hunter lowered himself into the pit before dawn and waited. When an eagle finally landed to take the struggling rabbit, a dark human hand flashed up from beneath the bird, grabbed it by both legs and dragged the giant bird into the pit. There the hunter wrestled with his captive until the bird was secured.

The eagle bait sometimes attracted other, more dangerous animals. In *The Mystic Warriors of the Plains*, Thomas E. Mails tells of a grizzly that was angered when a warrior drew his bait into the pit by the attached string to keep the hungry bear from taking it. The grizzly promptly tore the covering off the pit, dragged the hunter out, and killed him.

Perhaps the most important bird in the life of the Indians was the wild turkey, which in various subspecies densely populated the country. These giant birds were, first of all, a source of protein, especially for the woodland people. But the parts we throw away were often put to use. The woman who plucked a freshly killed turkey was careful with the feathers for they had many uses. By tying the feathers to strings made of hemp, then tying the strings together so the feathers overlapped like shingles, she could make a fine jacket, warm and rainproof. The hunter saved the tail and wing feathers for making headdresses for ceremonial dances. He checked each feather carefully and selected the finest of all to make fletching for his arrows. When the turkey was cooked, the bird's bones were saved. The wing bones could be fashioned into awls for stitching garments together. Or should the hunter be so inept that he had never mastered the fine art of calling wild game by mouth, he might keep a large wing bone to make a turkey call.

But customs varied among the tribes. Some Plains tribes believed that warriors should never eat the flesh of the turkey. They believed that the cowardly traits of these birds that ran or flew off at the first sign of danger would become manifest in those who consumed their flesh. One early traveler told of a party of white hunters who shot a turkey too old and tough to chew. They boiled it hour after hour and still could not render it palatable. Before they could toss it out, however, a little group of hungry Indians arrived begging food. They were offered the contents of the pot which gave off tempting odors. The aging chief peered thoughtfully into the pot for some time. He looked saddened by what he saw. He shook his head, then spoke in his native tongue to his fellow travelers. "You must not eat this cowardly bird," he explained. "You are brave warriors and you must not eat food that will make you timid in battle. You must remain strong and brave to overcome our enemies. But I am no longer young. My fighting days are over, and, although this brings me great sorrow, there can be no harm in my eating the meat forbidden to warriors." He then fell upon the contents of the pot and consumed most of it.

The Indians hunted turkeys in many ways. Their methods are well outlined by A. W. Schorger in his classic book *The Wild Turkey*.

WILD TURKEY by John J. Audubon. As the deer was the most important mammal in the Indians' life, so the wild turkey was the most important bird. They hunted the turkey for its meat, made clothing, headdresses, and fletching for their arrows from the feathers, and fashioned the bones into awls and turkey calls.

Sometimes agile young hunters simply forced the turkeys to fly, followed them, and eventually ran them down. This was easiest when snow was on the ground. They also drove turkeys into trees where they could be spotted against the sky, then shot them with arrows. For night hunting some Indians learned to use a long pole to poke at the feet of roosting birds until the turkeys stepped onto the top of the pole. Then, slowly and carefully, they lowered the pole, plus turkey, to the ground and picked the bird off by hand.

Indian hunters also used the turkey's fanlike tail as a decoy. Holding it up from behind a log, the hunter would cluck, putt, and gobble. When a turkey left the flock to investigate this stranger, a dusky hand reached out in a lightning-fast move and grabbed the bird by its legs. Other turkeys were caught in traps made of poles. A line of bait, often the tuberous roots that turkeys fancy, led the hungry birds toward the trap and down a trench beneath the wall, then up into the trap.

Indian turkey hunters even caught the birds on baited fish hooks. But perhaps the most widespread turkey-catching device was the snare. A turkey walking through the woods was often in danger of kicking the loop of a snare and finding itself snatched into the air where it was suspended on a limber sapling until the hunter came to claim it.

Jonathan Alder, one of the earliest white people to invade the Ohio country, became another white captive who left us his observations of the Indian's hunting methods and the red man's relationships with the wild animals around him. Before returning to his blood relatives in 1805, Alder spent more than twenty years living with the Indians.

AN INDIAN TRAPPER by Frederic Remington (1889). By the 1820s, the mountain men had begun to explore the Rocky Mountains in their search for beaver and traded with the Indians at their annual rendezvous. In this magnificent painting, Remington portrayed an Indian hunter with a Hawkin rifle he probably acquired from a mountain man.

Alder's captivity began one spring day when the eight-year-old boy was sent to the woods on his family's western Virginia farm to fetch the horses. Suddenly he was surrounded by five Indians accompanied by a white renegade. After many days of travel he and his captors arrived in the distant land of the Shawnees in central Ohio. Alder, young and adaptable, gradually became accustomed to the Indian life-style and grew up among his captors as part of the tribe.

In due time his Indian "parents" sent him out to hunt, and by the time Jonathan was fourteen he was known as an outstanding hunter. He gradually lost all desire to leave the Indians and return to his own people. "I was an expert hunter," he later said, "and took great delight in the chase. . . ."

Alder was especially fond of bear hunting in the fall, when he could sometimes find a female with three or even four cubs. He recalled how he once came upon a female black bear and her four cubs. "I shot the old one and then took my ramrod and chased the cubs until they treed and then shot them down." On other occasions he would shoot the mother, then kill the young bears with his tomahawk, a method he characterized "as more real fun than treeing and shooting them."

During the summer he practiced fire hunting for deer. Fire hunting was an early version of jacklighting. The deer came to the streams to wade the shallows and eat the aquatic mosses, and the hunter approached by floating downstream in his canoe, equipped with a burning pine knot in the bow. Behind the fire he arranged a "shade board" to hide himself. While the mesmerized deer stood staring into the approaching light, the hunter moved in close for an easy shot. Alder mentioned a couple of hazards inherent in this method. During the summer months snakes often crawled into the canoe with him. Sometimes the deer were also a threat. "I have seen them jump into the canoe and sink it," Alder recalled.

In spite of the Indians' constant hunting, whether for bison on the plains, deer in the eastern woods, moose in the North, or salmon in the Northwest, fish and wildlife remained abundant. The land was wilderness. There were no massive alterations made in the landscape. Probably no more than a million people were spread across this vast land, drawing their sustenance from the forests, marshes, and grasslands, and from the lakes and streams.

The human population had simply not reached levels that threatened many wild species. That threat would wait for a new breed of hunters, farmers, and developers driven by a relentless urgency to conquer the wilderness and people the land.

The white man would bring a revolutionary new concept—the conviction that, instead of simply using the land or its products, people could divide land up among themselves and claim absolute ownership of it. The Indian believed that the land did not belong to people, but that people—like the bison and deer, the eagle and the wild geese—were part of the land. Now foreigners would arrive claiming personal ownership of land they wanted, building fences around it, and destroying the trees, grasses, soil, and water that had given life to the wild animals and the Indian people over seasons beyond counting. The face of North America was about to change for all time.

2

Pioneering Hunters

Into this red man's wilderness of broad green spaces, deep-shaded forests, and sparkling waters came the vanguard of the European invaders. The earliest to move beyond the Appalachians were frontier squatters living off the land. They came out of the forests of Pennsylvania and Virginia and crossed into the valleys beyond. Often they were rough-cut scoundrels, willing to ignore the Indian threats of death by fire and hatchet and paying no heed to the King's soldiers sent to keep them out of the Indian hunting lands.

These solitary woodsmen found the game trails through the deep forests and up and down the rivers—the Monongahela, Kanawha, New, Muskingum, and Ohio. They stopped and built their scanty shelters where they chose and lived by trapping, hunting, and sometimes trading with the Indians. This scattering of scruffy backwoods hunters, tough and independent, was the stock from which rose the hardy and bold frontiersmen. Their offspring would open the land and become the backbone of the western movement—the rivermen, Indian traders, wilderness surveyors, scouts, guides, and mountain men. The wealth of open land and wild game, an abundance unequaled on any other continent, drew them westward to new scenes.

Behind them, even before the land was secured and the peace established, came the tidal wave of settlers. The earliest were half-farmer, half-hunter, supporting families on venison, wild turkey, and

The first settlers in Virginia were astonished at the abundance of fish and game they encountered. This 1618 print reflects the sense of wonderment they must have felt on arriving in this land of plenty. Even after two centuries of hunting, there was still game aplenty for Appalachian frontiersmen in the early 1800s.

In the 1800s the eastern forests teemed with whitetail deer. Hunters sometimes floated streams, searching the banks for drinking deer. Others still-hunted in the first snow when tracking is easy and the deer, in the midst of the rut, have lost some of their normal caution.

A GOOD CHANCE by Arthur F. Tait (186?).

FIRST SNOW by Arthur F. Tait (1855).

corn from the family patch. But even as farming became vital to family survival on the frontier, these pioneering men could not get the lure of the hunt out of their minds. With the coming of autumn, thoughts turned to the pursuit of wild game. The season of falling leaves, frosty mornings, and occasional snow flurries beckoned them to the woods. As one writer put it, "They became uneasy at home. Everything about them became disagreeable. The house was too warm. The feather bed too soft, and even the good wife was not thought for the time being a proper companion. The mind of the hunter was wholly occupied with the game and the chase."

The constant pursuit of game, the land clearing, and the absence of regulations would take their toll. By one count, more than nine hundred flatboats floated down the Ohio River in 1787 alone, carrying eighteen thousand men, women, and children, and their belongings, including twelve thousand head of livestock. The wild animals of the forest would help provide for these families as they struggled in the wilderness, and the hunt was constantly on their minds.

Older boys sometimes carried their guns to school and bagged game along the way. An aging ex-schoolteacher on the Illinois frontier recalled the early 1850s when he "went west and became a school marster." He stood speechless on opening day when the larger boys arrived, dropped a dozen prairie chickens on the floor and, as was their custom, stacked their guns in the corner. The teacher responded by fixing a place in the woodshed to hang the game out of reach of local dogs and the guns out of reach of smaller children. Then he entered into the spirit of the community and began carrying his own gun to school and helping supply food for the families with which he "boarded around." "Many a good bag have I made of a morning and evening," he wrote in *Forest and Stream*. "Quail were very abundant; hares so plentiful that no one thought of shooting them; grouse in sufficient quantities, and the ducks—mallard and teal—why the ponds were alive with them."

As the size of the pioneers' clearings grew, and their unrestricted hunting spread, game sometimes grew scarce. Eastwick Evans, who traveled through northern Ohio in 1818, wrote that "game cannot always be found." Colonel Richard Henderson, a Kentucky contemporary of Daniel Boone, noted sadly that "settlers drove the game out of the country quickly." But in the early and mid-1800s there were still some species flourishing in such abundance that they seemed of little value, and that was the age of throwaway wildlife.

An unforgettable example is the extermination of the wild pigeons that crossed the North American skies in astonishing numbers, bringing gunners the most fantastic wing shooting the world has ever known. Early explorers called these birds "turtle doves" because of their outward resemblance to European doves or, as they called them, wood doves. We know them as passenger pigeons, and find it difficult to imagine how many once lived here.

John James Audubon wrote of one flock that darkened the sky and required three days to pass overhead. "The air was literally filled with pigeons; the light of the noon-day sun was obscured as by an eclipse." He recalled that the roar of their wings "had a tendency to lull my senses to repose," and the pigeon droppings fell like wet snow.

Audubon computed that these birds cruised at sixty miles an hour, and, as they exhausted their food supplies, their speed on the wing carried them swiftly to new feeding areas.

After visiting a six-mile-wide pigeon roost in Tennessee about 1819, an English traveler wrote that "the birds roost in the high trees, which they covered . . . piled one on the other from the lower to the topmost boughs which, so laden, are continually bending and falling with their crushing weight."

One respected observer, studying the flocks moving up the Mississippi Valley on their spring migration in the 1860s, calculated that they passed at the rate of a hundred and twenty million pigeons *an hour*. For five hours the flight continued—involving perhaps six hundred million birds in a fraction of a day!

A noted Indian chief named Simon Pokagon studied the pigeons in the final years of their abundance. He visited nesting grounds in Michigan, Ohio, and Indiana between 1840 and 1880. He wrote that the nesting areas were commonly up to thirty miles long and four miles wide, and within these areas every tree was spotted with nests. Moritz Fischer, writing in 1913 in *Bird Lore*, then the Audubon Society magazine, calculated that such a nesting ground would harbor fifty-seven million adult breeding birds.

These concentrations attracted Indians from miles around. They came with their families and stayed on the pigeon nesting grounds for a month or more, feasting on squab and turning the fat young pigeons into "squab butter" for spreading on other foods. They smoked and dried supplies of the birds to take with them.

The pigeons fattened on nuts, acorns, chestnuts, berries, weed seeds, and insects. Beechnuts were a favorite, and as the nuts ripened in the fall the pigeons came thundering into the big woods for

Swarms of passenger pigeons darkened the skies in the 1800s. One observer calculated 120 million pigeons had passed over him in one hour, and the flight continued for five hours. Hunters believed the supply was inexhaustible and shot the pigeons into extinction.

the harvest. Audubon wrote that the sheer weight of the pigeons, crowding in to feed, broke off trees two feet in diameter near the ground or brought large limbs crashing down, killing many pigeons in the process.

Wherever they went, whether nesting, feeding, resting, or moving, the highly social pigeons stayed together. Once the flock had fed, it took off toward the end of day for its favorite roost, and soon the rookeries became known to the pigeon hunters. Everywhere the birds appeared they were attacked by people. In the nesting areas, where their nests bent the tree limbs, both nests and squabs were knocked to the ground by the thousands so the nestlings could be sent to market. Pigeons were also killed at their watering places and on their roosts. Audubon often visited a giant roost along the banks of the Green River in central Kentucky, and he described one night's hunt there.

Two hours ahead of sunset the air around the large, open woods was empty. Not a pigeon could be seen. But the people were already waiting. Men and boys from miles around had brought guns, poles for knocking down the pigeons, pine-knot torches, sulfur for smoking them out of the trees, fire for burning them out, and grain soaked in alcohol as bait to intoxicate the pigeons, which could then be gathered up by hand. People slid about under the trees in pigeon dung inches deep.

Someone shouted, "Here they come," and the whispering wings soon roared like a waterfall as pigeons began settling into the treetops in the dusk of evening. Wave after wave arrived, crowding onto the branches until they were landing on the backs of other birds and hanging on the branches in clusters like swarming bees.

By this time the pigeon harvesters were hard at work. The birds made such a commotion that the explosion of guns fired into the mass of birds could not be heard except by the gunners themselves as they fired. Long poles reached into the trees and knocked hundreds of pigeons to the ground to be gathered into heaps. Others set sulfur pots beneath the trees and moved upwind to wait until the suffocating pigeons began raining to earth. As the pigeons showered about them, men lit fires so they could see to work. The birds seemed indifferent to the tragedy of the roost.

As the new day dawned on the banks of the Green River, the surviving birds began leaving the roost, while behind them people gathered up the dead and wounded. Audubon said the pigeons were heaped up "until each had as many as he could possibly dispose of.

. . ." Any they missed were cleaned up by the hogs brought in by farmers to fatten on the remains. One large herd of hogs had been driven nearly a hundred miles to reach this bonanza.

What did the people do with these rich harvests of pigeons? They sold all they could at market. Pigeons were shipped to the East Coast where they were offered at a few cents, sometimes a penny, each. As late as 1840, they sold on an Indianapolis market for as little as twenty-five cents a bushel.

For seventy-five years—as long as the birds lasted—they were also taken for trap shoots. One marksman, in a seven-hour shoot in Chicago in 1868, hit six hundred and five birds. As many as half a million birds a year may have been used by trap shooters because, despite their sixteen-inch wingspread, the pigeons' swift and darting flight made them difficult targets.

The passenger pigeon was a social creature living in flocks so large that a pigeon hunter could easily bring down several birds with most of his shots. A rifle bullet shot into a mass of pigeons might bring a dozen of them to earth, and a blast from a muzzle-loading shotgun was sometimes known to drop forty or fifty of them. If they flew low, as they often did, they were simply knocked from the sky with branches.

One Pennsylvania pigeon hunter was known to have killed up to six thousand pigeons in a day using a clap net whose broad wings snapped shut on as many as two hundred and fifty birds at a time. Netters baited with grain and acorns. They also decoyed the pigeons with blind stool pigeons that had their eyelids sewn shut to keep them perched.

Another method of capturing the birds was to set a limber pole into a ridge where the birds passed at low elevation. The hunters attached a rope to the pole, then hid at a distance and kept the pole whipping back and forth as the birds flew over. With this device they knocked pigeons from the sky by the dozens. Sometimes the pigeon hunter would dig a long trench and scatter grain along the bottom. Then, taking cover in a nearby blind, he would wait until the ditch was crowded with pigeons and fire down the length of it.

Live decoys were often used to lure pigeons into range, as shown in the print above. To supply the market, pigeons were trapped in large nets (below).

Some hunters preferred testing their marksmanship against flying pigeons. One Wisconsin market hunter famous for his wing shooting averaged some twelve hundred pigeons daily. His one-day record was fourteen hundred and fifty-eight pigeons.

Any weapon seemed fair. A. W. Schorger, who wrote the authoritative book *The Passenger Pigeon—Its Natural History and Extinction*, tells of the soldiers on Lake Ontario who fired into a flock of pigeons with a cannon loaded with grapeshot, killing "hundreds." In Wisconsin the Sparta *Herald* reported that a merchant sold three tons of powder and sixteen tons of shot during the 1871 pigeon nesting season.

Shooting, concludes Schorger, became the most destructive of all the pigeon-killing methods. Gunners far outnumbered trappers, and, as the pigeons grew scarcer, the shooters traveled farther to find them. Sometimes special trains carried parties of shooters to the nesting areas. "Time and again," says Schorger, "the birds were driven away before their young were raised."

By the best estimates, the market hunters took ten to twelve million adult breeding pigeons a year between 1866 and 1876. With the combination of direct killing and destruction of the forests, the end came quickly. Concerned people began forecasting the pigeon's doom. In 1876 a writer in *Rod and Gun and American Sportsman* wrote, "I was speaking with an old pigeoner who had followed the business for 21 years, and his opinion was that the birds were rapidly decreasing. . . . it is high time to do something for their protection."

In 1878 remnant flocks in Michigan and Pennsylvania were still large enough to attract the last of the commercial pigeon takers. Between April and September that year thirty million more pigeons were taken from their nests and shipped to the cities. After that, the birds may still have assembled a million strong in a single Michigan location near Grand Traverse. Again they were attacked, and twenty thousand of the last of the great pigeons were shipped to Coney Island, New York, for a trap-shooting tournament. Finally, by the 1890s the last of the passenger pigeons were gone from the wild. People who had seen the pigeons by the hundreds of millions in their youth saw them no more.

Passenger pigeons had been so abundant that they were not even considered a game bird until the mid-1800s, when they began to

In some parts of the country, prairie chickens flourished in astounding numbers. This print depicts a hunt in Kansas with dogs to retrieve downed birds.

diminish noticeably. By the turn of the century they were so rare that they were prized possessions in a few zoos, where they lived out their final days in cages. Zookeepers in Cincinnati kept these symbols of the American wilderness alive longer than anyone else. The world's last known passenger pigeon died there in 1914. Her name was Martha, and on the zoo grounds today, her little stone house stands as a memorial to her kind, telling the story of the passenger pigeon and of other species that have slipped into the last great darkness.

Meanwhile shorebirds, too, were being killed for the market. Plovers, sandpipers, and Eskimo curlews were vanishing. Said one writer, "No hope can be held out for the future of these birds until our markets are closed to the sale of native wild game."

Our attitude toward a wild animal often depends on that animal's abundance. If we had walked in the boots of the first settlers coming into the eastern forests, many unprepossessing wild animals would have been seen as a threat to our survival. Gray squirrels, for example, weighing just a pound or a little more, could strip a field of grain intended for a family's winter food.

The struggling farmer developed squirrel nerves in September and October, the season when the squirrels began their migrations. These mass movements are rare today, but earlier writers left numerous records of waves of gray squirrels moving like a plague across the land and swimming the lakes and rivers. "Onward they come," wrote the Reverend John Bachman more than a century ago, "devouring on their way everything that is suited to their taste, laying waste the corn and wheat fields of the farmer." As their numbers were thinned by gun, dog, and club, more squirrels filled the ranks.

Bachman told of millions of squirrels swimming the Hudson and Ohio rivers, and other waters, and wondered at their feat, because they are poor swimmers. Old records tell of rafts of drowned squirrels washing up on the banks and against logjams in the rivers, and still the squirrels kept coming to the water's edge and launching themselves.

Whatever triggered the movements, the massive die-offs reduced the squirrel population and perhaps better fitted their number to their environment. This was no regular migration of the squirrels, but simply a mass movement. Durward L. Allen in *Our Wildlife Legacy* said, "They were going nowhere, and they got nowhere." He added that the migrations served to recycle "a million animals back into the humus of the earth."

Early local governments paid bounties on squirrels in an effort to reduce their numbers. Some counties in Ohio set up a system calling for people to pay their land taxes in squirrel scalps, allowing them from one to three pennies each. One Ohio hunter was said to have shot a hundred and sixty squirrels in one day, and that in the season when they were *not* moving.

Faced with these hungry armies of rodents, the early farmers fought back as best they could. Everyone became a squirrel hunter, and any method of taking the creature was acceptable. If his own dogs, wife, and children could not fend off the invaders, the farmer tried to hire expert shooters to help in the emergency. Virginia hunter Meshach Browning learned of a neighboring farmer willing to pay a dollar a day to "any good gunner who would shoot the squirrels that were destroying his corn." He and a friend, both excellent shots, decided to take advantage of the offer "and have fine sport besides being paid for our services.

"The next day we started off to the corn field before daylight, and as soon as we could see, found ourselves surrounded by the greatest number of squirrels I ever saw, which were running by the hundreds in all directions. At them we went, shooting sometimes half a dozen on one tree. My partner would place himself on one side while I would take the other; and between us we killed and took home so many squirrels that Mr. Foot would have no more brought to the house. We carried away as many as we wished, but after two or three days we left them lay where we shot them."

This was a normal situation around ripening grain fields. Browning and his companion shot for nine days, reducing the squirrel population enough to save some of the corn crop.

Enormous flocks of wild turkeys strutted about the forests. Early writers called them more common than barnyard fowl. One writer, amazed by flocks of turkeys near the homes of colonists in Massachusetts in the 1600s, was told by the Indians that in the forest they might see a thousand a day. Flocks of five hundred turkeys were seen leaving their roosts in the North Carolina swamps at sunrise. A Maryland hunter told of seeing flocks of fifty to a hundred young turkeys chasing grasshoppers in a forest opening. In eastern Kentucky wild turkeys roamed the forests in such numbers that one hunter recalled times he could have killed forty in a single day at the mouth of Big Sandy. In 1784 a traveler wrote of turkeys in the Ohio Valley, five thousand to the flock.

Today's turkey hunter can be forgiven for questioning these early reports. The approaching turkey season instills high fever in the modern hunter. As the season draws near, he checks every detail of his readiness. He has his license and special turkey permit. He plays it safe by discarding and replacing old shells with new. He has taped camouflage cloth over the stock and barrel of his gun to keep the sharp-eyed turkey from spotting it. In addition, he has checked his camouflage outfit from the ground up: dark green or brown boots to match the forest floor; coveralls in the broken pattern of camouflage;

THE TURKEY SHOOT by Tompkins H. Matteson (1857). This painting was inspired by the novel "The Pioneers," by James Fenimore Cooper, which is placed in upstate New York in 1793. Cooper's hero Natty Bumppo, the prototype of the American frontiersman, is reloading his musket after having killed a turkey for the demure young woman in red.

brown, black, and green greasepaint for the face and hands. He adds camouflage gloves for the crisp spring mornings and a head net of flimsy camouflage to keep the alert turkey from distinguishing the size and flesh tone of his face. He wears a hat camouflaged to match the rest of the outfit. Nowhere is there a shining button, a glint from eyeglasses, a flash of bare skin. He fits into the background as surely as a woodcock hen on her nest or a snowshoe hare in winter.

He has also bought the latest turkey calls—slate, box, and diaphragm, perhaps one of each, plus recorded tapes of the voice of the wild turkey in all its moods. For weeks ahead of the season's opening as he drives to and from work, this modern turkey hunter listens to his tapes and practices using his assorted calls. Finally, opening day is but two weeks off. Now comes the vitally important matter of "scouting." Where do they roost? Where are the turkeys at daybreak? Can he find the territory of the old gobblers that welcome the spring mornings with their rattling calls? Gobble-obble-obble-obble! He is in the woods at daybreak to meet the sounds, but hides his presence so the strutting gobbler does not suspect that his realm has been invaded.

If the turkey hunter has done everything right, has great good luck, and is not disturbed on opening morning by too many others of his own kind, he may call up a displaying bird and reduce it to possession. That's it for the year. In most states the modern hunter is permitted one turkey annually, a limit that would be as difficult for those old-time hunters to understand as it might be for their descendants to visualize the hunting opportunities of yesterday.

Audubon, for example, told of a morning he called a flock of some thirty splendid gobblers to him. They came bowing and strutting and spreading their fine feathers for female inspection "toward the very spot where I lay concealed." When they were so close that Audubon could see the glint of "light in their eyes," he fired and killed three in a single shot. He explained that he could have taken more as the live ones strutted around their dead companions, but that would have been wasteful.

In Missouri two men spent the day husking corn but took their guns to the field with them and by evening had killed a hundred and thirty-two turkeys. Along the Texas-Oklahoma border, and elsewhere, turkeys were so abundant that men on horseback took them by running them down. One writer told of being with a group of Indians who flushed a large flock five times until they could fly no more. At this point they could catch them by the neck and gathered up a hundred and sixty of them. In parts of the West turkeys blackened the trees, as roosting starlings would in a later age.

Turkeys, like squirrels and other wild animals, could do their share of damage to the early farmer's crops. One settler decided to get even with the turkeys that were parading down the rows of emerging corn and pulling the little green shoots to get the grain. He dug a trench big enough for turkeys to enter, then sprinkled shelled corn in it. In due time the turkeys followed a line of corn into the trench. Meanwhile, the farmer brought forth the large punt gun he used for his mass killing of ducks and set it up pointing down the trench. When the trench was black with hungry turkeys, he touched off the cannon by means of a long string that reached to his hiding place. The blast scattered turkeys and turkey parts in all directions, and the survivors avoided the corn field for the remainder of the season.

Farmers also used traps to collect turkeys. They built a pen of logs covered with brush and poles. They dug a trench under the wall of the pen nearest the woods, then sprinkled a row of yellow corn from the woods into the trench and the pen. Turkeys following the bait into the trap could seldom find their way out.

The supply of turkeys dwindled soon after the settlers came, and their distribution became spotty. John Josselyn wrote of New England in 1672, "I have also seen threescore broods of young Turkies on the side of a marsh, sunning of themselves in a morning betimes, but this was thirty years since, the English and the Indians having now destroyed the breed, so that 'tis very rare to meet with a wild Turkie in the woods."

In Massachusetts, turkey numbers fell lower and lower until the last one was gone by 1851. According to A. C. Bent, whose multivolume life histories of North American birds were first published by the Smithsonian Institution, turkeys were not seen in Connecticut after 1813. In Kentucky, where they had once been so abundant, they were gone from large parts of their former range by the beginning of this century. They had already disappeared from much of the East, although they did persist in some areas, including Pennsylvania and West Virginia. However, in many states that once had flocks of turkeys hundreds strong, the clearing of the woods and overshooting had brought about the turkey's demise.

As the game bird became scarcer, hunters sometimes went to greater lengths to take a turkey for the pot. One noted hunter who

Turkeys were as common as barnyard fowl when the first settlers arrived on these shores, but their numbers dwindled rapidly as uncontrolled hunting and habitat destruction took their toll. Even as late as 1871, when this Currier & Ives print was published, hunters evidently encountered good-sized flocks.

tramped the fields and forests of Maryland and Virginia in the early 1800s, told of taking his friend Sam Vansickle along to "help carry the game." They sat beside a large oak tree on a riverbank, and a gobbler soon answered the hunter's call; there was no question that this bird was hot on the trail. He flew in but saw the two men as he landed, whereupon he wheeled and attempted to become airborne once more.

At the same time, the hunter's gun fired, and his shot broke one of the bird's wings. The turkey jumped into the river and swam across. The hunters could see him on the other side in the bushes, but our storyteller decided that they had lost this bird. After all, it had crossed a stream forty yards wide and maybe twenty feet deep. But even though a scattering of snow still lay on the ground and the river carried chunks of ice, Sam said danged if that turkey was going to make a fool of him, and he commenced stripping off his clothes until he was, as the saying goes, "naked as a jay bird." He dived into the water and swam across, which made both the injured turkey and Sam's hunting partner highly nervous.

The chase through the thicket went on for some time, with the naked hunter getting a tail hold on the bird now and again but the big turkey always escaping once more into the heavy cover. Both of them disappeared for some minutes, but when Sam returned, scratched and bleeding, to swim back across the stream he towed his turkey by the neck. In time, his scratches and bruises healed, and he could speak proudly of the turkey that didn't get away.

There has probably always been an element of sport in hunting wild game, even for those pursuing animals out of hunger and desperation. The Stone Age hunter returning to his shelter smiled with pride when he dropped his brace of grouse before his mate. The Plains Indian also knew pride when honored by his people for his superior hunting skills. The woodsman in the wilderness preferred the challenge of the chase to hoeing corn. Wherever men have hunted they have found pleasure in taking record animals, large and dangerous and bearing spectacular racks or horns. This is part of the ritual that traces its roots to the earliest days of man's hunting, when his skills as a predator became the foundation of survival. The ancient urge to hunt still draws modern hunters to forest and field long after there is need to hunt for food.

Just as the motivations for hunting and the methods of taking wildlife changed over the years, so the types of firearms used by outdoorsmen also evolved. The earliest firearms to arrive on our shores came with the Spanish explorers, beginning in 1513 when Ponce de León discovered the coast of Florida. The Spaniards, whose major interests were collecting gold and other treasure and converting Indians into Christian slaves, astounded the native people with the guns they carried.

Their firearms were matchlocks. The fire needed to ignite the powder was supplied by a cord impregnated with saltpeter, which, once lighted, smoldered or glowed. Both ends were kept lighted when possible, enabling the gunner to relight the match if dampness should extinguish it.

These guns were seldom used for hunting for a couple of reasons. First, the Spaniards were not good hunters. Instead of gathering their own food, they made the Indians supply them. In addition, the musket then standard issue to Spanish soldiers weighed between fifteen and twenty pounds and was commonly supported by a forked stick while shooting. The Indians did not adjust easily to Spanish

Spanish explorers carried matchlocks when they discovered the coast of Florida in 1513. The matchlock employed a slow-burning fuse held by a metal arm, and a small pan to hold priming powder. Pulling the trigger brought the fuse into contact with the primer, which ignited gunpowder in the barrel and propelled the ball. Too heavy and inaccurate for hunting, the matchlock served primarily as a weapon of war.

Pilgrims in Massachusetts Bay were equipped with snaphances, the first rifle action that utilized a flint-and-steel principle. When the shooter pulled the snaphance's trigger, an arm holding the flint snapped forward, striking a steel battery and showering sparks into the flashpan holding the priming powder.

subjugation, and the constant conflict between the invaders and the natives made it inevitable that the Indians would replace their bows and arrows with captured guns whenever possible.

Flintlocks began replacing matchlocks in the mid-1600s and would remain in use for more than a hundred and fifty years. The system used in this gun was more reliable than the matchlock's had been. The flintlock mechanism, which evolved from the earlier snaphance, struck a piece of flint against steel to create sparks and at the same instant removed the cover of the flashpan, so the sparks could touch the priming powder. The early flintlocks used in this country varied considerably. Perhaps typical of those first appearing in the East was a .50 to .60 caliber smoothbore with a full stock and a barrel fifty inches long.

Early double-barreled shotguns were flintlocks and so heavy with their long barrels that they were not widely accepted. In the early 1800s British gunsmiths developed new breech designs, which permitted more efficient burning of powder, and therefore shorter barrel lengths. As a result the double barrel became highly popular among sportsmen. Then came the percussion system and eventually breech actions. A decade or so after the Civil War the hammerless model ushered in the age of modern shotguns.

Although smoothbore guns were sometimes carried westward by the trappers and settlers, the man going across the plains and into the mountains relied most of all on his rifle. Rifling, a system of spiraling grooves on the interior of a gun barrel that cause the bullet to spin, had its origins in the mid-1600s. A good rifle meant improved accuracy on the long shots, and that was important in the open country of the West. Early trappers heading west carried Kentucky-Pennsylvania-type flintlock rifles, which were typically .45 caliber with an overall length of about fifty-five inches.

As a plainsman gained experience, he wanted to replace this rifle with a shorter one having greater shocking power. He needed a rifle that could be more easily carried on horseback and was more effective against grizzlies and buffalo. Fifty caliber, thirty-inch barrels became popular, and the demand was met by creation of the plains-type rifle typified by the Hawken.

Modern firearms really came onto the scene with the introduction of smokeless powder ammunition just a few years before the dawn of the twentieth century.

3

Point the Small End Foremost

Meshach Browning, a lanky, freedom-loving backwoodsman, was born in Frederick, Maryland, in 1781 and lived most of his life there and in Virginia. His father died when he was two weeks old, leaving young Meschach to be raised by his mother. Much of the time he had to be farmed out with an aunt and uncle who were sometimes unkind to him, and this may have played a major role in bringing him to his chosen career. Possibly to get away from home, the boy spent his days roaming alone in the woods. His growing love of the outdoors was so profound that it would eventually make him the most famous hunter in that part of the country. When he was twelve, he went to school for a few months and learned to read and write. By the time he was sixteen, he considered himself to be a skilled hunter.

He could hardly have found a better place to pursue his profession. Many years later he wrote in his autobiography, *Forty-Four Years of the Life of a Hunter*, "the country abounded with deer, bears, panthers, wolves, wild cats, catamounts, wild turkeys, foxes, rabbits . . . partridges, wild bees, and in all the streams trout without number."

From this idyllic world young Browning had taken enough raccoons and bobcats to pay for his first gun, a secondhand flintlock that "carried a one-ounce ball." He had tagged along on many a hunt, but others had done all the shooting. Now, carrying his old gun, the tall, gangly Browning set off on his first deer hunt alone, still smarting under the constant warning of older hunters that "Sure's Hector's a pup, you'll score a clean miss the first deer ever you shoot at."

He soon spotted two deer, supported his gun against a tree, pulled the trigger, and found that by dumping powder down the muzzle without benefit of a measure he had loaded her with twice what was needed. The blast staggered him. When he recovered, he saw that one deer was down and kicking, while the second one was standing there dumbfounded looking at it.

Unable to reload the gun, which was now snow covered, Browning, drawing his knife as he ran, dashed over and leaped onto the wounded deer. Taking a firm grip on the animal, he cut its throat, thereby killing the first deer he ever shot at and setting a pattern of success which would hold good throughout most of his life. Ahead of him would be many opportunities to practice his knife-wielding act.

If not for the testimony of trusted witnesses, much of what Meshach Browning accomplished in the woods might today be viewed as tall tales from the frontier. But Browning's good friend Edward Stabler, who edited the old hunter's memoirs, insisted that he was "devoid of egotism." He credited Browning with "integrity, strong intellect, generous feelings and heroic courage, whether in combatting with savage beasts of prey or struggling against the stream of poverty. . . ." His praise was seconded by Judge Thomas Perry of the Fourth Judicial District of Maryland, who once said, "You can rely on any statement he has made or may make."

Browning said solemnly of himself that he had never "departed from the known truth." When he was approaching eighty, and still going out occasionally to hunt or trap, he recalled the more dramatic encounters with the large wild animals of the Alleghenies. His estimated totals—he kept no written records of animals he took—may have been conservative. He told Stabler that he had killed perhaps two thousand deer, maybe four hundred bears, and fifty cougars, along with "scores" of wolves and bobcats.

When he was eighteen, Browning married his pretty childhood sweetheart. He installed his new bride in an unimpressive little cabin far back in the woods, and now began his long career of

Unable to reload his gun, which was now snow covered, Browning, drawing his knife as he ran, dashed over and leaped onto the wounded deer.

supporting his family from the wealth of wild animals around him. Bear, turkey, and venison became their common fare.

By then Browning's reputation for coolness—some folks called it foolhardiness—in close encounters was already becoming legend. He had still been young and unmarried when he killed his first black bear in his own freestyle manner. A group of visitors in the home of the people with whom the fourteen-year-old Browning was then staying saw a large bear run across the yard and disappear into the woods. Some of them had never seen a bear before. Running people, accompanied by a couple of yapping little poodles, took up the chase. Browning, upon hearing that a bear was the cause of the commotion, grabbed his gun and raced off in hot pursuit, forgetting for the moment that he had left his pouch of balls behind.

He quickly outran all the other bear chasers, raced up the wooded slope, and eventually came upon the bear engaged in battle with the dogs. In the scuffle, the shot from his rifle was poorly placed, and the bear, under severe pressure, took to a tall tree.

The rest of the party came huffing up the hill, offering to shoot the bear with the little bird guns they carried. Finally a neighbor, said to be a bear hunter, arrived with a good gun and supply of balls. He managed to hit the bear a few times but not very effectively. Hours passed. Darkness came on. Browning finally convinced them to let him take a shot with the bear hunter's gun. He also injured the bear, and this time it came scrambling down from the tree, scattering fourteen people in all directions. Among them was an Irish immigrant who, as Browning recalled it, added to the confusion when he ran into clusters of twelve-inch-long thorns on a honey locust tree, and began screaming, "O Jasus! O Jasus! I'm ruint! I'm ruint. It's ruint that I am!"

The bear and dogs carried the fight on as they half-ran, half-tumbled down the steep hill away from the crowd. While the dogs worried the bear, Browning waded into the tangle of animals, carrying a heavy club picked up along the way. He managed to miss the dogs and brought the club thudding down on the bear's head, thereby doing what bullets had failed to accomplish; the bear died on the spot.

The woods grew strangely quiet. The scattered onlookers began calling to each other in the darkness like a covey of scattered quail. As they reassembled, they realized that the only one missing was young Browning.

"It's no use to call," one of them said. "He's as dead as hell."

Then out of the darkness came Browning's soft, "Whadaya want?" Mostly they wanted to know about the bear. Then they wanted to know how Browning had killed it without a functioning gun or tomahawk. "I beat him to death with a club," Browning said. Then each of the visitors took the club in turn and gave the dead body a whack or two so they could claim, as Browning recalled, "they had helped to kill a bear."

Having cut the throat of his first deer and clubbed to death his first bear, the budding frontier hunter was now ready to tackle the cougars that still lived in the Alleghenies in considerable numbers. The opportunity struck one snowy morning when Browning and his dog, Gunner, were off in pursuit of deer. He was tracking four deer when he saw them suddenly scatter in four different directions.

He worked his way in between the deer expecting them to reassemble and allow him a shot, but after a few minutes he discovered that he was not alone. The face of a cougar materialized from behind a log. This was the first time Browning had ever seen a cougar, or mountain lion. In that instant, when they looked each other in the eye, Browning fired. The giant cat leaped and ran off through the brush, with Gunner in hot pursuit. Browning caught up with them, shot the cat again, and finally killed it. From the tip of its tail to its nose it measured eleven feet three inches, making it the largest of the fifty or so cougars Browning killed in his lifetime.

I n season, Browning stayed out of the woods long enough to plant his crops and work his garden. But as fall came on he would tell his wife that the time had come to put up a stock of meat for winter, pick up his gun, call his dogs, and head out for the woods. She worried about his hunting methods and had visions of his being killed in close-up combat with a bear or cougar. She begged him not to "get into their clutches." He assured her he would give them a rough time if they tried to attack him. Mary fretted because she was afraid that, given the opportunity, he would simply wade in and try to finish the job by hand, which, of course, he did. In such encounters he took comfort and pride in the knowledge that he was a swift runner, possessed of lightning quick reactions and powerful muscles.

One early fall day as Browning left his own clearing, his dogs hit a bear trail. When they brought the animal to bay, Browning shot it, but not too well, and the fight was on. Dogs and bear were tearing up the bushes and Browning couldn't do much about it for fear of killing a dog. But his dogs needed his help badly, and when he couldn't find a suitable club for the job, he drew the butcher knife from his belt. While the embattled dogs hung onto the bear, Browning rushed in and delivered enough thrusts of the blade to finish the fight. He considered this an excellent contest. "The harder the fight," he admitted, "the better I liked the fun."

Another animal that never failed to attract this hunter's attention was the wolf. There was genuine loathing of these animals, and bounties were paid to hunters who delivered evidence of a kill to the proper authorities. One of the first opportunities Browning had to take a wolf occurred one February day when he thought he was fox hunting. He came upon the trail of a three-legged wolf and unleashed his dogs so they could follow the scent. They caught up with the wolf where it had lain up in a rock shelter. The dogs dragged the wolf from its bed, while Browning killed it with a club. He gave the eight dollar bounty money to Mary. "That was the way I served every wolf . . .," he said, ". . . for every trespass they made on me."

Typically for the hunters of his day, he held wolves accountable not alone for the sheep and calves they might take but also for the deer they killed and ate. The frontier spirit was strong in Browning, and he assumed the wilderness was there to be subdued. It never occurred to him that people coming to the hills trespassed on the age-old territory of the wolves.

Browning had a way of turning bad luck to his advantage. When the land on which they lived was claimed by another man who appeared to have rightful title, Browning and Mary, with their infant daughter, loaded up their horse and headed for an area known as the Glades. The area appealed to Browning because of the rich wild hay growing there, as well as the fact that it was home to uncounted numbers of wild turkeys, bears, deer, and other creatures on which he could draw as others might go to the pantry or root cellar. The country was still so little settled at the beginning of the nineteenth century that there were no roads into that area wide enough for wagons or carts. They moved by pack horse.

They fixed up their cabin, killed rattlesnakes, and otherwise began to make the new home livable. Browning had his own way of warding off snakes when he was in the woods. He would gather long grass, twist it, and wrap it around his legs thick enough that snakes could not bite through. At night when lying out in the woods, he slept with his head on his dog and his feet and legs wrapped in grass.

The Brownings had come into a land of plenty. The hunter soon began taking his extra deerskins to the mill where others less successful at hunting would trade grain for the hides. He sold bear meat for "four dollars a hundred" and used the cash to buy flax and wool for Mary to card, spin, and weave for making clothing.

Browning would take his gun, powder horn, and pouch down from the pegs in the early morning, kill a couple of deer, and be back in time for breakfast. He once took twenty-two deer in two weeks of fall hunting. On a normal day's hunting he would see ten or twelve deer. The family was never short of meat. Mary could place an order as other wives might send to the grocery store.

Once, when her sister came for a visit, Mary dispatched Browning to bring back "some young turkeys for supper." Four hours later he returned with nine of the big birds loaded on his horse. He claimed that it was easy enough once Gunner chased his prey into a tree. Browning was careful not to make eye contact with the turkeys, but instead would walk past as if he didn't know the birds were in the tree, and the turkeys would perch motionless. Then Browning would stop, wheel about, and before the turkey could fly, shoot off its head.

There were days when bears were almost as thick as deer or turkeys. He and his brother-in-law once chased nineteen from a single laurel thicket. One autumn he killed seventeen bears and eighteen deer and saw nothing unusual about his feat.

There were bad times mixed with the good. One year, in preparation for moving his growing family west to Ohio, Browning sold off his livestock and goods, but then could not collect any of the money owed him. He was despondent until Mary reminded him that on the day they married he had told her that he was strong enough to make a living anywhere. Browning, thus inspired, set off to see what he could shoot.

His dog soon struck a bear trail, and Browning, who knew the bear trails about as well as the bears did, headed off at his swiftest pace, shortcutting across thickets to come out ahead of bear and

Browning would walk past the turkeys as if he didn't know they were in the tree, and the birds would perch motionless. Then he would stop, wheel about, and before the turkey could fly, shoot off its head.

dog. As the bear drew near, Browning spoke softly to it, a custom Browning had adopted to make a bear or deer pause and investigate. This momentary hesitation was just enough to give him a clear shot. At five paces Browning dropped the bear in its tracks, and before it could move he was upon it with his knife.

He opened the stomach, noted that it had fed heavily on "red acorns," and knew where to hunt for more bears. Beneath the red oaks he soon encountered the largest bear he had ever met and killed that one, too, knowing now that his family would have meat enough for several weeks.

By this time, it was quite dark, and Browning, his spirits lifted considerably, headed back to where his horse was hobbled. On the way his dog treed another bear, and, sighting at its outline against the sky, he shot his third bear in four hours. He had to return with a second horse to help carry the meat back. The weight of the largest bear was estimated at four hundred and twenty-five pounds. This contributed to the payloads of venison and bear meat that he hauled to market, along with wild honey, butter, and furs, to rebuild his fortunes.

This backwoodsman's reputation continued to grow. Folks said there wasn't a bear in the woods that Meshach Browning was afraid of. But he was not without feelings for the animals he killed, except for the wolves. One bear fight in which he had to stab the animal seven times left him downcast and feeling that the bear had died bravely in an uneven fight. He wondered if he had "committed a crime against an unoffending animal."

There are always those willing to challenge a noted marksman, and Browning was not against accepting a little wager for the fun of it. One of these matches continued over two days. Two teams of two hunters each set off to see which could bring in the most game. The other team came home with a small doe. Browning and his companion brought back a buck, three bears, and two turkeys.

In another test of his skill Browning speculated that he could kill two deer in one day. A bystander said, "I'll bet you a gallon of whiskey you can't." Browning quickly accepted the bet. A large part of his success grew from his knowledge of the habits of the game he hunted. He could read sign better than most people could read books. He had met so many animals of all kinds, and studied them under such a variety of conditions, that he possessed an uncanny ability to anticipate how an animal would act. He knew how and when to bleat like a fawn or snort like a buck. He could stand perfectly still for a long time and outwait the puzzled bear or deer that might be looking directly at him. He knew when to let a patch of his somber-colored buckskins show from behind a tree to convince a wary deer that this was one of its own kind so it would step into the open. Browning returned at the end of that day, not with two deer, but five.

Furthermore, he said, there was enough light left that, for another gallon, he could bring in one more. This became one of Browning's more humbling memories. In the near darkness, he shot at a deer at close range and did what he almost never did—missed his target cleanly. He charged the miss off to "vanity."

On occasion others wanting "to learn how to hunt" would accompany Browning. George Riley joined him on a hunt, and in two days they killed twelve deer, so many that Browning had to take a sled and team of horses back the next day to haul in the meat.

Eventually he began to wind down. He could no longer broad-jump twenty feet or race a bear. But still he went hunting, often in the company of his sons. He remembered a week-long hunt in 1836 during which he and a son took twenty deer, ten each.

When the "fun fever," as he called the almost uncontrollable lure of the chase, really began to rise in him, Browning might go without food in his relentless trailing of an animal. On one hunt he went with two sons to the headwaters of the Potomac. Having become separated from camp and his sons while trailing a deer, he went all day without eating. That night he had to stay out alone in the woods. He had done this a thousand times, knowing that as long as he had powder, a supply of balls in his pouch, and a horn of salt he could survive.

That night it rained hard, then snowed, and he spent the night sitting against the trunk of a large pine tree. He needed a deer for his breakfast and soon came upon a herd of about twenty. He selected a buck and shot it. But by this time the old man was so overwhelmed with the "fun fever" that, although he quickly field-dressed the deer, he forgot to eat.

He trotted off through the woods, convinced that he could overtake the herd and kill half a dozen before the day was over. He had gone only a short distance, however, when he heard his sons coming on his trail and calling. They talked him into giving up the hunt and returning to camp for a breakfast of buckwheat cakes, stewed fat turkey, potatoes, and turnips. Having stayed on the trail two days without eating, Browning declared this breakfast "the best meal I ever tasted in my life."

If there was one animal that could keep him all day on the trail, it was the cougar. He begrudged the giant cats every deer they took. He once ran, with his dog, all day, traveling some thirty-five miles on a cat trail before he finally shot the cougar from a tree in the gathering darkness.

As he grew older, Browning sometimes asked himself if it might be "sinful" to hunt deer for amusement. But old habits die hard, and the "fun fever" still ran strong in his blood. The increasing shortage of game, perhaps more than any newly acquired sense of values, finally brought on his retirement.

People were crowding into the country. Farmers ran herds of livestock where wild beasts had roamed. Unfettered by game laws, people shot whatever they saw—and in this they were no different from Browning. But they also cut down the forests, and all these pressures combined were taking their inevitable toll. There came a time when Browning knew that the cougars were gone, and so were the wolves. Bears were no longer abundant, and even the deer were harder to find.

But always he had his memories. He recalled, for example, the day he fell on his gun, broke the stock, tied it together, and used it to shoot another deer. He also told about the most dangerous fight he ever had with a large buck and the unorthodox manner in which he took it. His dog drove a buck into a river, then followed it. Rather than have the buck go over a waterfall into the deep pool below, Browning put down his gun and dived in, knife in hand.

As soon as Browning grabbed an antler, his dog stopped fighting and swam to shore to watch. Nothing Browning could say brought his dog back into the deep water to help.

Browning did not dare relax his grip for fear the buck would eviscerate him. Winded and weakened, he realized that he had to gain the advantage soon. Grabbing both antlers and twisting hard, he threw the deer off balance in a manner that made it fall with its feet pointing away from him.

Eventually he managed to put a foot on one antler. Using all his weight, he held the deer's head under water, and sometimes his own head as well. Gradually the deer weakened, and Browning knew he had won the hardest fight he had ever had with a big game animal.

He also recalled the time his wife suggested that he go shoot a deer because she had a hankering to taste venison again. He told her that he had been busy on the farm so long that he might have forgotten how to hold a gun. "When you see a deer," she coached him, "just keep saying, put the small end foremost, put the small end foremost."

He returned having added five deer to his total, all because, he explained, he had remembered to put the small end foremost.

Meshach Browning lived into his eighties. He had eleven children and more than a hundred and twenty living descendants. But none among them ever approached grandpa's hunting skills or the old man's experiences among the wild beasts when the American frontier was young. About the same time he was roaming the woods of Virginia, another frontier hunter was perfecting his peculiar deer-hunting technique on the south shore of Lake Erie.

4

Bucking the Waves

Frontier hunters were resourceful people always willing to adapt their hunting practice to meet the situation. The hunter who discovered a more effective way to take the animals around him quickly changed his methods. This was what Solomon Sweatland did, and his willingness to pursue deer in an unorthodox manner brought him the wildest ride of his career.

His adventure had its origins in his love for deer hunting. If he had not been so fond of deer hunting, his sobbing wife would have had no reason, one autumn day, to be all red-eyed and dressed in mourning. Folks in her neighborhood understood that in a frontier community people have to stick together. They spoke quietly of her loss and offered words of condolence. They promised help with her field work. Life was going to get mighty hard for the young widow Sweatland and her little family now that they no longer had Sol's strong back and his skill in bringing meat to the table.

Wild game was still abundant around the Sweatland's clearing in the northeast corner of Ohio in 1817. The promise of unlimited hunting had been one thing that drew Sol from New England to take up uncleared land along the shore of Lake Erie. There were turkeys, deer, bear, and smaller animals for the taking. The big canvasback ducks, as well as mallards, black ducks, and a host of smaller waterfowl came in by the thousands in autumn, and anybody wanting to shoot, trap, or otherwise take them did so without limits because there were no laws to say he couldn't. Lake Erie also held tons of perch, walleye, lake trout, and other fish available for the catching.

But of all these wild foods, Sweatland's favorite was always venison. In addition to adding fine vittles to the family table, he knew that the hide of a deer was valuable. What the Sweatlands didn't need for their own jackets and other items of clothing, he could swap for salt, lead, and sugar.

Most likely, however, his preference for venison was closely linked to the excitement of deer hunting, which added zest to a life of toil on the frontier and which could get into a man's blood. Sweatland and his neighbor, whose name was Cozens, worked out a highly efficient system for taking deer. In later years, after the coming of game laws, their method would have been viewed as both illegal and unsportsmanlike, but on the frontier anything went.

Cozens had a little pack of scruffy hounds that would rather run deer than eat ham scraps. Sweatland, on the other hand, had a boat, of sorts. According to the 1878 history of Ashtabula County, Ohio, which recounted the story of Sol Sweatland's best remembered deer-hunting adventure, Cozens would call his hounds in the early morning and jog off behind them into the swampy thickets outside the settlement where deer bedded for the day. The dogs sniffed about until they cut a fresh trail, whereupon their mournful howling would rise from the cattails.

This was enough to set the deer running, and deer in those parts knew from experience that the broad waters of Lake Erie, lying a mile or so to the north, offered them refuge when the hounds were hot on their trail. They would lead the hounds directly north and splash into the big lake while the frustrated dogs ran along the shore baying for a while before giving up the chase.

Sweatland, busy with his morning chores, always kept a keen ear open for the voices of Cozens's hounds. Although he knew that his neighbor was off deep in the swamps, unable to keep up with the dogs, Sweatland was there to watch where the deer entered the lake. When they took to the water, Sweatland would be in full pursuit in his canoe before they had any chance to slip back ashore and escape.

This system had worked time after time. Ordinarily, the hunt ended quickly enough as Sweatland's canoe, driven by the force of his hand-carved hickory paddle, drew abreast of the deer. At close range, his old flintlock could scarcely miss.

On this September morning the hound music first sounded

HOUND AND HUNTER by Winslow Homer (1892). Like Sweatland, this hunter took his deer in the water with the help of his dog. Homer often hunted in New York's Adirondack Mountains, a long way from Sweatland's home near Lake Erie; but evidently hunting with a canoe was common practice in both regions.

shortly after daybreak. Sweatland didn't even take time to pick up his coat, or the battered old felt hat that normally sheltered him from sun, wind, or snow. Grabbing up his long gun and his powder horn, he raced for the lakeshore. He arrived in time to see a big buck, eyes rolled back so the whites showed, swimming off in the direction of Canada.

His canoe, tied to a stake at the edge of the lake, was rocking gently on the ripples. Although the dugout looked more like a big wooden shoe than a canoe, and as Sweatland admitted, "warn't much for purty," it had served him well ever since he hollowed it out

of a big tulip tree log with his felling ax, gutter scorp, and adz. The dugout was fourteen feet long. A man had to be a mite careful how he balanced her, but Sweatland had developed a genuine sensitivity for his canoe's moods. Standing up in her was a little like a log-rolling contest, but Sweatland could anticipate the slightest tilt and correct it by a subtle shifting of his weight. The way he had squared her off a little on the bottom was a help in keeping the canoe from rolling over—most of the time.

With the big buck pulling away from shore, Sweatland hurried to untie his canoe. He laid his loaded flintlock in the bottom of the boat and, his paddle in hand, jumped in and pushed off into the lake in full pursuit.

He soon noticed that the wind was coming out of the southeast. That was uncommon. It should have been a warning. But the hard-swimming deer was not far out of range, and Sweatland figured the job could be wrapped up quickly—the same as always.

He knew all about Lake Erie's well-deserved reputation as a widow maker. The most dangerous of the five Great Lakes, Erie is the shallowest and a storm can quickly roll its waters into mountainous waves. It has claimed countless lives of the careless and the unfortunate, as well as numerous boats, large and small. But Sol Sweatland didn't sense the real danger in his situation, leastways not yet. Besides, he had no intention of getting far from shore.

But the buck was a strong swimmer and the promise of fresh venison lured the hunter and his canoe farther and farther out into the lake. Moving the sluggish canoe with a single paddle was heavy work, even for a tough young frontiersman, but the wind, pushing from behind, helped delude him into believing that he could easily overtake the buck.

Then the force of the wind began building. Sudden gusts sometimes made it difficult to keep the canoe on course. Sweatland began to grow uneasy. Maybe he should be turning back. But he hated to give up the chase with the deer almost in range.

His decision was made for him when the buck finally reversed course, swam around him, and headed back for its home country on the lake's south shore. Sol promptly turned around and paddled as hard as he could. He noticed almost immediately that, with the wind against him and the deer riding low in the water, the animal was increasing the distance between them. On this morning, he never did get close enough for a shot at the buck.

But the loss of the deer soon became the least of his worries. No

Before the practice was outlawed, hunting from a canoe was widespread in America. This drawing from the Illustrated London News of 1858, over an article on "Frontier Life in America," shows that swimming deer were fair game at this time.

matter how hard he paddled, his little cabin in the clearing gradually grew smaller in the distance as the gale force of the mounting wind pushed him farther out into Lake Erie.

The storm now had his full attention. It had come up with frightening swiftness, and it was a dandy. His unresponsive little dugout rose to the crest of each new wave, then slid down into the deep trough like a piece of driftwood. Sweatland, rain soaked and wind battered, struggled to keep her upright, expecting each new wave to dump him into the cold, turbulent waters.

One after the other, the waves came, sweeping across the lake toward the distant Canadian shore some fifty miles away. Sweatland could no longer see land in any direction, even from the crest of the highest waves. Furthermore, the waves were washing sheets of water

into his canoe, making it almost impossible to control. He looked around for a bail, but there was none. Finally, in desperation, he pulled off one of his boots and used it frantically to dip water from the canoe.

Back on shore, meanwhile, Cozens had come out of the woods in time to watch the early part of the chase. The sudden strength of the southeast wind made him uneasy. When the buck turned back, Cozens had seen enough. He ran for help. He rounded up a couple of neighbors and the three of them set off paddling madly in a larger boat.

They worked furiously trying to reach Sweatland's canoe. They passed the returning deer and kept on going. Finally, they completely lost sight of poor Sol and his canoe. Muscles tired and time passed, and still there was no glimpse of Sweatland. Hours later, the neighbors admitted sadly that their rescue effort had failed. They turned back and, laboring against the wind, gained distance, foot by foot, until late in the day they reached shore, weary and defeated.

There they were met by Sweatland's grief-stricken wife and wailing children huddled with assorted neighbors on the lakeshore. Without question, Lake Erie had claimed another victim.

In due time the circuit rider arrived at the little Sweatland cabin to console the widow and finalize the funeral plans. At the appointed hour, on a beautiful autumn day, folks dressed in black gathered from miles around. The preacher read the Twenty-third Psalm. He spoke kindly of the dear departed, praising him as a devoted father and husband, and a good farmer. He may also have mentioned that Sol Sweatland was a noted hunter, whose skills were much respected on the frontier.

The assembled mourners joined voice in singing "Amazing Grace" through its last verse.

> Yes, when this heart and flesh shall fail
> And mortal life shall cease
> I shall possess within the veil
> A life of joy and peace.

It should have been all a man could ask of his funeral, but something was missing; without a body and a grave to receive it, Sol Sweatland, friend, neighbor, and deer hunter of note, somehow seemed not to be really dead. The fact was, and those assembled could not know it, ole Sol wasn't dead—not yet at any rate.

Out there in the middle of Lake Erie, he had never given up hope. He knew that his situation was desperate. He would have been a consarned fool to think otherwise. He was soaked with the rain and spray. Wearing neither coat nor hat, he felt the cold wind biting into his thoroughly chilled body. Only constant vigilance kept the canoe upright among the rolling waves. He had no food, could not tell direction, or know where he was headed.

At one point in the afternoon his hopes soared. Off in the distance he saw the large sail, then the smaller foresail of a schooner come into view. Trying to stand tall in his unsteady canoe, he waved his arms and his paddle in the air and shouted against the howling wind. Gradually the ship pulled off in the distance. Her crew had not expected to see anyone out here in the middle of the storm-driven lake, and were unaware of Sol Sweatland's plight. Later a second schooner came into view, but this one, too, failed to spot the deer hunter in his log canoe.

He had noticed of late that the days were growing shorter, and on this stormy fall day with its low, scudding clouds, darkness settled over Lake Erie even earlier. If the wind held its direction, it would eventually bring him to Canada on the north shore. That was his only hope.

That night was the longest Sol Sweatland ever knew. Hour after hour, in almost total blackness, he fought waves, wind, hunger, and exhaustion.

At last, he thought he could detect a faint light in the eastern sky. He strained his eyes staring into the blackness. There was still no sign of land. As the rainy, gray day came on, however, he made out a thin, dark line off to the north. His spirits soared. There could be no doubt; he was being blown toward the Canadian shore.

As he drew closer, however, he could see no sign of human life. There were no cleared fields, no boats, no cabins by the water's edge. He finally drew his canoe up on the swampy shore. His body was stiff, his legs unsteady. No doubt he stood for a few moments, enjoying the solid footing and savoring his delivery from the watery grave with which he had flirted for the past thirty hours.

Off in the distance he saw the large sail, then the smaller foresail of a schooner come into view. He waved his arms and his paddle in the air and shouted against the howling wind.

Soon he began pushing his way inland, through the swamps and forest, searching for a settlement. He walked all day. Toward evening, he came to a lane, which led to a cabin on the edge of a settlement. The people shook their heads in wonder. "Crossed the whole lake in that storm! In the dead of night, and in a log canoe?" They welcomed him as a hero and gave him food and dry clothes.

One more piece of good fortune had come his way that day. On the edge of the lake he had found a stock of salable goods from an earlier shipwreck. His new Canadian friends accompanied him there, perhaps with horses, and helped him bring in his find. Within a few days, he caught a boat headed back across the lake for Buffalo. There he traded his goods for new clothes. Then he began looking around for a way back to his own settlement at the mouth of Conneaut Creek. The schooner *Fire Fly* was headed in that direction, and Sweatland, with broad smiles and high spirits, took passage on her.

He had been gone for nigh onto a week. Back at his clearing, his family and friends were adjusting to the routine of life without him. The records leave us no hint, but chances are that some were already thinking about matching up the widow Sweatland with a new man.

Then the *Fire Fly* came riding down the wind. She was obviously putting into shore. As she drew close, Sweatland's wife and neighbors couldn't help noticing the unusual activity on board. Men were gathered on the deck waving and shouting and shooting off guns, as though in joyous celebration.

In the midst of the uproar, Solomon Sweatland jumped ashore, a big smile on his face. His stunned family and friends gathered around him. He had come back from the dead! They could scarcely believe that he had somehow escaped Lake Erie's deadly grip.

Almost certainly, he soon began casting about for a suitable tree from which to fashion a new canoe. And as he went about his morning chores, he continued to listen for the beckoning call of Cozens's hounds. It is believed, however, that henceforth whenever Sol Sweatland pursued a deer into Lake Erie, he was a mite more cautious about the south wind. After all, coming home from a hunt and finding your wife wearing mourning in your memory is enough to make a sobering impression on a man. As for missing his own memorial service, he allowed that he had no regrets. "Hell," he said, "I never wanted to go to my funeral nohow."

5

Daniel and the Long Hunters

One winter day early in 1769, John Finley rode his scrawny horse down the Yadkin Valley of what is now North Carolina looking for the cabin of a man he hadn't seen for more than thirteen years. The Yadkin Valley road looked no more promising to a peddler than a thousand others he had traveled, but Finley had come here with a special purpose in mind.

Some years earlier he had been with General Edward Braddock in the disastrous effort to take Fort Duquesne, which the French had built on a spot that would later become the heart of Pittsburgh. Finley was a wagoner on Braddock's ill-fated expedition. Around evening campfires, he made the acquaintance of another wagoner, a considerably younger man, a backwoodsman named Daniel Boone.

Boone was fascinated by Finley's wanderings, which had carried him all the way across the mountains into the mysterious wilderness of Kentucky. Finley had once led his pack horse down the Ohio as far as the Kentucky River, which empties into the Ohio about halfway between the modern cities of Cincinnati and Louisville. There he had enjoyed perhaps the most prosperous wilderness trading he had ever known. The Indians brought him valuable beaver and otter pelts as fast as they could collect them and bartered for the

61

lead, powder, and fancies the trader offered. Then Finley came back up the valley and converted his furs to cash.

Traveling along the narrow road through the deep wilderness of Pennsylvania toward Fort Duquesne, he had told young Boone of the wonders of Kentucky. He spoke of buffalo by the hundreds, along with elk, deer, and wild turkeys beyond counting. He explained how these animals concentrated by the thousands around the salt licks, which were choice places to hunt the large herbivores. On his way down the Ohio, Finley probably visited the greatest salt lick of all, the mysterious graveyard of the giants, called Big Bone Lick today. Here, twenty miles downstream from Cincinnati, in a small marshy area two miles east of the Ohio River, large animals had come for salt since prehistoric times, and the bones of many were preserved in the bog.

As Finley explained to Boone, a man traveling the frontier country could easily kill as many animals as he chose. Such tales were certain to appeal to the man on the frontier. Theodore Roosevelt later wrote of these Appalachian people: "Each backwoodsman was not only a small farmer but also a hunter; for his wife and children depended for their meat upon the venison and bear's flesh procured with his rifle.

"Wild turkeys were plentiful. Pigeons and squirrels were everywhere. The hunter's standard game was the deer, and after that the bear; the elk was already growing uncommon. . . . He lived out in the woods for many months with no food but meat, and no shelter whatever, unless he made a lean-to of brush or crawled into a hollow sycamore."

Roosevelt added, "The West would never have been settled save for the fierce courage and the eager desire to brave danger so characteristic of the stalwart backwoodsman."

For more than a dozen years, Boone had worked and hunted in the Yadkin Valley, but the vision of Kentucky and the dreams of wilderness were heavy on his mind. He had seen people crowding into the frontier settlements. The forests were cut. The wild game was harder and harder to find. In two years he moved his family three times, trying to stay ahead of the waves of settlers. This land east of the mountains was no longer where a true hunter belonged—and Daniel Boone had been a hunter since boyhood.

By the time he was eight years old, he was killing rabbits and bobwhite quail with a throwing stick made from a sapling. When he was twelve, his father bought him his first rifle. He was soon expert

In the late 1700s, the flintlock musket became famous in the mountains of Pennsylvania and Kentucky. A vast improvement over the matchlock and snaphance, it came to be known as the Kentucky rifle. Its action was simple and sure-fire. When the trigger was pulled, the flint hit the metal arm of the pan cover, forcing it open and throwing sparks into the powder in the flashpan, igniting the gunpowder in the barrel through a small hole in the pan. The Kentucky also had a rifled barrel, which enabled frontiersmen like Boone to shoot with astounding accuracy.

with the gun—small wonder because he spent every hour that he could escape his father's fields and blacksmith shop roaming the woods in search of game.

The Boone family move to the Yadkin, when Daniel was eighteen, had put him within hunting distance of a high plateau where wild game fed on luxuriant grass and took refuge in the nearby cane-brakes. Of this area the historian Reuben Gold Thwaites wrote, "At first, buffaloes were so plenty that a party of three or four men, with dogs, could kill from ten to twenty a day. . . . An ordinary hunter could slaughter four or five deer in a day; in the autumn, he might from sunrise to sunset shoot enough bears to provide over a ton of bear bacon for winter use; wild turkeys were easy prey; beavers, otters, and muskrats abounded; while wolves, panthers, and wild-cats overran the country." Boone began spending long periods in the woods collecting furs for the market.

Along the Yadkin it was common knowledge that the Boone boy was perhaps the best rifle shot in the valley. He became the family's chief hunter. He was fond as any frontiersman of the shooting matches that tested his skills against those of other hunters. One day he journeyed to the town of Salisbury to trade his deerskins. A pair of frontier con men, seeing his furs and not recognizing him, proposed a little target competition, suggesting that a small wager would add zest to the match. Boone promptly won ten dollars from one of the men, which may have been part of their plan.

Then they closed in for the kill. The challenger said he would risk one more shot, and he would just bet a hundred dollars against Boone's load of furs. They had set up the trapper. There was a previously made bullet hole slightly off-center of the bull's-eye. When the con man shot, Boone noticed that he moved the muzzle of his gun to one side, just enough to miss the whole target, and immediately understood the scheme. All the challenger had to do was miss the entire target, then claim as his own the hard-to-see hole that touched the edge of the bull's-eye. To win, Boone had to place his bullet in the very center of the bull's-eye—and that's what he did.

Years later, when Boone was in his seventies, he chanced to meet the famous artist John James Audubon, also a crack shot. Boone offered to show the artist how he shot squirrels. Boone and Audubon stood where, as Audubon later wrote, "squirrels were seen gamboling in every tree around us. . . ." Boone carried a heavy rifle. Said Audubon, "The gun was wiped, the powder measured, the ball patched with six-hundred thread linen, and the charge sent home with a hickory rod."

Boone aimed, not at the squirrel some fifty yards distant, but at the limb beneath it. His bullet hit the limb and sent the squirrel "whirling through the air." Audubon soon learned that "barking" squirrels to avoid damaging the meat was a common practice among top marksmen in Kentucky and Tennessee.

Hunting was the one thing Boone really lived for. The approach of autumn was his summons to the woods, and he hunted as a professional who relied on what he took to help support his family. Within a fair season he might take between four and five hundred deer, sometimes killing thirty in a day. To the deerskins he added the hides of beaver and otter, which were more valuable. He knew the fine points of stalking deer, of setting and baiting beaver traps, and setting traps in the otter slides.

But as the hordes of settlers seeking land and freedom pushed westward, the game quickly thinned out, and hunting became increasingly unrewarding. All this was nagging the restless Boone that winter day when John Finley pulled up in front of the cabin where Boone lived with his wife, Rebecca, and their children.

Both men recalled vividly their narrow escape when Braddock's forces were ambushed by eight hundred French and Indians. As the leading elements of the military formation broke for the rear, Boone slashed the harness to free his team from the wagon; he leaped onto one of the horses and beat a retreat as fast as he could, with Finley close behind. A dozen or so less fortunate men, drilled in the formal battlefield procedures of the British, simply surrendered to the approaching Indians and, one by one, were burned at the stake.

Finley longed to return to Kentucky, that wilderness land of deep green forests, sprawling canebrakes, swift, clean rivers, and the promise of wealth from furs. He had come out of his way to present Boone with a plan. He stayed on into the winter, and every night the menfolk, including Boone's brother Squire Boone and his brother-in-law John Stuart, sat before the fire and talked and dreamed of the land beyond the mountains.

Finley explained his thinking. "I'm just a trader, not a woods-man, and dasn't go out there alone again and get myself lost or kilt. Now, you could find your way. You know how to live on what you find and what you shoot. I'll tell you this much, I learned from the Indians that there's a trace called the Warrior's Path as leads you once you're across. The Warriors' Path is the trace the Cherokees and Shawnees follow when they go off to fight each other. Following the Warriors' Path, we can get down into Kentucky sure."

The talk shifted gradually from the speculative stage to the planning. This was to be a hunting trip, a long one, with the extra lure for Boone of finding and claiming new land. When they set out from Boone's cabin on the first of May 1769, there were six of them: John Finley, Daniel Boone, John Stuart and three local men hired as camp tenders. Daniel's brother Squire also had a strong hankerin' to go, but somebody had to stay back to tend the crops and look out for the families, so Squire agreed to join them later. The travelers set off with extra horses and plenty of lead, powder, and traps, as well as food and supplies enough to tide them over until they found game abundant beyond the frontier.

Boone and his companions probably wore the typical backwoods outfit, a buckskin hunting shirt that came nearly to the knees, buckskin pants and leggins, moccasins that sponged up water, a broad-brimmed hat rather than the common coonskin cap, and a belt in which were tucked butcher knife and tomahawk. Hanging from a shoulder strap were bullet pouch, powder horn, and a few gun tools.

In the hour of departure on the long hunt, Rebecca and the other women folk stood surrounded by their children in the middle of the dirt road that ran in front of their cabin. They watched their men ride off slowly out of sight and had no way of knowing when they would see the hunters again, or if they would ever see them. Daniel Boone was tasting adventure. The wilderness beckoned. He would be away from home in the Kentucky country for the next two years. He was the advance guard for the parties of settlers who would follow him over the mountains into the green hills of Kentucky.

The trails they followed had felt the moccasins of earlier hunters, little known and long forgotten. The earliest white woodsman to give the crossing place a name, and make it known, was Dr. Thomas Walker of Virginia, who, leading five other hunters, crossed the mountain pass in 1750 and named it Cumberland Gap, honoring the Duke of Cumberland. For six months Dr. Walker and his party

In the hour of departure on the long hunt, Rebecca and the other women stood surrounded by their children in the middle of the dirt road that ran in front of their cabin. They watched their men ride off slowly out of sight and had no way of knowing when they would see the hunters again, or if they would ever see them.

explored the wilderness, but their trip was not an easy one. Bears wounded three of their dogs and bit one of the men. One dog was killed by an angry bull elk. A bull buffalo charged them. Copperheads and rattlesnakes often bit their horses. The records show that they killed thirteen buffalo, eight elk, fifty-three bears, twenty deer, and one hundred and fifty wild turkeys, plus assorted other game.

Boone and his party followed the trail leading across Cumberland Gap, then they found the Warriors' Path and were deep in the wilderness. For more than half a year, Boone's party hunted this "dark and bloody ground" without incident. Boone later claimed that these months, when he tramped the forest unfettered by responsibilities and surrounded by natural wonders, were the happiest months of his life.

Their business was hunting, and they steadily added skins and furs to their collection. They had come into big country, sparsely populated. But there was always the possibility of encountering hostile Indians. Although no Indian tribes lived permanently in Kentucky, it was a favored hunting ground over which the tribes fought and where the "white faces" were unwelcome trespassers.

Then one day, when he and Stuart were hunting, they were surprised by a party of Shawnees who had come down from the Ohio country on a hunting expedition. Finding two lone white hunters was a bonus, and there was precious little that Boone and Stuart could do to avoid capture. They were quickly surrounded by the warriors and a chief who called himself "Captain Will."

Captain Will, with a big grin on his dark face and a tomahawk in his hand, demanded that the two hunters lead him to their camp. There was only one commonsense answer if the Yadkin Valley hunters wanted to go on living, so Boone grinned back and said, "Come along, Captain Will," and he and the reluctant Stuart set off at a slow pace leading the column of Indians back toward their camp and their accumulated furs.

There the jubilant Indians took everything of value to them. Then they lectured the trespassers sternly against hunting on lands that belonged to the red man. Finally, they told them that they should go back home across the mountains and tell other white men to stay home. Captain Will graciously gave them just enough supplies to make the trip.

The loss of their furs was serious enough, but having their horses taken was an even greater blow. The others in the party promptly voted in favor of jogging off through the forest homeward bound, but Boone and Stuart talked them into waiting while they tried to recapture some of their horses.

A couple of nights later the two woodsmen slipped up on Captain Will's camp and quietly led four of their horses off into the forest. They stopped to listen for sounds of pursuit, mounted and rode hard for the next twenty-four hours. Finally, believing that they had made their escape, they stopped for a brief rest.

Then, as Stuart bent low to tie his moccasin, he could hear a distant rumbling—the unmistakable sound of approaching horses. Minutes later, he and Boone were again surrounded. This time the Indians decided to have a little fun with these white hunters. They tied a horse bell around Boone's neck. "Make bell ring big." Boone, a realist, grinned at Captain Will, and went into his dance, while the Indians whooped and shouted with glee.

But getting out of this tight spot was not as simple as dancing the jig. Captain Will said they would take "Wide Mouth" and the other paleface along to the banks of the Ohio so they could usher these white hunters out of Kentucky. The leisurely march took seven days. At night Boone and Stuart were tightly bound. In the land south of where Maysville, Kentucky, stands today stood broad stretches of cane, growing thick as hair and sometimes twenty feet high. One night Boone and Stuart escaped, grabbing a couple of rifles, and made it safely into the brakes.

The Indians hunted for them, but looking for a man in the canebrakes was like looking for a raindrop in a waterfall. Captain Will and his troops soon crossed the Ohio back into their own country, perhaps thinking that they had scared "Wide Mouth" so thoroughly he and other trespassers would indeed go home and stay there.

But Boone had another idea. He and Stuart traveled hard, returning to their camp to search for the other four members of their party. However, their companions, now convinced that Daniel and John were "deadern ary doornail," had, like the three wise men, followed their star to the east.

Boone and Stuart eventually caught up to the party. To Boone's

delight, his brother Squire was with them. His younger brother had come out to Kentucky bringing extra horses and traps for Daniel. The new equipment gave Boone a choice: he could either stay in Kentucky and try to gather a new pack of furs, or he could turn tail and head back across the mountains. For Daniel Boone, the decision was easy enough. He, Squire, and John Stuart, along with Alexander Neely, who had come out with Squire, would stay on in spite of Indian threats or British edicts.

The winter trapping season was coming on, and through the following weeks they collected a good stock of furs. Stuart and

Boone agreed to trap separate areas and meet later. Stuart was never seen again.

The following May, Squire Boone loaded their heavy packs of furs and started off for home to market their catch. He was to bring back a new stock of supplies.

Other hunters off on trips were now invading the Kentucky hills, and a party of Long Hunters (so called because of their extended absences from home) one day heard a strange sound. Their leader, so the story goes, motioned them to silence while he crept forward to investigate. There, in the wilds of the Kentucky forest, he found Daniel Boone, thoroughly relaxed, stretched out on his back, gazing at the blue sky and singing a country ballad to pass the time until Squire arrived.

Finally, after another successful winter hunt the two brothers loaded their catch and headed for home. They had almost made it to safety when a band of Indians again robbed them. Boone had little to show for his two years in the wilderness. He was deeper in debt than when he had set off. But he had blazed a trail. He now understood the richness of the land beyond the mountains—and he knew Kentucky's rivers and trails.

Another frontiersman whose hunting experiences brought him lasting fame was a Tennessecan named David Crockett, who when not politicking or in military service kept a pack of special hounds to help him hunt bears and "painters." Come fall, he and his dogs gave the bears no quarter. Following his hounds to the woods, he would begin taking bears to provide his winter stock of meat and oil. Soon he would have all his family could use. Then he might go off hunting to help a friend or neighbor and be in on the kill of a few dozen more bears.

One evening Crockett and his young son killed three bears, dressed them, and stored the meat on wolf-safe platforms. The next morning they killed three more in half an hour and the following day killed four more. That week they took seventeen bears and didn't slow down until the last of the bears took to their winter beds. Bears were so common in western Tennessee that Crockett in one six-month period killed a hundred and fifty-five.

David Crockett

His fame as a bear hunter spread across the frontier. Friends put his name up for public office, perhaps as a joke. He won local offices, then served three terms in the United States Congress, proving that hunting skills alone were enough to start a frontiersman on the climb to high public office.

The early hunters were not the only ones exploring the frontier wilderness. Several groups of hunters left their homes in Virginia to cross the mountains and follow the game trails to the salt licks. If they managed to elude the Indians and return with good packs of furs, they could accumulate $1,500 or more for a season's hunt.

Boone had been a year away from home when Colonel James Knox led a party of forty Long Hunters through the Gap and down into Kentucky on a two-year hunt. Although Boone was also in Kentucky at the time, the paths of the two parties never crossed. Years later one of Knox's hunters recalled that he had killed eighty-one deer on that trip. Another Long Hunter, an older man, whose sight was so poor that he had to tie white paper to the front sight of his gun to aim, recalled shooting numerous deer.

One day Isaac Bledsoe, a prominent Long Hunter, rode out of the hunting camp and came upon a buffalo trail, which he followed for thirteen miles to a salt lick. There he found buffalo and other animals so numerous that he was afraid to dismount. He shot two deer, but the buffalo tramped them into the mud before he could reach them.

The Kentucky wilderness was the traditional hunting ground of various tribes, the Creeks, Cherokees, and Catawbas from the south and the Shawnees, Delawares, and Wyandots out of the north. Daniel Boone appeared to have enjoyed a somewhat different relationship with the Indians than did most of the Long Hunters. He was captured, held, and robbed, but there must have been an element of mutual respect between Boone and the Indians. More honor seemed to have come to the Indians who held the famous hunter captive than they could expect by taking his scalp.

Most of the early hunters invading the Kentucky country, however, looked upon the Indians as mortal enemies. It became established policy "never to suffer an Indian invasion to go unpunished." Lewis Collins in his *History of Kentucky* recounts that Colonel George Rogers Clark once led a force of one thousand riflemen into the heart of Indian country: "Their towns were reduced to ashes, their corn cut up, and the whole country laid waste with unsparing severity." Travelers coming on a vacant cabin in the wilderness might find food waiting there for them, but before eating any of it, they had to look carefully. Sometimes a notice was posted, warning that the food was laced with arsenic for "trapping" Indians.

Typically the Long Hunter studied the features of the land wherever he went. He took special note of the stream crossings, springs, and scenic hollows where the soil was rich, thinking often of returning to claim land on which his family could settle. Boone was among these hunting settlers, and he claimed extensive acreages in Kentucky. But his claims were later ruled to be improperly registered, and he lost everything.

Later Boone moved his family out of Kentucky and on to Missouri, where he was welcomed. As he grew older, he continued to take his gun and dog and go hunting. But he never forgot crossing through Cumberland Gap and the fair land he had found beyond the mountains. As an old man looking back on those days, he called Kentucky, "The Garden of God, unequaled on our earth."

The land where the Long Hunters roamed sharpened the skills of a special breed of men. Out of this frontier would come the rugged individuals—men like George Drouillard—who would move on west to meet the Plains Indians and the grizzly bears in the land of the mountain men.

6

Of Men and Beaver

George Drouillard, a tough, powerfully built frontiersman, was known for his lightning-quick reactions, resourcefulness, and excellent judgment. Meriwether Lewis heard about this master outdoorsman while floating down the Ohio River with his newly built keelboat in 1803. Lewis, who was recruiting men for the historic trip he and William Clark were about to lead to the West Coast, also learned that Drouillard, who was part Indian, had mastered the universal Indian sign language. The party was certain to need a skilled interpreter as they moved westward and met the new tribes. Consequently, when Lewis and his keelboat reached Fort Massac on the Illinois shore of the Ohio, he tied up and had a talk with Drouillard. He never regretted it. As events developed in the coming months, Drouillard's hiring was probably the wisest bit of recruiting Lewis or Clark did in all their preparations for their grand adventure. Drouillard, whose pay was set at twenty-five dollars a month, was enthusiastic about the western adventure. Whether he would have been as eager to go if he could have foreseen his eventual fate we will never know.

Drouillard's father, a British subject, worked for his government in Detroit as an interpreter. Young George was probably born in the 1770s. His mother was a Shawnee, and the blood of generations of proud woodland hunters ran in the youngster's veins. Although little is known about his early life, Drouillard must have been an accomplished hunter by the time he met Lewis. Not every male living near the frontier was a premier hunter who was always at home in the wilderness. With hunting, as with most enterprises, there were the superior, the average, and the incompetent. But in Drouillard, Lewis had found the master outdoorsman. He was perfectly comfortable in the wild places and possessed a natural aptitude for hunting, trapping, and exploring. He quickly became the main hunter for the Lewis and Clark party.

Drouillard had spunk. He was comfortable alone in the wilderness; he could live off the land day after day. He was a tireless traveler, on foot or horseback. He was also a man who could get along well with others. Writer and historian M. O. Skarsten described him as "sensitive, alert, imaginative." In time, Lewis and Clark would come to look upon George Drouillard as indispensable to their mission, and he probably was.

As the party moved westward across the plains, Drouillard was sent out almost daily to hunt. Lewis and Clark had acquired a couple of horses for their hunters to use. Often Drouillard would take along another hunter, and they would bring their game to the riverbank each evening to meet the main party moving up the Missouri. By one estimate, they needed a buffalo a day to keep the men in meat. How well the hunters did in providing this food depended on where they were and sometimes on weather and luck. Often there were swollen streams to cross, long days of cold rain and blinding snow storms.

Lewis and Clark soon realized that Drouillard was their best shot and most capable hunter. Captain Clark wrote in his journals that Drouillard and one helper returned one day with two deer, one bear, and a horse they found wandering wild on the plains. Another time he wrote, "Several hunters sent out today on both sides of the river, *Seven* deer killed today, Drewyer [Lewis and Clark's name for Drouillard] killed six of them." There were times when he was gone for several days at a time, operating twenty or thirty miles from the main group.

One winter day Lewis dispatched Drouillard and one other hunter to hunt elk. Wrote Lewis in his journal, "They returned in the evening Drewyer having killed 7 elk; I scarcely know how we Should Subsist, I believe but badly if it was not for the exertions of this excellent hunter. . . ."

While Drouillard had his own favorite Kentucky rifle for hunting, we know that he probably also had access to one of the early U.S. regulation Model 1803 rifles produced at Harper's Ferry. This rifle

As the party moved westward across the plains, Drouillard was sent out almost daily to hunt. Lewis and Clark had acquired a couple of horses for their hunters. Often Drouillard would take along another hunter, and they would bring their game to the riverbank each evening to meet the main party moving up the Missouri.

had a thirty-three-inch barrel, accommodated a .54 caliber ball, and was charged with ninety to one hundred grains of powder. Lewis and Clark carried several rifles of this model on their westward journey, and no doubt they permitted Drouillard to use the weapon if he found it superior to his own muzzleloader.

As they moved deep into the West the captains were sharply aware of the odds against them. "We are now several hundred miles within the bosom of this wild and mountainous country," wrote Lewis in July 1805, "where game may . . . become scarce and subsistence precarious . . . without knowing how far these mountains continue. . . ."

Eventually, they came into the land of the Shoshone. If their trip were to be successful, they needed Shoshone guides to lead them through the mountains and over the Continental Divide and horses to carry their equipment. The Shoshone were the people of the Indian girl Sacajawea, who was serving as a guide. Although her presence helped in the negotiations, Drouillard still had to interrupt his hunting long enough to interpret for the captains, buy the horses, and arrange for the guides.

On one occasion, the camp was host to a large party of hungry Shoshones. Drouillard and another hunter were dispatched to bring in food. Even though a crowd of curious Indians trooped along to watch him hunt, Drouillard killed three deer to feed the delegation.

All across the country the party had transported the iron framework of a collapsible boat, which Lewis had devised to use when they could find no trees for making canoes. When the time came to test this iron canoe frame, they were deep in Montana country. Lewis and Drouillard went hunting for the elk whose skins would cover the iron skeleton. In one day they killed six elk, two buffalo, two mule deer, and a bear, which, as Lewis wrote in his journal, being "all in good order we therefore took as much of the meat as our canoes and perogues would conveniently carry."

The bear they killed that day was a grizzly. It had charged Drouillard and come within a few paces of him before the hunter rendered it a fatal shot in the head. Lewis noted in his journal that the brain shot was the only shot "that will conquer the ferocity of those tremendous anamals."

Drouillard's superior marksmanship, as well as that of others in the party, impressed the Indians. Lewis noted that the Indians watching Drouillard shoot formed a "very exalted opinion of us as marksmen and the superior excellence of our rifles . . . this will deter

Regulation Model 1803 rifles, made at the Harpers Ferry Arsenal, were issued to the Lewis and Clark expedition. Drouillard used his own Kentucky for hunting, but occasionally switched to a Harpers Ferry flintlock.

CAPTAIN WILLIAM CLARK MEETING WITH INDIANS OF THE NORTHWEST by Charles M. Russell (1897). In this recreation of an incident that occurred before his birth, the famous western artist captured an extraordinary moment in history when two alien cultures met for the first time.

them from any acts of hostility if they have ever meditated any such."

Wherever an encounter with a grizzly is mentioned in the journals, Drouillard is usually on hand—as he was on a summer day in 1805. Some members of the party decided to get even with the bears they believed slept during the day on an island in the Missouri across from their camp. The island was covered with a jungle of willows from which the bears were thought to foray into camp at night. Lewis wrote that the bears had "annoyed us very much of late. . . ." Had they not been "annoyed," chances are the men would have gone bear hunting anyhow.

The hunting party split into groups of three and began pushing into the thick-growing willows. But for all their tramping around, they flushed only one bear. This bear, it seemed, made a bad choice and charged Drouillard, crashing through the brush chuffing and snorting. At twenty paces, Drouillard shot the grizzly, according to Lewis's journals, giving the hunter time to leap out of the animal's path. They then followed the bear a hundred yards or so into its refuge, where they found it dead.

At times even Drouillard could not bring game into camp. Meat was scarce for three hundred miles down the Columbia until they arrived at the Dalles. The water was fast, and the lure of seeing the great Pacific Ocean at last was strong. Instead of stopping to search for game, they often subsisted on berries and the flesh of dogs purchased from the Indians.

Drouillard's most difficult hunting assignments came when the Lewis and Clark party was in its winter camp at Fort Clatsop near the Pacific. There were no longer the herds of buffalo and other game they had met while crossing the plains. They were now in a gray world, where rain and dense fog blanketed the forest nearly every day. The forest floor was littered with deadfall trees, and hunters struggled knee-deep in the waterlogged duff. They sometimes wandered for hours without knowing where they were. Even Drouillard could become confused, but he seemed to be guided by an uncanny sense of direction that soon brought him back on course.

There were days in this country when Drouillard tramped from morning until night without firing a shot. The hunt might keep him out for several days at a time. But still, in less than four months, during the winter of 1805–1806, the hunters brought to camp a hundred and thirty-one elk plus assorted other game. On one occasion Drouillard and another hunter spent three days following a herd of elk, gradually moving them closer to camp so the meat would not have to be carried so far. They then came into camp to report that they had butchered and hung eighteen elk some six miles from camp.

These elk were needed for their skins as well as the meat. The crew spent much of their remaining time in that camp preparing clothing for the trip back across the mountains. They tanned the skins and converted them to blankets, leggings, and three hundred and fifty-eight pairs of moccasins.

The trip up the Columbia and back into the mountains began in June, with Drouillard leading the way. When they again needed Indian guides, it was Drouillard who was dispatched on the ticklish mission of dealing with the natives.

There were disappointments. One night, ten of the party's finest horses disappeared. Drouillard and a companion were sent to search for them. They soon split up to cover maximum ground and, in due time, Drouillard picked up the trail. He located the camp where fifteen lodges of Indians, with their horses, had rested long enough for the horses to consume all available grass.

Knowing the size of the band, Drouillard could have turned back. Instead he followed the Indians, carrying his sheathed rifle across his legs. But Drouillard had to face facts: if he came upon the Indians what could he do against the warriors of fifteen lodges? At last he did what George Drouillard never liked to do, he turned back without completing his mission and retraced his route, traveling alone through another fifty or sixty miles of wilderness to learn that Lewis and Clark had about given up hope of seeing him again.

George Drouillard was happiest when off by himself in the wild, lonely mountains of the West. To such a man, the boisterous riverbank welcome that greeted the explorers in St. Louis, the shouting and gunfire, must have brought mixed feelings; how could a wilderness traveler be a contented part of this crowded scene? Drouillard needed something that promised to feed his hunger for adventure. He soon found it.

The travels of Lewis and Clark were of special interest to the budding fur industry. With high-quality fur much in demand in the United States and Europe, trappers and traders listened carefully to the expedition's reports of unlimited beaver. Lone trappers and small parties were already pushing deeper and deeper into the western wilderness. The Lewis and Clark party had overtaken some of them along the river as they came downstream headed for St. Louis, and the trappers' canoes rode deep in the water under their packs of furs.

Drouillard conferred with Manuel Lisa, the aggressive little dark-complexioned trader who had formed a fur-gathering partnership with some other St. Louis businessmen. Lisa was headed into the mountains to take charge personally of the beaver-trapping and fur-trading mission. His partners, less adventuresome than Lisa, wanted a representative to go along and watch out for their interests. They chose Drouillard.

The party established a fur-trading post on the Yellowstone, from which Drouillard and John Colter, another noted Lewis and Clark crew member hired on by Lisa, made long solitary journeys into Indian territory. Their assignment was to encourage the Indians to bring their furs into the new post to trade for guns, lead, knives, blankets, and other goods.

Drouillard returned to St. Louis, but in the spring of 1810 he was back in the mountains once more, this time working out of a new trading post at the Three Forks, where the Missouri River is born in western Montana. This idyllic situation had one sour note: the presence of the trappers invariably aroused the Blackfoot Indians, who killed and mutilated any trapper they caught. Bold trappers, however, took the risk and set their traps. But they had to stay in close to the fort for safety, and they chafed under the Indian threat. Mountain man Thomas James, who kept a journal, wrote, "We all became tired of this kind of life, cooped up in a small enclosure and in perpetual danger of assassination when outside the pickets."

Understandably, men who had penetrated that far into the wilderness, with its Indians and grizzly bears, would eventually refuse to allow the Blackfeet to dictate their behavior. Thus, in early May twenty-two trappers, including Drouillard, set off up the Jefferson River, determined to harvest a paying crop of beaver plews.

The Indians did not bother them, and the trappers grew more complacent. Their boldness allowed them to split into still smaller groups to work the tributaries and beaver ponds. Days passed. The trappers were moving out farther and farther from the main camp.

THE PRAIRIE HUNTER by Arthur F. Tait. This painting, published as a Currier print in 1852, depicts a situation similar to the one that led to George Drouillard's death at the hands of the Blackfeet. The artist may have had the incident in mind.

Even that did not satisfy Drouillard. He was at his best when traveling and working alone. So the veteran mountain man, the Indian negotiator, half-Indian himself, set off for the day. He said that he would see them all later, and he tramped off upstream, perhaps a couple of miles, and put out his traps.

Drouillard returned to camp without having seen any sign of Indians. The following morning he ran his trap line and brought in six fine pelts, one for each trap. The following day was a repeat performance. Drouillard, grinning, said, "This is the way to make the beaver come." More cautious companions warned him that he might be the one that got caught. Drouillard had the answer to that one too. "I'm too much Indian," he'd say, "to get caught by Indians."

But the following day the Blackfeet slipped up on him. Earlier they had overwhelmed two other trappers who had taken courage from Drouillard's success. When none of the three trappers returned, a party went searching for them. What they found was not pretty. First they came upon the two hunters, dead and mutilated. Then they discovered what remained of Drouillard's horse, and of the mountain man himself, beheaded and eviscerated. The tracks made it plain that Drouillard had battled to the last, and taken his toll of the raiders.

George Drouillard, master woodsman, had earned his place as one of the most important hunters in the history of America. His violent end against insurmountable odds was predictable.

7

Naturalists with Guns

In those magic times when much of the broad American wilderness lay untouched by the feet of white men, frontier hunters were sometimes joined by a curious breed of explorer traveling in the interest of science. Naturalists wandered wide-eyed into the remote places. They found strange birds and mammals, fantastic plants, and unbelievable insects and reptiles. They rushed about collecting specimens. They preserved them as best they could and shipped them back to eastern cities and on to Europe. There, scientists pored over these new American discoveries and lovingly stored them away for later study.

Most of these frontier scientists had been hunters before they became naturalists. Hunting was their earliest impetus to studying the ways of animals; the pursuit of game gradually led them into serious study. While they collected specimens to compare or paint, they also loved the excitement of the chase. In that they were little different from any other hunter on the frontier.

Today's anti-hunters sometimes insist that nobody who really respects wildlife can be a hunter, whether for meat, scientific studies, or the excitement of the chase. But the evidence tells us otherwise. Many noted naturalists, with a deep appreciation for wild animals and natural ecosystems, have been skilled and enthusiastic hunters.

The urge to hunt most likely goes back to the dawn of humanity when there was no luxury of choice; a man hunted, or his people starved. The fact that we are here tells us that there were skilled hunters among the ancestors of all of us. This is our heritage, and naturalists going afield with their guns have long known that man is not apart from nature, but is part of it.

Hunting has become a matter of individual choice. No longer must each of us be a hunter to survive, because now we hire others to kill the animals we eat. Some of us eat only plants and ignore questions about the morality of killing plant life. Because most people grow up without the opportunity to hunt in this crowded world, some become anti-hunters, renouncing our heritage and seeking to forget that we, too, belong to a predator species.

Among the earliest of America's pioneering hunter-naturalists was a young man dispatched on his greatest adventure by the President of the United States. Meriwether Lewis, although more often thought of as an explorer, was, as one writer said, an "instinctive naturalist." Once he understood that Thomas Jefferson expected him to study the wildlife encountered on his historic journey, Lewis began taking instruction from learned scientists in Philadelphia. These cram courses helped prepare him for describing newly discovered plants and animals in his journal and for selecting important specimens to send back east.

Lewis had been a hunter since the age of eight, when he began roaming the woods with his dogs in pursuit of raccoons and opossums. But his pioneering journey across the plains and mountains brought him rare opportunities to see a new world. He and William Clark found tribes of previously unknown Indians, unnamed mountain ranges and rivers, and hundreds of yet undiscovered plants and animals. Lewis and Clark gave the world its first knowledge of mule deer, white-tailed jackrabbits, bighorn sheep, magpies, and more. They captured and sent back preserved skins and skeletons of animals new to science, as well as crates of living prairie dogs, magpies and prairie chickens. Traveling over the plains, Lewis noted in his journal that "game is still very abundant. We can hardly cast our eyes in any direction without perceiving deer, Elk, Buffalo or Antelopes. The quantity of wolves appear to increase in the same proportion. . . ."

Of all the western creatures he met and described, however, the most impressive was the grizzly bear. Indians had warned the party about the great white bears. Following initial, and relatively unexciting encounters, Lewis innocently described the giant bear as "by no means as formidable or dangerous as they have been represented."

Lewis dashed about eight yards, saw the bear was gaining on him, and in desperation jumped into the river.

He soon changed his mind. In one attack after the other on various members of the party, the giant bears demonstrated that they were never to be trifled with.

Lewis wrote in his journal of the adventures that began one day after he shot a buffalo. Instead of loading his gun at once, as frontier hunters usually did, he stood watching the great beast die. As he stood there, "a large white, or rather brown, bear crept on me within 20 steps before I discovered him." Lewis was not certain how best to deal with this dicey situation. "I thought of retreating in a brisk walk until I could reach a tree about 300 yards below me, but I had no sooner turned myself about but he pitched at me, open mouth and full speed." Lewis dashed about eight yards, saw the bear was gaining on him, and in desperation jumped into the river. He sloshed out until he stood waist deep in the icy water. To his relief, this grizzly changed its mind, wheeled about, and ran until it disappeared over a hill three miles away. Grizzlies were, and still are, highly unpredictable.

Later the same day Lewis met a brownish yellow animal he did not recognize, but which he took to be "of the tiger kind." It was "standing near its burrow, and when I approached it thus nearly, it crouched itself down like a cat looking immediately at me as if it designed to spring on me." Lewis braced his gun on his espontoon, aimed, and fired, but the animal vanished into its burrow. He was never certain he had hit it. But he thought he had because, as he wrote, "My gun is true."

Shortly afterward he was charged by three buffalo bulls that broke away from a herd. They slid to a halt in the dust a hundred yards distant, wheeled, and departed. This series of encounters coming in rapid succession left a shaken Lewis wondering if "all the beasts of the neighborhood had made a league to destroy me." It was, he recalled, somewhat like a dream, until the prickly pears piercing his moccasins convinced him that the situation was real enough and that it was time to "make the best of my way to camp."

On the heels of the Lewis and Clark party, and inspired by the richness of their discoveries, came other flintlock-bearing scientists. In 1832, two naturalists joined the party of trader Nathaniel J. Wyeth, who was then headed for Oregon and the Columbia River country.

One of them was Thomas Nuttall, who was originally from England. He had studied minerals and was a recognized authority on plants and a Harvard faculty member. He had already made one

Thomas Nuttall

trip west in 1811, traveling part way up the Missouri River searching for new plant species. Now nearing fifty, he was older than most of the western adventurers and about twice the age of the party's other naturalist, John Kirk Townsend, a youthful physician and ornithologist from Philadelphia.

Moving along with the party of seventy men, the two naturalists kept busy searching for new plants and animals. Nuttall wandered off so often "dreaming of weeds," Townsend said, that others worried about his safety among the Indians and bears. Townsend, meanwhile, was busy collecting birds with his double-barreled muzzleloader. Walking together one day on the prairies, Nuttall and

Townsend came upon an unbelievable concentration of golden plovers, eleven-inch-long birds that breed in the Arctic and winter in the Southern Hemisphere. The shorebirds were feeding over acres of the grasslands. The two scientists did the natural thing; they took a good bag of the fat birds for their supper.

Townsend, on one occasion, even admitted his guilt in shooting a female antelope for which the party had not the slightest need. She ran along beside the riders within easy range. To shoot her would be an immature act, but the youthful Townsend, finally yielding to temptation, hung back, dismounted, and killed her—then left her where she fell. Shooting animals for practice, or for no good reason at all, was commonplace on the plains. In a land seemingly overflowing with wildlife, ethical standards were slow to evolve. But Townsend was immediately sorry for what he had done and agonized for days about his wanton waste.

Townsend's journal, *Narrative of a Journey Across the Rocky Mountains to the Columbia River*, captures some of the excitement these gun-carrying naturalists found in the West. On one occasion Townsend wrote, "I had determined to kill a buffalo. . . ." Rounding a high point, he saw directly before him a resting herd of some twenty animals. "There were so many fine animals that I was at a loss which to select. . . ." He did as many an inexperienced hunter had and picked the largest and grandest of the old bulls, when a far more practical choice would have been one of the fat young cows. After hesitating several minutes, during which he fought down a bad case of "bull fever," Townsend centered his sights and squeezed the trigger.

The herd scrambled to its feet in confusion and ran for the distant hills. Running with them was Townsend's bull. But the bull soon slowed, then stopped, and stood bleeding until it fell. Townsend cut out the tongue, which was as much of the old bull as he and his companions considered fit for human food. There was nothing unusual in this either. "I have seen dozens of buffalo slaughtered," he wrote, "merely for the tongues, or for practice with the rifle. . . ."

By this time he and his hunting companions, one of them a missionary accompanying the party, were extremely thirsty, but there was no water to be found. A more experienced western traveler among them opened the buffalo with his knife to view "the great stomach, and still crawling and twisting entrails." While Townsend backed off and the missionary covered his mouth with one hand, the hunter pressed his tin cup to the edge of the warm, green mass, collected a serving and, after offering it first to his companions, drank heartily, "smacking his lips and drawing a long breath after it with the satisfaction of a man taking his wine after dinner." Townsend did drink the blood, thereby satisfying both his hunger and thirst. Lifting his face from the source, Townsend saw the disapproving look on the missionary's face and smiled broadly until the grotesque sight made the man of the cloth roar with laughter. But the missionary still did not follow the example, and Townsend said that he never again drank blood.

Somewhat later that summer in Idaho, Townsend had an encounter with a grizzly bear. He was with a group returning to camp in the soft evening light. A huge grizzly came snorting out of a willow thicket, scattering horses and riders in all directions. Mountain travelers customarily attacked any bear they saw, and this beast immediately felt the impact of several lead balls in various parts of its body. Each shot added to his fury, and the bear attacked the men one after the other, racing off in the direction of each new shot. Finally he was cornered and held at bay. Guns continued to crack, and the bear continued to flinch.

Then, the grizzly dashed for the river and tried to swim away to safety. But a better marksman, arriving late, leveled a shot into the bear's brain, and it died "instantly." Four men dragged it from the water, figuring its weight at six hundred pounds. The bear had been shot perhaps thirty times. Said Townsend, "There did not appear to be four inches of his shaggy person . . . that had not received a ball." Before the afternoon was over the hunter who delivered the fatal shot killed two more grizzlies.

By this time, another of America's early gun-carrying naturalists was becoming a legend. In time, he would become the best known of all frontier hunter-naturalists. His father, a French sea captain and owner of a plantation in Santo Domingo, had formed a liaison with a young Creole girl, who gave birth to a son, John James Audubon.

Young Audubon's father took him back to France, where his wife accepted the boy as if he were her own. As he grew, he spent increasing amounts of time in the outdoors watching birds, which his father, the captain and landholder, considered somewhat frivolous. One cannot fault a prominent man for wanting his son to amount to something or insisting that there was little future in chasing birds.

Audubon's father decided that his son would become a sailor. But at sea the lad was so often seasick that the French navy discharged him. There remained the probability that young Audubon would be drafted into Napoleon's army, and to help him avoid this fate his father bundled him off to America. He was eighteen when he arrived at his father's country estate in Pennsylvania.

In Pennsylvania, Audubon was free to roam the fields, hunting. He went fishing. He socialized and took full advantage of his training and skills as swimmer, horseman, dancer, musician, fencer, taxidermist, painter, and marksman. He also had an eye for pretty girls, particularly the neighbor's daughter, Lucy Bakewell. Audubon later married Lucy, and she stuck with him through more than most present-day wives would tolerate.

About the time of Audubon's marriage, his father's business failed. Young Audubon was on his own. Moving west to the Ohio Valley, he entered a partnership operating a mill in Hendersonville, Kentucky. His partner complained that Audubon was off hunting and chasing birds when he should have been tending to his grinding, instead. Audubon said that *his* partner spent too much time worrying about money. Audubon had a knack for getting away from problems. When things were troublesome at the mill, he would pick up his gun and go off to the woods, stalking birds either to eat or as models for his painting.

As a result, he failed in business. He was put in jail as a debtor. After declaring bankruptcy, he went to Cincinnati, where he found work as a taxidermist in the museum. But then the museum fell on bad times. Eventually Audubon and his little family drifted downstream to New Orleans. There, Lucy supported herself and their children by working as a governess and teacher, while Audubon occasionally earned money painting signs and portraits or teaching French and dancing.

All this time he continued to roam the forests. He had painted hundreds of birds and had begun to dream of going to Europe to have his pictures published. He and Lucy together saved enough money to pay for his trip. The journey abroad eventually led to the publication of his full-sized elephant portfolio containing what, in time, would become the world's best known bird pictures. Although

John James Audubon

Audubon barely survived on what he made from his pictures, one of his elephant portfolios on the market today might bring a million dollars.

The eccentric Audubon became highly popular in England. He did what he could to enhance his image as an American woodsman by walking the streets of London wearing his frontier clothes, including a wolfskin coat, while his long, wavy hair fell onto his shoulders.

Upon his return home, he spent several months traveling west into the Missouri River country. With the help of his son, John Woodhouse Audubon, he gathered specimens and made paintings for a new volume on mammals of North America. He was by then well acquainted with influential people both in the United States and Europe. But he still had not lost his interest in shooting nor tempered his compulsion to roam the wild places.

There were wild animals wherever he looked. One evening he shot five ducks and had wild duck and prairie chicken for his camp meal. The following day he wrote, "Saw three bighorns, some antelopes, and many deer, fully twenty; one wolf, twenty-two swans, many ducks." To top it off, he killed two fine bull elk. Another day he reported "wolves howling, and bulls roaring, just like the long continued roll of a hundred drums." Here he saw fresh sign of Indians as well as bear tracks, and "thousands upon thousands" of buffalo.

But his wild adventures were not limited to the raw frontier. His journals contain an account of a bear hunt he remembered in the Ohio Valley. He was staying the night with a friend when a messenger from a farm five miles distant arrived, saying that his boss had sent him for help. The bears had invaded his cornfield, and the crop was in jeopardy.

Guns, shot pouches, and powder horns were gathered, horses were saddled, and soon Audubon, his host, several farmhands, and a pack of hounds were racing through the dark, sultry night to rescue the neighbor's corn crop. The battle plan was to slip up to the field from various directions, then, on signal, rush into the field making maximum commotion. This was designed to send the startled bears up the dead trees which the settlers had girdled, and which stood like skeletons in the field among the corn stalks.

Horns, howling dogs, galloping horses, and shouting people brought a new dimension to the world of the peacefully feeding bears. As predicted, the bears climbed into the trees, and what followed would never earn high marks for sportsmanship.

First, two small bears were shot from the trees. "They were cubs of no great size, and being already half dead, we left them to the dogs, which quickly dispatched them." Another and larger bear was spotted in a different tree. This tree was cut down because, Audubon wrote, "we were anxious to procure as much sport as possible." The dogs would now "tug" the bear, while the shooters stood by to make sure that it could not escape. One cur grabbed it by the snout and hung on, but the bear threw all the dogs off. It then killed two dogs with its lightning-fast swats and turned on one nearby horseman, who was without a gun. It grabbed the terrified horse and hung on until the rider dispatched the bear by laying open its skull with his ax.

As dawn broke, two more cubs were found cowering in a tree. Brush was piled around the tree and set afire, turning the tree into what Audubon described as a "pillar of flame." The two cubs crashed to the ground where the dogs were encouraged to worry them to death. "The party," said Audubon, "returned to the house in triumph." Audubon's role may have been more observer than participant, but the vengeful and inhumane treatment of bears he observed was in keeping with the prejudices of the times, which made it acceptable not only to kill bears but also to torture them.

Typically, the hunter naturalist explored and hunted the wildest places he could find, and few chose more rugged country than Charles Sheldon did. Vermont born in 1867 and educated at Yale, Sheldon was a civil engineer. But in his thirties he gave up his business career to spend full time in the outdoors and headed for Alaska's craggy peaks, where the wild sheep live. There he climbed cliffs of loose rock, forded turbulent icy streams, and, as Dr. C. Hart Merriam, Chief of the Bureau of Biological Survey (now the U.S. Fish and Wildlife Service), once said, "risked his life a hundred times—day after day and week after week."

Sheldon, who was never guilty of bragging or given to loud talk, always claimed that he was a mediocre shot, but the evidence says otherwise. In the rugged Alaska Range, one of his assignments was to collect a group of impressive ram heads for display in the National Museum in Washington, D.C. On this day, he made his way carefully along a narrow cliff, following goat trails up the treacherous slopes of loose stone, with the Arctic world stretched out before him in silent splendor.

At last, he topped the ridge and spotted in the distance below him a band of old rams, fat and content in their high-country domain. Between hunter and rams lay two valleys and steep fields of loose stone that, if dislodged, would spook the whole band. If just one of the sheep saw him move, all would quickly disappear. Sheldon began his stalk and during an hour and a half of tense maneuvering eased steadily closer.

He reached the second canyon but was still three hundred yards from the sheep. Foot by foot he advanced, moving only when the rams had their heads down. Crawling forward, he chose carefully each spot he placed a knee or elbow. A golden eagle soaring overhead screamed. A marmot sounded its alarm. But the rams fed on.

At last Sheldon was close enough for a shot. He lay still for a few minutes allowing his nerves to settle. From a sitting position he squeezed off his first shot, and the ram fell. A quick second shot brought another ram down. At this, the confused creatures began running in various directions. In the next few minutes Sheldon had more good shots, and when it was over he had shot eight times and killed seven old rams.

By the time Sheldon got back to his camp that night, it was nearly midnight. He had been on the mountain since early morning, soaked to the skin from wading icy streams and staying out in the rain. But he paid little attention to personal comfort when hunting or studying wild game. The following day he spent more than sixteen hours working on the rams, skinning them, cleaning the skulls and skins, and packing them all, including the massive heavy horns, down to the foot of the slope to be shipped to the museum. Five of the seven had been shot through the heart.

Mt. McKinley's distant white snowfields held a magnetic attraction for Sheldon, and he spent much time mapping and studying that area and its mammals. His work eventually played a major role in having the area set aside as Mt. McKinley National Park, now Denali National Park, and a major Alaska tourist attraction, with grizzly bears, wolves, caribou, and ptarmigan protected along with their habitat.

Sheldon became a leading conservationist. He helped establish the Great Smoky Mountains National Park. He worked for stronger laws to protect waterfowl and other migratory birds. In the Boone and Crockett Club he was long-time chairman of the conservation committee. He was also a member of numerous professional scientific associations.

The hunting naturalists have been keen observers and careful reporters. They introduced the world to everything from grizzly bears and pronghorns to delicate prairie flowers. And through their understanding of natural systems and their writings and teaching, they awakened respect for American wildlife and the animals that people hunt. Their works encouraged hunter and nonhunter alike to become conservationists, and their influence in saving wildlands and wildlife is beyond measure.

8

Thunder on the Plains

On a typical day's hunt, buffalo runner Frank Mayer would be out on the range at first light, creeping up on a herd of buffalo. His horse was tied somewhere half a mile away, while he made his cautious approach, first on foot and finally on elbows and knees.

The way Mayer figured it, three hundred yards was close enough to make killing shots without worrying about the noise of his gun spooking the herd. Once in position, he waited until the beasts had grazed on the lush grass and settled down to rest. Then, when at least some of the animals had lain down and none seemed to suspect danger, he went to work. Some hunters in the early days of the hide business ran the buffalo on horseback instead of shooting from a stand, but that scattered the animals across the plains and reduced the kill.

Mayer positioned a pair of hickory sticks to form a shallow V that supported his "Buffalo" Sharps. He studied the band of buffalo carefully and picked out the cow that was the leader. Drop her first and the others would likely mill about aimlessly as he shot them one by one.

Mayer had already determined the direction of the wind by dropping a blade of grass or a feather and watching it settle. He elevated the gun to compensate for the distance and squeezed off his first shot of the day.

A group of buffalo runners. These professional hunters rode into the West in the early 1870s and shot buffalo for the eastern markets. So efficient were they that within a dozen years the herds had almost vanished from the western prairies, leaving room for domestic cattle.

With that first sharp crack of the rifle, the lead cow jerked up her head and maybe ran a few steps. Mayer knew that a heart shot might send her dashing off three or four hundred yards before she fell, setting the whole herd to running and leaving no choice but to start all over and set himself up in another position. So, just as he had intended, he shot her through the lungs.

Mayer watched carefully. If another member of the herd moved toward the edge of the group, she was next. In the following minutes the sound of his Sharps continued to resound across the plains, as one after the other the giant buffalo fell.

Like most buffalo runners, Mayer aimed to get his killing done early, giving his skinners time to finish their heavy work by day's end. If possible, he simplified their work by killing all his animals within a small area. When all went well, he would shoot every member of a band of up to fifty or so head, which was as many as his team of skinners could handle in a day.

He was among the most skilled shooters in the business, but there were other famous marksmen, and stories of their best scores spread rapidly. Buffalo runners far and wide knew of Tom Nixon's record day when he killed two hundred and four buffalo from one stand. It was said that Brick Bond killed two hundred and fifty buffalo from one stand. But perhaps none ever equaled Nixon's record of a hundred and twenty buffalo killed in forty minutes. These market hunters took pride in the number of animals they could kill without a miss. One "buff runner" killed a whole band of fifty-four animals with fifty-four shots.

These, and a long list of less skilled shooters, were the gunners working the buffalo range in the early 1870s. They were a rough and bloody lot, sweeping westward to get in on the big kill while the market was right and the buffalo were there for the taking. They became a major factor in clearing the range of wildlife and leaving it for the use of domestic cattle.

By then, buffalo runners had excellent breechloaders for their work. Some preferred the Remington Buffalo Rifle, which came onto the scene at the peak of the buffalo-hide business in 1872 and was manufactured until 1890 in miscellaneous calibers. The 44–90 cartridge with a 400 grain bullet was a favorite. Others, like Frank Mayer, swore by the .45 caliber "Buffalo" Sharps. Mayer estimated that 120 grains of powder in this gun gave the 550 grain slug a muzzle velocity of about 1,400 feet per second.

The earliest white men arriving on the eastern seaboard soon discovered buffalo, or more properly, bison. Together, the plains bison and its cousin, the wood bison, had spread from Canada's Northwest Territories south into Mexico and from eastern Oregon as far east as New York State, Virginia, and the Carolinas. Across the heart of the continent these wild cattle flourished in unbelievable numbers.

Among the early travelers who actually saw the herds stretching

The .45 caliber Sharps rifle was favored by many buffalo runners. Invented by Christian Sharps, a mechanic once employed at the Harpers Ferry Arsenal, it was the most successful breechloading rifle of the time. Early Sharps rifles used cartridges with paper or linen cases; when metallic cartridges were invented, the action was modified to accept them. Union troops were issued Sharps rifles during the Civil War.

off to the horizon like a dark blanket drawn across the grasslands was naturalist and hunter John Kirk Townsend. As part of the Wyeth expedition up the Missouri in 1834, Townsend recorded the sight in the valley of the Platte River: "Towards evening, on a rising hill, we were suddenly greeted by a sight which seemed to astonish even the oldest among us. The whole plain, as far as the eye could discern, was covered by one enormous mass of buffalo." Townsend figured that the herd stretched solidly over an area at least ten miles long by eight miles wide. The group made camp, and its hunters soon brought in "the choice parts of five that they had killed."

One hunter was rebuffed when he suggested that his companion share the animal he had shot. Going off in a tiff to find his own meat, he promptly came upon a little herd of seven bulls. He slipped up close to them, using the gullies as cover until in good position, then began to shoot. He shot them one after the other until all seven lay on the ground, then rode back to camp with the tongues hanging on his saddle horn "as testimony of his skill."

Nowhere else in the world, including Africa, had men ever seen such concentrations of a single large species of wild animal. Travelers reported seeing loosely assembled herds that took several days to pass and stretched on for fifty miles. Such herds were believed to total in the millions. Early steamboats on western rivers were sometimes caught in the midst of crossing buffalo herds and locked in place for hours until the beasts had passed. After the railroads came, the herds sometimes massed on the tracks, bringing locomotives to a halt.

Figures of the total number of buffalo inhabiting the continent must remain imprecise, because they can be no more than estimates. Tom McHugh, author of *The Time of the Buffalo*, computed, after careful investigation, that there were as many as thirty million of them. Others have estimated a number twice that, or even more. Whatever the figure, McHugh concluded, "buffalo wandered across the land in astonishing multitudes."

The giant herds were no more remarkable than was the individual animal viewed close-up. The buffalo is a massive creature. An adult bull, ten feet long and six feet high at the shoulders, commonly weighs eighteen hundred pounds, but sometimes a ton or more. His massive shoulders form a hump, and his back slopes downward. The broad head is draped in shaggy, dark hair. Although not blessed with the lithe form of the antelope or the streamlined shape of the deer, a buffalo is capable of propelling its huge body across

Buffalo hunters at work were caught by Remington in this fine drawing. Behind them are the prairie schooners they lived in for months at a time.

An 1874 magazine cover registered a critical comment on buffalo hunting. Entitled
"Slaughtered for the Hide," the drawing was a stark reminder to eastern readers of the
bloody business of market hunting that provided them with meat and warm robes.

the plains at enormous speed. The man on foot should never make the mistake of thinking he can outrun one of these beasts. People have been gored and trampled for that mistake. Only the swiftest buffalo ponies can bring a rider abreast of a hard-running buffalo.

Stampeding buffalo were a deadly hazard faced by early western travelers. Thousands of frantic animals, pushing the leading ranks forward, could trample wagons, cattle, men, and horses beneath their thundering hooves. Major Richard Irving Dodge, speaking of the stampede that threatened him, wrote, "There poured down upon me . . . one immense compact mass of plunging animals, mad with fright and as irresistible as an avalanche."

Sometimes the lead animals could be shot and used as shelter for the threatened men, perhaps causing the herd to split and flow around the island of people and horses in their path.

One tenderfoot hunter who had ventured west from Ironton, Ohio, to work in the buffalo-killing business reported to his home-town newspaper on how it felt to be caught in a stampede. He was creeping up on a small group of animals to get into shooting posi-tion when, "Hark, a roar in the distance like a terrific storm. The noise of their hooves is something fearful. They rush upon the herd I hoped to destroy. On they come. I realize my critical position."

He leaped to his feet, dashed off toward a small tree a hundred yards distant, and scaled it "with the dexterity of a squirrel. They soon are under me and on all sides of me, going with a noise like thunder." He had dropped his gun in the rush for the tree but now remembered his revolver and "managed to empty it among the panic stricken buffaloes, killing one old shaggy-headed bull. How many I wounded I am at a loss to say."

He was walking over the field surveying the scene of recent events proudly when, in the distance, he saw his companion rolling on the ground in fits of laughter. The jokester had stampeded the herd purposely to see how the newcomer would manage his escape.

These sprawling herds of grass-eaters replenished their numbers each spring with countless little reddish-brown calves, and the an-nual increase was more than sufficient to feed the Indians, as well as the wolves and other predators dependent on them. Even after the Indians acquired horses from early Spanish explorers and became as skilled as any mounted hunters in the world, the great herds withstood the added drain on their numbers.

Then came the white invaders who, from the beginning, spelled

THE STILL HUNT by James Henry Moser (undated). This painting gives us some idea of the huge herds of buffalo that darkened the plains in the 19th century. Stampeding buffalo posed such a hazard for hunters on horseback that often they shot from cover to avoid spooking the herd, and used a rest to make every round count.

disaster for the American bison. The white man first encountered the buffalo in Texas in 1533, when Cabeza de Vaca saw on the plains "oxen with little horns and long hair." Seven years later Coronado, who marched all the way to Kansas in his fabled search for the Seven Golden Cities of Cibola, found buffalo in large num-

bers. His troops killed eighty of the animals in their first encounter, thereby setting a pattern that would continue as long as the great herds lasted.

The earliest white hunters and settlers found in the buffalo an animal offering abundant meat as fine as the best cattle, and all belonging to those who could take them. But by the early 1800s the buffalo were gone, or nearly so, from the eastern states as well as the Ohio Valley.

Early western travelers scarcely made a dent in the supply. Lewis and Clark, and soon the beaver-trapping mountain men, figured nothing was better than fat cow, and if you had to eat it three times a day, things could still be worse. There followed the soldiers moving west to subdue the Indians, and the army had hunters to bring in more buffalo. Still the grand herds withstood the pressure.

F inally the railroads pushed their steel ribbons deep into the very heart of the buffalo country, which was the beginning of the final chapter for the giant wild cattle. The railroads sent their agents eastward, and even to Europe, drumming up trade and telling about the unbelievable buffalo herds to be found where their new tracks ran. As the buffalo-shooting fever grew, railroads, hungering for business, organized expeditions into the plains from St. Louis, Kansas City, and other cities. They promised their riders the once-in-a-lifetime opportunity to shoot a buffalo. Furthermore, a man need not even get dust on his walking shoes to make his kill.

The trains rolled west, and in due time the distant black specks on the plains grew into buffalo. Soon the cars were surrounded by the beasts crossing the tracks, or running along beside the noisy smoky train, and the dudes shot until their ammunition was gone. Sometimes they had time to recover a tail or some other trophy for a souvenir, but usually not. They left the remains for the fattening wolves, coyotes, and ravens.

The railroad construction companies also had their professional buffalo hunters supplying meat for their workers. Among the more famous of these meat hunters was William Frederick Cody, a tall handsome man of slender build, with hair that fell in ringlets to his shoulders, a mustache, and a trim goatee.

Railroads often organized hunting expeditions for eastern dudes who wanted the thrill of downing a buffalo. They didn't even have to muddy their shoes, but shot from the train's roof and windows until their ammunition was gone.

Born in Iowa, he moved with his family to Kansas Territory as soon as it was opened to settlement in 1854. In due time young William tried various kinds of employment, including riding for the Pony Express and serving the Union cause in the Kansas cavalry. He might not have joined the army had he not one afternoon, as was his frequent custom, drunk himself into a stupor. When he sobered up, he remembered nothing of what had transpired during those previous hours and was mighty surprised to find that he had enlisted. But, having taken the big step, he decided that the honorable thing to do was make the most of it.

Later, he drifted from one job to the other and eventually moved west, where he began his buffalo killing career, supplying meat for Union Pacific construction crews. So successful was he at this work that the railroad workers began saying, "Here comes Buffalo Bill." From the beginning, Bill figured that the name had a nice ring to it, and he lived up to it by shooting fantastic numbers of buffalo.

Next came service as a scout for General Phil Sheridan, whose troopers were fighting Indians. In the Texas panhandle, during the winter of 1868–1869, Cody's superiors dispatched him to gather meat for the troops. With him went twenty empty wagons and assorted enlisted men to bring back the meat. On one occasion, Cody stampeded the herd directly into a box canyon. His two-day score stood at ninety-six, and after a couple of days of butchering the heavily loaded wagons headed back to camp.

Before long, famous visitors coming west to sample the buffalo hunting were asking specifically for the guide services of Buffalo Bill Cody, and Bill loved the spotlight. A writer of the time made the popular hunting guide the hero of a dime novel adventure story. The story was then dramatized, and Cody played himself in the production. This was his introduction to public appearances, and he gravitated easily into producing his own show—"Buffalo Bill's Wild West." The show further publicized the killing of buffalo. As the dashing Cody rode at full gallop onto the scene, shooting glass balls from the air, not with a shotgun but with his rifle, he brought the crowds to their feet.

Understandably, when General Sheridan entertained a dozen or so prominent newspaper editors and other notables on a buffalo hunt in 1871, he wanted Cody along. The visiting hunters were much impressed with Buffalo Bill, who, wearing a crimson shirt, a suit of light buckskin with fringe, and a broad-brimmed hat, rode out on a galloping snow-white horse to assume leadership.

In ten days, under Cody's influence, this party killed more than six hundred buffalo and two hundred elk. Had they waited a couple of years longer, their hunt could not have been as successful because the downfall of the great plains buffalo came with terrible swiftness.

Until 1871, limited technology held down demand for the animals. The meat, mostly tongues and hind quarters, was shipped east by railroad. The heavy robes were sold for use in carriages and sleighs. But tanners had never perfected a system for treating these

William "Buffalo Bill" Cody

heavy skins to make them into useful leather. Then a German tanner worked out such a successful system that the demand for buffalo skins skyrocketed. The leather found a ready market for making belting, seats for carriages, and various other goods.

The ensuing demand for buffalo hides ushered in a gold-rush

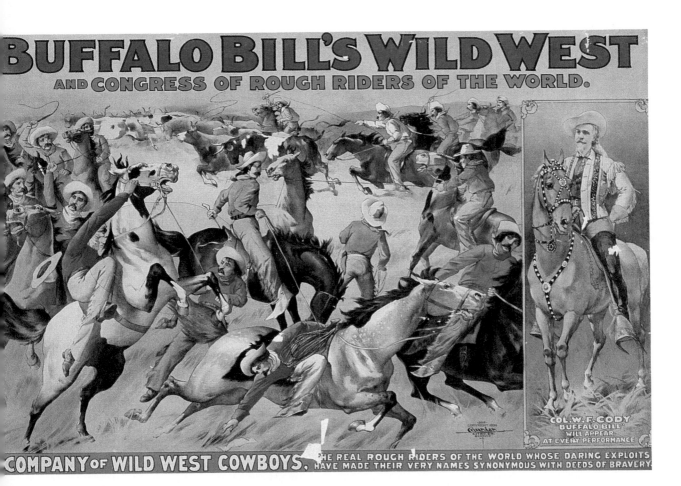

A poster for Buffalo Bill's Wild West Show. Cody would amaze crowds with his marksmanship by shooting glass balls in the air—with a rifle.

atmosphere. The buffalo shooters fanned out across the country, seeking what remained of the great herds. Instead of running the buffalo down on horseback, Frank Mayer and other buffalo runners soon learned to shoot from a stand. As the few aging beaver trappers must have said, "They made the buffer come they did."

Once the shooter had done his day's work, his skinners began removing the hides. This was heavy work, and sometimes it was aided by a team of horses helping to strip the hides from the carcasses. The hides were stretched out in the sun, hair side down, and staked in place so sun and wind could dry them flint hard.

Then, they were bundled and loaded on wagons to be hauled to the train depot, ready for transporting to the eastern tanneries and factories.

After half a dozen years the giant herds were almost gone. The buffalo had vanished throughout the West, making room for domestic cattle and the ranchers who owned them. The army was pleased to see the buffalo go. With their age-old source of food gone, the Plains Indians were pauperized and could now be easily herded onto miserable reservations.

Out on the sunbaked plains there remained only the buffalo bones and the horns, and these too soon found a commercial market. The horns could be made into glue, the bones used either for fertilizer or processing refined sugar. Destitute families fanned out from their sod homes, gathering the bleaching bones and moving them off to be piled high beside the railroads.

Ravens, wolves, the forces of putrefaction, and the human bone pickers soon cleaned up the remnants. Soon the only evidence that the remarkable American bison had ever walked over the plains were, here and there, a rutted trail, where generations of the beasts had walked, a wallow, where they had rolled in the mud to soothe itchings and control the insects, or a huge field boulder rubbed smooth as they walked around and around it, scratching their heavily furred bodies. The buffalo was nearing extinction. Poachers were shooting the last of them to sell the heads to taxidermists and collectors.

At the last moment, enough survivors were brought together to stock the Wichita Mountains wildlife area in Oklahoma. A couple of dozen or so had been saved in Yellowstone. To the north a few hundred still remained in Canada's Wood Buffalo National Park.

Today there are again perhaps as many buffalo as this world has room for. Nearly all are in fenced areas. The exceptions are in Wood Buffalo National Park and in Yellowstone. It is often written that the Yellowstone buffalo are the only wild, free-roaming buffalo left in this country. How free these animals are to roam is questionable, because the land beyond the park boundaries belongs to cattle and sheep.

But if it makes us feel better, let us call them "free roaming"— all eight hundred of them.

9

A Proper Adventure

As word spread abroad that the North American frontier harbored spectacular numbers of large wild animals, foreign sportsmen, often of noble birth, arrived to test themselves against the wilderness. In the American West they could have once-in-a-lifetime adventures mingling with bison, grizzly bears, and honest-to-god Indians. The idea held obvious appeal. On an American safari the wealthy foreigner could escape the boredom and idleness of his daily life. He could buy excitement and, if he chose, surround himself with comfort as well. He could shoot as many animals as he chose, with little concern for any restrictions imposed by law, custom, or common sense. Quite simply, in the 1880s, America's West offered as exciting an adventure as the world's outdoorsmen were going to find. The success stories of foreign noblemen coming here to shoot buffalo, or whatever other animals they met, fed the legend.

Prominent among the earliest European visitors on the western plains was Captain William Drummond Stewart. Beginning in 1833, he spent six years traveling and living with the beaver trappers in the most remote valleys of the West. Each summer he joined them in their wild, free-wheeling rendezvous, visiting with the Indians and mountain men and studying their ways. He braved the mountain weather, fought the Indians, and took Indian women, as did his beaver-trapping companions.

The grubby mountain man in his dingy buckskins might snicker at Stewart's fancy Panama hat and white jacket, but when he saw the Englishman ride and shoot he soon gained respect for this foreigner's outdoor skills. Sir William later wrote of his adventures, and although he cast his story as fiction he and others are easily identified. His book, *Edward Warren*, tells us much about what the mountain men said and how they lived and hunted.

Stewart grew up in the family manor in Perthshire, Scotland, where he was the second-born of five children. This accident of birth made him the victim of the rule of primogeniture, which passed the family estate to the eldest living son, leaving Sir William shy of responsibility as well as limited of funds. After a reluctant marriage to a servant girl he had pursued too successfully, he decided to escape to America to see the West.

After half a dozen years among the fur trappers, Stewart returned to Scotland to take care of family business. But he was hooked on the West. He could not get the grand, sweeping landscapes out of his mind or forget the wild animals and wild-spirited people he had found there. He decided to return for one last hurrah. In 1843 he arrived again in St. Louis. There he arranged for his friend William L. Sublette, a seasoned trapper and brigade leader, to lead his eight-man party of greenhorns into the wilds. Bill Sublette was an excellent choice, and with the beaver-trapping industry now winding down he was available for Stewart's adventure. Also included at Stewart's invitation was Alfred Jacob Miller, whose paintings made on that journey offer us a unique view of the western scene at the time.

By this time, the death of Sir William's brother had made him head of the family and far wealthier than he had ever been. He gave up the grubby life of the common mountain man and decided to live more in the tradition of the titled European. With him when he departed St. Louis were his servants, whose work included erecting his special tent with its carpeted floor and arranging the smooth linen sheets between Sir William's buffalo robes.

Buffalo were still so abundant upon the plains that members of the party could shoot as many as they chose and more than they needed. One day they saw an approaching herd, estimated at a million or more animals. The mass of huge dark bovines threatened to trample them into the Platte River. Stewart and his party managed to turn the leading animals aside and escape, but the herd needed two full days and nights to pass. Eleven years after his first

ROASTING THE HUMP RIB by Alfred Jacob Miller (1837). A New Orleans portrait painter, Miller accompanied W.D. Stewart on his western hunting trip and painted many pictures of the daily lives of the mountain men. Here two trappers are preparing to dine on their favorite meat, "fat cow."

venture into the western mountains, Sir William sailed back to Scotland for the last time.

Stewart had established himself as the forerunner of a long list of European noblemen to cross the ocean and travel inland to sample fabulous hunting. In northern Ireland, in County Donegal, Sir George Gore, then in his early forties, heard stories of chasing buffalo on the American plains, and the very thought of such adventure made him restless with desire. Furthermore, Sir George was blessed with the combination of wealth and idleness that allowed him to go to America and shoot buffalo if he pleased. He had precious little to keep him occupied, and earnings from his estates brought him a tidy annual income of $200,000 or so in an age when that amount of money went a long way. Because he was single, he could leave the castle when he pleased and absent himself as long as he liked. So Sir George, the titled nobleman who had been a pampered only son and Oxford educated, began arranging for what would become perhaps the most outlandish hunting safari ever to parade across the western grasslands and into the mountains.

By the time he reached St. Louis, Gore had a lengthy shopping list for his assistants to assemble. That year of 1854, Gore's wagon train moving up the valley of the Missouri River was the talk of the countryside. "I tell you, hoss, that's some, that is." Folks watching the safari wind out of sight allowed as how they had never before seen its equal. Sir George rode at the head of the column on a splendid Kentucky thoroughbred that he called "Steel Trap." Stretched out behind him were twenty-one carts, each drawn by a two-horse team of specially selected horses, four large wagons drawn by six-mule teams, and two more wagons, each powered by three yolk of oxen. Plugging along with the convoy were three cows to provide milk.

The party included forty people, counting Sir George's servants, gun bearers, teamsters, guides, and the dog handler who had come along to care for the fifty hunting dogs. Most of these canines were finely bred staghounds and greyhounds, brought from Ireland to run wolves, coyotes, and pronghorn antelope across the American grasslands. The shooters were ready for anything from grizzly bears to prairie chickens. One of the wagons was designated as the armory, and stored in it were guns ranging from pistols to a new Sharps breechloader, along with some seventy-five muzzle-loading rifles and twelve shotguns.

Everything was first class. Sir George was not some grubby fur trapper ready to live off the land or bed on the hard earth at night. The first night the outfit made camp, his companions watched in wonder as servants set up his special green and white striped tent, spread a plush rug over its floor, assembled the portable brass bed in which the master slept, then placed an iron stand beside the bed to hold Sir George's fine imported wines and his favorite copies of Shakespeare and Baron von Munchhausen.

If the weather was unfit for comfortable tenting, Sir George took lodging in his special wagon. Equipped with a canvas top that stretched over the wagon bed when a crank was turned, it was perhaps the first RV in the West.

Unlike most who traveled the West, Sir George was not an early riser. There was no "crack of dawn" foolishness. He arose along toward midmorning, had his breakfast, then relaxed until about noon, when he would set off hunting. Once on the trail of game, however, he hunted hard and might not come back until ten o'clock in the evening. Gore shot from a standing position, using a crossed stick gun rest. His gun bearer made it ready, then stood by with a second gun.

The safari got under way in June. The line of wagons, carts, livestock, and dogs stretched out along the route leading up the North Platte to Fort Laramie. There was still time to move on to a summer hunt on the slopes of the Colorado Rockies. In that enchanted setting, where the peaks provide a backdrop for rolling, sage-covered hills, Gore and his party found abundant game to shoot. There were elk, antelope, deer, and now and then a bighorn sheep. If he tired of shooting, he could fish for trout in sparkling mountain streams.

Before the winter, Gore's party was back at Fort Laramie to settle in for the cold months. There Gore met Jim Bridger, the pioneering fur trapper whose capabilities in the wilderness had become legendary. His photographic memory carried a wealth of information about western geography. He knew the streams and their branches and the tributaries large and small. He understood the weather, the Indians, and the wildlife, and he knew the mountain passes. There probably was no better guide a greenhorn could hire than "Old Gabe," and it is not surprising that Gore wanted to sign on Bridger to lead his group into the mountains. Bridger didn't see anything wrong with the idea, either. "Warn't doing much nohow, and this will be a site easier than fightin' bars and Injuns the way we use ter."

Bridger traveled with Gore for the next year and a half, leading him back to old trapping grounds through Colorado, Wyoming, Montana, and the Dakotas. As the party plodded along through the hills, Gore seemed never to tire of the hunting. He continued to take trophies, shooting hundreds of animals. The Indians viewed this excessive killing of game with long, sour faces. Officials all the way back to Washington began to hear of the discontent with Gore's unlimited killing.

But the safari continued for three and a half years before Gore eventually decided that he had accomplished whatever it was he had set out to do. He worked his way back to Fort Union, where the Yellowstone River empties into the Missouri. There he disbanded his outfit and sold off his horses, cattle, and other property. When the ice went out, and the river opened up again in the spring of 1857, Gore started back downstream for St. Louis. His odyssey was over. He had seen the American West, lived his comfortable version of the frontier life to the hilt, and collected memories enough to last the remainder of his life.

Intertwined in those memories were visions of the animals he had killed. He had taken more than any man should rightfully expect to kill in a single lifetime, even in those days. He admitted to personally shooting more than two thousand buffalo, sixteen hundred deer and elk, and a hundred and five bears, as well as uncounted antelopes, wolves, coyotes, prairie chickens, and other animals. William F. "Buffalo Bill" Cody, who knew him, once wrote that Gore was popular among those traveling with him, and that "he spent money with extraordinary freedom in the gratification of his passion."

It is only fair that we look at this unrestricted killing of game in the framework of the times. Those were the days when a one-ton buffalo was killed and left to rot because someone wanted its tongue. But whatever the times and customs, or the condition of the herds, Gore's two thousand buffalo meant perhaps a million and a half pounds of meat. His exercise was a gluttonous display of excessive killing of wild animals, simply because they were there. (Few people had yet seen the need to restrict their taking.) One wonders if the thought ever occurred to Sir George Gore, as he sat in solid comfort sipping his drink and admiring the western mountains, that he might have been indulging himself excessively in all that killing of North American game.

In the fall of 1871, official Washington was atwitter over the approaching visit of Grand Duke Alexis, one of Russia's legendary Romanoffs. Alexis nurtured no dreams of shooting long lists of game in the Gore tradition. But the promise of bringing down a genuine American buffalo excited him.

His adventure was set in motion when General Phil Sheridan was asked to make the arrangements and escort Alexis westward to the land of the buffalo. Sheridan, who was accustomed to getting things done upon command, knew exactly the person to show the Russian nobleman the proper American hospitality. He dispatched a message to "Buffalo Bill" Cody in Nebraska asking him to put Alexis within reasonable range of a buffalo. With more than four thousand buffalo to his credit, Cody, the professional meat hunter, seemed just the person to accomplish the task.

Grand Duke Alexis of Russia (right) posed for a studio photo with General George Armstrong Custer before setting out from St. Louis to hunt buffalo and other game on the western plains.

THE GREAT ROYAL BUFFALO HUNT by Louis Maurer (1894). This painting shows Grand Duke Alexis galloping into a buffalo herd armed only with a pistol, with Buffalo Bill Cody riding nearby. Unable to hit anything with his pistol, Alexis finally brought down a buffalo with Cody's rifle.

Cody had extensive help in preparing for the grand hunt. Everyone from President Ulysses S. Grant to the common soldier and average citizen seemed to want all to go smoothly for Alexis. The Grand Duke, along with assorted Russian diplomats, arrived in St. Louis and from there moved on to North Platte, Nebraska, in a special train. In addition to the luxurious sleeping cars and a diner, there was a supply car carrying meat and fowl, eggs and butter, gin, bourbon, and champagne. Also aboard was the flamboyant General George A. Custer, age thirty-two, already known for his long, blond curls and beautifully fringed buckskins.

At North Platte the expedition changed from the train to a long line of wagons. Behind the wagon bearing Grand Duke Alexis and, from time to time, his companions General Custer and General Sheridan stretched a parade of several hundred people, among them entire companies of soldiers, a military band, and assorted Indians.

Soon the party leaders began to spot the great shaggy forms of grazing buffalo on the distant plains, and all was made ready for the Grand Duke to experience, for the first time, the atavistic satisfaction of bringing one of these famous beasts to the ground. At this point Buffalo Bill took charge. The Grand Duke was riding a special horse, fully trained for running buffalo. His mount carried the dignitary to within twenty feet or so of a fine bull, as Alexis bounced over the prairie firing in the bull's general direction with his pistol. After listening to half a dozen shots from the royal weapon, Cody could plainly see that the Grand Duke's handgun was unlikely to bring down the bull, which was now lumbering off in the distance.

The Grand Duke kept shooting at other bison with similar results until Cody, in desperation, rode in at full gallop and handed him his own favorite buffalo rifle, a .50 caliber Springfield. Cody yelled to the Grand Duke to ride in close and not shoot until he gave him the word. Whereupon Cody whacked the Grand Duke's horse with his quirt, and the horse, knowing the drill, swiftly carried Alexis to within ten feet or so of a fine, large bull racing over the plains under

One cartoonist's humorous view of the royal hunt. Alexis is portrayed as a gangling and inept hunter who couldn't even hold a rifle properly and was chased by his quarry. Finally (lower right), the duke and his companions take a vow to keep their bungling a secret.

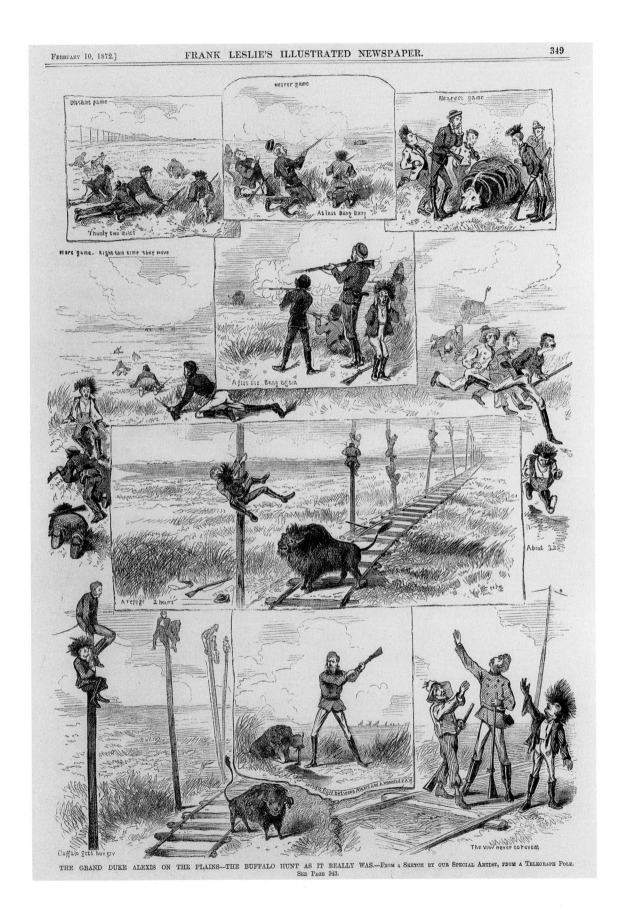

THE GRAND DUKE ALEXIS ON THE PLAINS—THE BUFFALO HUNT AS IT REALLY WAS.—FROM A SKETCH BY OUR SPECIAL ARTIST, FROM A TELEGRAPH POLE.
SEE PAGE 343.

a full head of steam. "Now," yelled Cody, and the Grand Duke fired point blank at the broad, hairy side of the beast. The bull came tumbling to earth, thereby setting off a round of jubilation that amazed Cody and the accompanying Indians.

The Grand Duke brought his horse to a dusty, skidding halt and leaped from the saddle, cheering wildly in his excitement. He dropped his gun, drew his knife, and cut off the bull's tail. Then, waving his trophy overhead and yelling all the while, he called for his servants, who came rushing forward with a case of champagne. The Russians, shouting congratulations in their native tongue, danced, hugged each other, and spilled copious amounts of champagne onto and into themselves.

Later in the day, Alexis repeated the performance by bringing down a cow, and the servants once again rushed forward with champagne, which, appropriate or not, added an air of gaiety to the whole adventure. By the time the hunt ended and the soldiers and Indians rode off into the sunset, Alexis had killed another half-dozen buffalo. He had killed a fair share of the entire party's fifty-six animals, but his toll could scarcely match that of Sir George Gore.

Buffalo Bill also remembered Sir John Watts Garland, another English sportsman who arrived around 1869. Sir John alternated his hunting between the American West and Africa, where he pursued lions and elephants. "At different points on the plains and in the mountains," wrote Cody, "he established camps and built cabins, to which he would return regularly about once every two years. In his absence, his horses and dogs were left at these camps, in charge of men employed for that purpose."

Sir John was especially fond of hunting elk in the wild manner then common. "Elk were hunted in much the same way as buffalo, the perfection of the sport being found in the saddle," said Cody. Typically, half a dozen elk hunters would ride out at dawn on their fastest horses. Eventually they would spot a herd of elk, "two or three hundred perhaps," and begin moving in on them. When they were still half a mile or so distant, the elk would "give a mighty snort and dash away after their leader." If horses and riders performed well, they could eventually race in among the panic-stricken elk. Then, dropping the reins, the hunters shot with their .50 caliber Springfield breechloading military rifles. The shooting was restricted to the master of the hunt and his guests, while lesser members of the party amused themselves lassoing the young elk so they could be taken back to camp alive.

Like that of Grand Duke Alexis, the party of another noble-man who hunted with Cody had its own military escort. This was not uncommon. The U.S. Army post in the region to be hunted frequently assigned escorts to these visiting parties and might send along wagons to haul the meat back to camp. Lord Adair, who became the Earl of Dunraven, arrived in 1869 at Fort McPhearson on the Platte River. His party, with its soldier escort, made various forays, staying in the field for several weeks at a time, then returning to the post, re-outfitting, and heading out again for bear, buffalo, and elk. Lord Adair may be best remembered for having purchased his own "hunting park." This enchanted area, spreading over a hundred thousand acres or so, lay north of Denver and is today known as Estes Park.

The pioneering outdoor publication, *Forest and Stream*, in 1874 told of organizing the hunt that might have become the grandest yet, larger even than Sir George Gore's extravaganza. This one was spawned in the mind of an American sportsman, Colonel W. C. McCarty, then described as "a gentleman whose experience as a soldier and huntsman extends over three continents." The Colonel, who had fought with Maximilian's forces in Mexico, joined France in the Franco-Prussian conflict and then traveled in Egypt. He finally returned to the United States, where he worked for the U.S. Bureau of Mines and Mining. That was the job he resigned so he could devote full attention to organizing his grand hunt.

While overseas, the Colonel had discussed over many a social drink the splendid shooting available on the western frontier. The enthusiasm his stories generated convinced him that he could as-semble an impressive list of wealthy sportsmen eager to spend large amounts for "the purpose of chasing the wild animals so numerous in the West and Southwest, and dallying among the game fishes so abundant in many portions of the country," said *Forest and Stream*.

As the scheme ripened, Colonel McCarty planned a guest list that would include one hundred European gentlemen, plus their servants, dogs, and horses. After sightseeing in New York and Chi-cago, they would be off to Dallas, where their ranks would be reinforced by a hundred Texas Rangers, who promised to stay with them throughout the hunt, and some sixty Comanches. The Indians' role would be to drive big-game animals toward the hunters during the day, then as evening came on to amuse the hunters with demonstrations of their native dances.

In making his plans, the Colonel overlooked few, if any, wild species that might enliven the chase. As reported by *Forest and Stream*, the party would invade north Texas to chase deer and antelope before the hounds and learn how this sport might compare with the stag hunts of England and Ireland. Once they sated their appetites for this brand of hunting, the sports would "take dashes after the shaggy buffalo . . . engage bruin . . . beard the cougar in his leafy retreat, pursue the gaunt wolf over hill and dale, or take a run after reynard to the wild music of a pack of hounds. The jackrabbit will also afford sport as it will be chased by greyhounds. . . ." Nor was wing shooting neglected in the plans. Shotguns would be carried along for the taking of wild turkeys, quail, prairie chickens, and ruffed grouse, or whatever else flew and attracted their attention.

By the end of summer the party would move on to Kansas for fall hunting, then to the Great Lakes for whatever hunting and fishing it could find, after which the sports would make their way back east and off to England, warmed by memories of a grand adventure that lasted half a year.

McCarty knew that an enterprise of this magnitude called for meticulous planning. He scurried about engaging the finest cooks he could find, arranging for quality horses and completely stocked wagons of provisions, solid and liquid. We are told with a dash of sarcasm that "to drive care away, a full brass and string band will accompany the expedition, so that when the weary hunters return from the chase, their fatigue may be banished by the dulcet notes of sensuous music."

If all went well, the Colonel expected to see stretched out across the prairies the grandest hunt ever staged in America—thirty wagons, ten ambulances, a hundred and sixty horses, and some two hundred and fifty men.

As word of the approaching "Big Hunt" spread, some American sportsmen expressed their opinions of the hunt and its organizer. For some it inspired expletives. Samuel A. Mead, Jr., of Fort Sill, Oklahoma, wrote to say that the Colonel appeared to know little about either the game or the country he proposed to hunt. As for the summer hunt in Texas, Mead said, they might as well go to Cape

Cod and predicted that any visiting Englishman trudging through the hundred-degree heat would "dig his grave in the bottom of Red River." As for the Colonel's assurance that there would be golden plover in countless thousands, Mead remarked inelegantly, "I say stuff."

While there can be no doubt that the "Big Hunt" was seriously planned and seriously considered by numerous sportsmen who dreamed of collecting their own trophy buffalo, the whole project began to fade away as summer came on. *Forest and Stream*, which had been so enthusiastic in the beginning, began taking steps to distance itself from the whole scheme. There were hints that Col. McCarty was considered by some to be of shady character. Had the Big Hunt taken place the literature of the day would surely have recorded the adventure and the results. But all mention of it dies out, and we must assume that the plan finally came apart. However, as the very concept of such a hunt testifies, America's abundant wildlife in the 1800s could inspire grandiose plans. The shooting of western game, especially buffalo, had become a dream adventure for sportsmen from distant lands.

10

New Deal for Ducks

Delbert "Cigar" Daisy, white haired and friendly, sits in his little green shop at the edge of the water, carving a new decoy while telling a visitor why he has changed his ways and become one of the good guys. "I used to think of ducks as God's given bounty," he says in his Outer Banks accent. "They were there, and we took as many as we wanted and didn't moind about the laws." His hatchet comes down on the block of white cedar, the chips fly, and the duck gradually takes shape.

"Moi people come here long time ago," he explains. "First come 'Old Man Dave of All,' they called him. He come down the beach on a horse and settled on Assateague. They had dirt floors. Lived totally off the land, hunting, fishing, and trapping. They took oysters, clams, and what have you. It was their loivelihood."

These scattered families of watermen on Virginia's eastern shore drew on the bounty of the tidal basins. There were clams and fish much of the year, and in fall flocks of returning ducks and geese dotted the sky everywhere.

Growing up in this atmosphere, young Delbert did what the rest of the people did, he took what he needed to make a living. He took ducks for his family, and he took ducks to sell, and he became known as one of the most able market hunters in the business.

His favorite method of taking ducks was to set out baited chicken-wire funnel traps for them. Trapping was easier and cheaper than shooting. It was also quieter in case the game wardens

DUCK HUNTERS ON THE HOBOKEN MARSHES by William Ranney (1849).
In this scene the artist has captured the freshness of dawn on wetlands that were once a
waterfowler's unspoiled delight. The gun is a percussion fowling piece of the period.

were around—which they seldom were. Besides, his ducks didn't
have any lead in them, and his customers appreciated that.

Then in 1943 the U.S. Fish and Wildlife Service established the
Chincoteague National Wildlife Refuge across the channel on the
lower third of Assateague Island—some of the finest waterfowl
habitat anywhere. Snow geese, brant, black ducks, pintails, can-
vasbacks, scaup, teal, old squaws, and more came winging into this
region as they always had. But the human population was becoming increasingly dense, and waterfowl needed protection from the
changes people were bringing to the land. Local people, however,
with roots deep in their own traditions, didn't like having the
government—especially "game wardens"—interfering with their
way of life.

The presence of the refuge accounted for Daisy's acquiring the
name by which he is now so widely known and with which he signs
his famous decoys. The refuge staff built a duck trap much finer
than Daisy or any of his market-hunting buddies dared use. The
government's duck trap was a big walk-in version, and Daisy no

131

This drawing from an 1850 issue of the Illustrated London News, which frequently ran articles on American wildlife, suggests the abundance of waterfowl along the East Coast at that time. Entitled "Wild Duck Shooting along the Potomac," the drawing shows a hunter in a sinkbox firing at a large flock of ducks attracted to his decoys.

sooner saw it than he recognized its potential. The refuge people caught ducks, banded them, and released them as part of their studies. Some mornings they were puzzled by the scant number of ducks that had come to the corn scattered in the big trap. Even given the ill-feeling among the local citizens, the refuge staff did not suspect that anyone was raiding their trap.

Then late one night Daisy and three companions were inside the trap, catching pintails, snapping their necks, and tying them up so they could carry them to their boats. "Twenty-eight ducks was as many as the average man could tote," Daisy recalls. Later, back home, he noticed that the cigars he carried in his shirt pocket were gone. He could not find them anywhere. He had a disturbing feeling that they might have slipped from his pocket when he bent over inside the duck trap, but he didn't dare return for them.

The night turned cold enough to freeze a film of ice on the water. When morning came, Daisy's cigars were locked on the surface inside the trap. They were lying there in plain view when the refuge manager arrived to band ducks. He asked around about who smoked cigars. People around town knew whose cigars were found in the trap, but they weren't going to tell the Feds. "That was when everybody started calling me 'Cigar.' "

Cigar Daisy puts down his hatchet and picks up his pocketknife to start the finish work on his decoy. As he carves, he speaks of how he converted from outlaw to conservationist. His visitor asks the obvious question. There were the law-abiding hunters, then there were the ones who, like Daisy, made their own rules. "Why didn't you feel it was wrong to violate the waterfowl laws?"

"We really didn't think on it. I never thought of it as violatin'. I just thought I would go kill me some ducks. There was ducks everywhere. There was creations of 'em. We sold ducks to lawyers and everybody, sometimes a hundred ducks a day. I sold ducks to the sheriff. I sold ducks to a lot of people. I reckon I sold 30,000 black ducks in my time."

Daisy could see, however, as early as anyone, that the ducks were dwindling. He blames some of this on the outboard motor, which allowed people to cover more territory faster. "You know what destroyed the whole East Coast? The outboard motor. It put a hurtin' on just about everything.

"I tell you we should all stand on our heads or do anything we can for the ducks. I think it's all over for the ducks today unless we do something different. That's why I've changed. I'd like for there to be ducks for moi grandyoungins."

Cigar Daisy is so convinced that duck hunting is seriously threatened that he has gone public. He appears on videotapes explaining how he has mended his ways and urging others to do the same. He even appears in person before audiences of duck hunters, fighting back serious attacks of stage fright, and tells his story.

Daisy is not the only former duck hunter to become a spokesman for waterfowl in recent times. U.S. Fish and Wildlife Service veteran

Market hunters in the Dakotas display their harvest on the side of a railroad car. Such excesses were common during the 19th century, when Americans thought the supply of ducks was inexhaustible.

special agent Dave Hall of Slidel, Louisiana, works with reformed duck hunters, who now do their hunting within the framework of the laws, and records their stories on videotape for wide distribution.

Hall is convinced that the old outlaw mentality is changing and that duck hunters must come to the aid of the ducks. "The change in duck hunting and in hunter attitudes in Louisiana," says Hall, "is really unbelievable." During one season in the late 1980s, Hall covered the marshes in six hours of helicopter time, searching for violators. He covered ponds and marshes where in recent years he had seen the water yellow with illegal corn and where he had made cases nearly everywhere he stopped. This time it was different: "It's hard to believe," he said, "but we didn't find a single baited pond. Not one! And we didn't make a single case. Not for overlimits, not for bait, not for lead shot, nothing."

Flouting the waterfowl hunting laws was once considered socially acceptable in the country's richest duck and goose wintering areas, but this attitude seems to be changing. Hunters have seen the disappearance of marshes and potholes, the drainage, and pollution. In Louisiana they have seen the canals that petroleum companies dig across the marshlands, and they've watched the invasion of saltwater destroying these ancient marshes steadily year after year. There is increasing concern about whether or not there will be ducks for tomorrow. Hunters who cherish the age-old traditions of waterfowling see no place in the duck blinds any longer for the shady characters who take more than the law allows or use such illegal practices as baiting and shooting during closed hours.

Hunters across the country had the opportunity late in 1988 to show their concern for the waterfowl. Columnist Dennis Anderson of the *St. Paul Pioneer Press Dispatch* went into the field with Hall to write a story about the ducks and hunters. The marsh country of southern Louisiana covers a vast area, and there are never enough conservation officers to patrol it all adequately.

At the time the federal agents working the vital wintering grounds in the Louisiana marsh country had no helicopter. There was no federal money for one, but few tools are more effective in curbing the illegal activities of outlaws. Anderson did a series of stories for his paper telling about the rampant outlaw hunting and urging sportsmen to chip in and buy a new helicopter for the federal agents working the marshes. His idea caught on quickly. Hunters saw in the helicopter project something they could do personally to help the ducks.

Word spread, and the money began to flow in. The Izaak Walton League of America became the collecting agency for the fund. As a result, the Fish and Wildlife Service agents working these southern marshes at the terminus of the waterfowl flyway now patrol from a new five-passenger Bell JetRanger on pontoons, purchased largely by hunters.

There is good evidence that duck hunters are sometimes ahead of public officials in efforts to protect waterfowl. "Cigar" Daisy and others saddened by the hard times faced by the ducks are willing to see the hunting seasons closed completely, if they must be, to give the ducks time to rebuild their numbers. They know that there can never again be the numbers of ducks there once were, because much of the wetland habitat has vanished and more disappears every year. But they also suspect that official government policies and competition between the states encourage seasons that allow shooting more ducks than should be taken.

We have been hard on the ducks, not just the hunters among us, but all Americans, including those who never hunt. We have taken over more than half the original wetlands, drained away their water and forced the ducks out. We have dispatched our market hunters to bring us fresh ducks in and out of season. In the quiet of an

Although we cannot reclaim our lost wetlands, most duck hunters today understand the necessity of obeying the law and taking only their limit of ducks in season. The old-timers depicted by A.B. Frost in his painting "Good Luck" belonged to another era.

autumn morning, when a damp mist blankets the marsh and ducks are moving on muffled wings, we have sometimes stretched the rules. It is difficult to bring back the wetlands, but the market shooting is largely gone, and, more than ever, hunters are recognizing the importance of doing their share to bring the ducks back to levels closer to what the habitat will support.

11

Outrun the Wind

As the buffalo were being pushed off the range, the American pronghorn antelope, North America's fastest runner, also disappeared steadily. A Wyoming homesteader, Perry Wallace, a tough, wiry little outdoorsman from Missouri, found no antelope when he arrived on the open plains east of Gillette, Wyoming, in 1913. Perry, dirt poor, had a .22 rifle, a few head of stock, some tools, and not much more. For some years he and his wife, like other pioneers before them, lived off the land and their garden. The fleet-footed antelope would have added variety to their diet of beans and jackrabbits.

Many homesteaders gave up and headed back east, but the Wallaces, young, optimistic and ambitious, proved up on their half-section and over the years saw it grow into several thousand acres graced with oil wells and herds of white-faced cattle. Because they stuck it out in that country around Gillette, they witnessed an American wildlife phenomenon: the pronghorn antelope began to increase, and Perry Wallace could at last see what they looked like.

A large buck antelope stands about forty inches at the shoulders and may weigh a hundred and twenty-five pounds or more. The legs are long and slender. The ears stand erect, giving the animal an alert appearance. The underparts and the rump are white, and there are white bands on the lower part of the neck. The upper parts of the body range from tan to reddish brown, with animals in the

PRONGHORN ANTELOPE by John J. Audubon. The fleetest animal in North America, the antelope has been clocked at sixty miles an hour. Both sexes have horns consisting of a bony core covered by a sheath of keratin. Near extinction at the turn of the century, antelope have been carefully managed and today are no longer in danger.

southern parts of the range being somewhat lighter in color than those in the north.

Both sexes have horns—true horns, not the antlers of bone carried by members of the deer family. The antelope's horns are covered with a black sheath of keratin, the material of which hair and fingernails are also made. This sheath forms over a bony core. The sheath is shed annually, a month or so after the autumn breeding season. Bucks may have horns a foot long, with forward-pointing prongs on them. The females have smaller horns or sometimes none.

The male's horns come into play during the breeding season, which, through much of the range, comes in September. The males gather females into harems, a system that assures that the strongest, most vigorous males sire most of the offspring. Following a gestation period of some two hundred and fifty-two days, the doe normally drops twin fawns.

Modern scientists agree that before the arrival of European settlers in North America some thirty-five million of these sleek animals ranged the western grasslands. They were found all the way from Saskatchewan south into Mexico. Their favored terrain was open, rolling grasslands, where they could find the wide variety of plants on which they fed and where they could spot a distant predator.

Among their enemies were blizzards and ice storms, coyotes and wolves, eagles that took the small kids, and ravens that pecked out and ate the eyes of the newborn. There were also the native people who took the pronghorn for food. These long-ago hunters had a variety of methods for killing pronghorns. A favored tactic was the surround. The hunters formed a broad circle around an antelope herd and quickly closed ranks, moving the animals into an ever smaller space. Meanwhile, a second line of hunters formed behind the first circle, giving a backup chance at any animals that slipped through the first line. In this way the antelope could be killed with ease, and few escaped. But the pronghorns were abundant enough, and the Indians few enough, that native hunters did not threaten the species's existence.

The pronghorn is an outstanding example of a wild animal evolving to fit a demanding environment. It survives the bitter cold of the plains winter protected by a coat of hair with hollow cells that hold pockets of insulating air. The hairs may overlap each other like shingles, keeping out the cold air. Biologists have also learned that the arrangement of the pronghorn's blood vessels is a further energy-saving feature for cold weather. Capillaries carrying blood in opposing directions to and from the extremities lie close together and help keep the blood warm, thereby saving energy. Then on midsummer days, when the sun beats down upon the plains, the pronghorn turns on its air conditioning. It cools itself by holding the individual hairs erect so that air can move against the skin.

Every antelope hunter knows about the warning system that apparently enables the pronghorn to flash messages across the grassland to every other pronghorn in view. The instant it senses danger, whether an approaching coyote or simply movement that it does not understand, the white hairs on the pronghorn's rump fan out. The message is picked up, and antelope begin running.

They can see these white flags from unbelievable distances, just as they can spot a threatening predator on the plains two or three miles off. Their eyes, as large as those of the much larger horse, are believed to give the pronghorn exceptional visual acuity. It is some-

BETTER THAN BACON by Charles M. Russell (1905). White rump hairs flaring, a herd of antelope speeds away at the sound of the rifle shot. One is down, though, and the lone hunter will feast on meat that is better than bacon. Note the saddle horse shying at the gunshot—a typical authentic Russell touch.

times written, although it remains unproven, that the pronghorn's vision compares favorably to that of a person using eight-power binoculars. The black eyes are set in a position that gives the animal a remarkably wide field of vision. They are also in deep sockets that protect them against thorns and sharp twigs as they browse. Heavy, dark eyelashes shade the eyes from the sun.

The feet and legs are also marvelous adaptations to the punishment they must absorb. There are no dew claws. The front hooves, which absorb most of the shock, are protected with a special cartilaginous padding, which, because it carries no nerve cells, permits the antelope to race across rough surfaces without discomfort to its

140

feet. Furthermore, its leg bones are constructed to take extreme punishment. At Oregon State College an engineering professor tested pronghorn leg bones against similar bones in cattle to see what their relative strengths might be. He found that, while a foreleg bone of a cow failed at 41,300 pounds of weight load per square inch, a comparable section of antelope did not fail until 45,300 pounds a square inch were applied. The antelope, however, weighs about one-seventh as much as a cow.

Still another adaptation equipping the antelope for its life of high-gear running is its ability to inhale maximum amounts of oxygen. An antelope's heart is twice the size of a sheep's of nearly equal weight, and its lungs are especially large for an animal of its size. Furthermore, it has a remarkably large windpipe for its body size. From the moment it starts running, it makes maximum use of this oxygen-burning capability by opening its mouth and inhaling oxygen in quantity.

And what does the pronghorn do if a long drought dries up the water holes? It simply goes without drinking, which it can do for weeks, providing it finds succulent vegetation.

Despite all these advantages, the antelope may still fall victim to plain curiosity. Modern hunters know, as did the earlier native hunters, about this chink in the antelope's armor. By waving a cap or piece of cloth in the air, or a handkerchief on a pole, hunters have sometimes brought the pronghorn into range. It is said that prairie wolves attracted pronghorns within striking distance by lying low in the grass and switching their tails back and forth.

It may be that, as people employed this trick more and more on the frontier, the antelope caught on to the danger involved. Teddy Roosevelt thought so. He said that the antelope were "getting continually shier and more difficult to flag. I have never myself shot one in this manner, though I have often seen the feat performed. . . ." Each time he tried it, Roosevelt found that his arm grew weak from waving his handkerchief back and forth and that the buck "suddenly took to his heels and made off."

As the 1800s wound down, neither game laws nor rules of sportsmanship had yet eased the hunting pressure on the pronghorn. Roosevelt told about two of his neighbors in the North Dakota ranchlands who chased the same band of antelope repeatedly throughout the winter. A band of thirty or so pronghorns remained on a two-by-five-mile plateau, which they would not leave, no matter how much they were pursued. The ranchers' horses could never

TOLLING UP ANTELOPE by Bob Kuhn. A hunter readies his rifle while his quarry stops to examine the fluttering white flag held by his guide. The antelope's curiosity, well known to the Indians, was often its undoing.

stay close to the speeding antelope, but at the edge of the plateau, the pronghorns always turned back into their adopted range, angling away from their pursuers. "When a favorable moment came," Roosevelt wrote, "the hunters would dash in as close as possible and empty their revolvers or repeaters into the herd." This shooting from horseback at swiftly moving targets brought them many misses, and no doubt some cripples, but the horsemen were out mostly for the chase and not the meat. During the winter, they hunted this band of antelope a dozen or so times and killed perhaps ten of its members.

In those years, covey shooting into herds of speeding game animals was common practice, even among shooters who viewed themselves as responsible sportsmen. One hunter told of shooting into a compact herd of racing antelope and bringing two down with one bullet. Teddy Roosevelt once topped a ridge and spotted a band of eight antelope a quarter mile distant and the chase was on. "I clapped spurs into Manitou and the game old fellow, a very fleet runner, stretched himself down to the ground and seemed to go almost as fast as the quarry."

Ages of experience has taught the antelope that it can outdistance its fastest pursuers. But this time, horse and rider traveled at an angle to the path of the antelope and the distance between them gradually closed—exactly as the rider had predicted.

With its neck stretched out and feet pounding the ground, the antelope does not bound like the deer but carries itself in an even gait, making it an easier target. When the two lead animals crossed his path and came within range, Roosevelt leaped from the saddle and ". . . blazed into the band as they went by not forty yards off, aiming well ahead of a fine buck who was on the side nearest me. The buck rolled over."

On occasion, the racing antelope seems an impossible mark. In *The Plains Of The Great West*, Colonel Richard I. Dodge wrote of the day he and a companion, riding in a light wagon, saw three specks on the distant horizon. The animals were coming directly toward them, and as they drew closer the two men stepped down from their wagons with their rifles ready.

When the antelope were within fifty yards, they made a complete circle around the wagon, while the rifles fired repeatedly. Col. Dodge was distressed to report that the animals ran off "unhurt." This surprised his companion also because the colonel was a noted marksman. On one occasion he was seen to get off right and left shots, killing two antelope running in opposite directions at three hundred yards.

The antelope, built to outrun its natural predators, has been clocked at nearly sixty miles an hour. It sometimes seems to make a game of racing along beside speeding pick-up trucks or automobiles; then, shifting into high gear, it cuts across in front of the vehicle.

Fitted as it is to its environment, the pronghorn antelope thrived for millions of years almost unchanged in form. It once shared its turf with dire wolves and saber-toothed cats, but survived long after those fearsome predators became extinct.

Hunting the antelope on horseback was a favorite pastime of western cowboys. In this superb Remington drawing, a rider gives his galloping mount free rein as he fires a shot at the flank of a speeding pronghorn.

Then the earliest white settlers brought a new threat, against which the antelope had no experience. Coronado saw them as early as 1535 on the plains of Kansas. Not until after Lewis and Clark killed one and preserved its skin, however, was the American antelope described by science.

Soon came the mountain men with their long guns. These beaver trappers were followed by settlers, traders, stockmen, and farmers pushing west all the way to the coast.

In 1834, naturalist and physician John Kirk Townsend, traveling west with the Wyeth party on a trading expedition, marveled at both the animals they met and the attitudes of the seventy men traveling in the group. In his journal, he recalled a May day in the Platte River country. "The antelopes are very numerous here. There is not half an hour during the day in which they are not seen, and they frequently permit the party to approach very near them." He tells of two sleek does that came near one afternoon "bleating precisely like sheep." The hunters mimicked the calls, bringing the does within fifty yards, and there they stood looking at the men until they were both dropped by the hunters. "We can now," said Townsend, "procure as many of these animals as we wish, but their flesh is not equal to common venison, and is frequently rejected by our people."

As the buffalo, that great provider of the plains, disappeared, the antelope took on growing importance as human food. Indian hunters had little choice. Settlers brought antelope meat to the family table. Ranchers fed their cowhands on it, sometimes seeing them consume an entire young antelope in a single meal. Wrote James B. Trefethen in his Boone and Crockett Club Book *Crusade For Wildlife*, "Where in 1880 ten men had been hunting antelope for meat, by 1890 there were a hundred or more. . . ." Meanwhile, the railroads were still trumpeting the wonders of western big-game hunting and urging eastern and European sportsmen to come west to add antelope, and other animals, to their trophy lists.

Under this undisciplined shooting, antelope numbers were steadily whittled down. Perhaps their numbers, including those in Mexico and Canada, then totaled fewer than twenty-five thousand.

As the frontiersmen moved west, they found their small-bore flintlocks inadequate against buffaloes and grizzlies, and adopted the Hawken plains rifle. The Hawken was a saddle weapon with a flintlock action and a thirty-inch barrel. It shot a .50 caliber ball, which had greater shocking power than the .32 caliber Kentucky.

Even scientist T. S. Palmer's estimate in 1908 of seventeen thousand antelope remaining in the United States was considered high by many people. So in 1912, the year before Perry Wallace went west, a report of the Boone and Crockett Club proclaimed the antelope "all but exterminated."

The age of free-ranging cattle was vanishing. Ranchers built fences around their herds, and the antelope had never learned to jump fences. Sometimes an antelope would scramble through or under a fence, and sometimes it hung itself on the wire until it died there. Later, coyote-proof fences, with woven wire buried in the ground, would become even more serious barriers, and such fences remain a threat today.

Early in this century the first state laws were passed to save the antelope; shooting was curbed. Gradually the antelope increased. In 1909 Wyoming closed the state to all antelope hunting, although some poaching continued. This premier antelope range was not opened to legal hunting again until 1927.

Wyoming's antelope population had climbed to some twenty-seven thousand animals by then. Today, the state figures that it has half a million antelopes, making antelope hunting a prime attraction for modern sportsmen.

As the pronghorn slowly rebuilt its numbers, ranchers worried that the animals were competing with livestock for forage. "Five antelope will eat as much grass as a cow," they told each other, although nobody really knew how much grass an antelope ate. As a result, ranchers even shot the pronghorns to save grass for their cattle.

This prompted big-game research biologist H. K. Buechner to study the food habits of Texas pronghorns. Trained observers with binoculars and spotting scopes stalked the herds for months, identifying the plants they selected and recording how much of their feeding time was spent on each species. They also collected antelope stomachs during the hunting season and did laboratory quantitative analysis on the contents.

The results of this study began to change ranchers' thinking. Buechner reported that the antelope spent much of its foraging time searching out and consuming, not grass, but weeds and shrubs. Of their summer forage, only fifteen percent was grass, and in fall the proportion fell to seven percent. Their diets included a hundred and thirty-five species, most of them forbs and shrubs. Sagebrush was an important winter food. Most important, Buechner found that the antelope actually improved the range for cattle; by consuming weeds that cattle wouldn't eat, they left more space for grass. Furthermore, in west Texas at least, they regularly ate, and relished, at least two poisonous range plants, one toxic to cattle and the other to sheep. One cow is now known to eat as much as thirty-eight pronghorns, and one sheep eats more grass than forty antelope consume.

When Perry Wallace was an old man, he was able to invite friends to come to Wyoming for antelope hunting. One of his guests later told of his first antelope hunt on Wallace's ranch. The rules had changed. He could take but one antelope a year, and there were strict modern guidelines setting forth how this was to be done.

"We spotted a lone buck off two or three miles in the distance," the hunter said. "He was lying down when we first put the glasses on him and at that distance did not seem concerned about us.

"Getting close enough for a shot involved a long stalk, much of the time along draws where I was hidden. I wasn't always sure that I was going in the right direction, or how close I might be coming to him. I had read somewhere that if you so much as lifted your head above the ridge, the antelope would spot you and be off.

"For the final two hundred yards I crawled on my belly. It took forever. I was always expecting him to leap to his feet and race away. Finally at about a hundred yards I eased my rifle into position and took careful aim. The shot was an anti-climax. The beauty of it was that this great animal had returned."

12

The Stately Elk

Today's elk hunter would probably be viewed as a mite peculiar by his great granddaddy. That long-ago hunter, watching all the preparations for a modern hunt, might say, "Sonny, if you gotta do all that to shoot meat it's pure wonderment that hunger don't set in terrible bad." And the longer he watches his descendant prepare to go elk hunting, the more he shakes his old gray head.

First come the long evenings devouring color brochures and other literature from Wyoming, Montana, Idaho, and Colorado. Then the calculations involving airline schedules and highway driving times. Arrangements must be made with guides and outfitters, and finally there's the checking of field clothing, guns, and the ammo supply.

To reach the hunting camp this modern sportsman may fly hundreds, and perhaps thousands, of miles. Then he may drive many miles over ranch roads, and finally ride on an unfamiliar horse deep into the mountain home of the elk.

Once in camp, hunter and guide begin exploring, watching, waiting, and plotting to outwit the game. There is no reason to expect an elk to come easily. If the hunter is lucky, he may get his elk after several days of riding and walking over America's most scenic but rugged country. His hunt has been a success. Or he may come off the hunt with no elk at all and still cherish the experience, as many do. Statistics from one highly productive elk-hunting state

149

BULL ELK AND COW by John J. Audubon. After the moose, the elk is the largest antlered animal on this continent, weighing from 700 to 1,000 pounds or more, and measuring up to 5 feet at the withers.

show that in the average year only seventeen hunters out of every one hundred are successful.

"Well, sonny," we can hear grandpappy saying from out of the distant past, "if that's what you've a mind to do, go fer it. But I'll tell you sure, time was when going fer elk was about as different from your way as Old Monongahela is from branch water."

By way of proving his point, the Old Man recalls his hunts and those of his contemporaries from days past. For example, James R. Mead, Connecticut born, had itching feet that took him west as a young man. There he became a successful trader and hunter. In the fall of 1862 he was elk hunting along the Saline River in Kansas.

One day while busy with camp chores, he glanced up to see a trio of huge bull elk walking single file against the skyline as they headed for water.

Mead abandoned his chores, reached for his rifle, and shot the lead bull. Even after the bull fell down, its curious companions stood there staring at it while Mead reloaded. He dropped the second bull beside the first. His third shot brought the last of the elk to the ground.

As he approached them, Mead was reloading his rifle, and it's good that he was. The third elk suddenly jumped to its feet and charged, holding its massive antlers low and coming on at full speed. Mead's shot stopped the angry bull when it was only five yards from him.

Elk hides were then bringing five dollars each, so Mead quickly skinned the animals. He left antlers and meat where they fell. He was in high spirits, having made fifteen dollars in half an hour.

There were times a century and a half ago when the white hunter simply ran the elk to earth. Beaver trapper Osborne Russell left a description of his brand of frontier hunting. The hunters, instead of chasing the individual animal, sought out a small band of elk, slipped up as close as possible, then applied spurs to their horses. Amid clouds of dust and considerable yelling, they set the frantic elk to running at full speed. A single elk could hold its own in such a race, said Osborne, but bunched closely and running for their lives, the frantic animals spent themselves bumping into each other and recovering their stride until, as Osborne observed, they soon "commence dropping down flat on the ground." The hunters then leaped from their mounts and dispatched the elk with their butcher knives.

To these early mountain travelers elk ranked next to fat cow as camp meat. Elk were so abundant that little thought was given to what we today call illegal "wanton waste." Often only the choice parts were taken and several hundred pounds of meat were left to the ravens, coyotes, and wolves. One mountain man, traveling in Dakota country in 1823, declared, "The best part of the animal is the udder, which, being hung upon a forked stick, was roasted before the fire."

Before European settlers came to this continent there were elk over most parts of the country. They were thriving from California to the Atlantic and from Canada into Mexico. They were soon gone from the East, then from the prairies as people moved westward. The mountains remained their last stronghold.

HUNTING ELK AMONG THE BLACK HILLS by *Alfred Jacob Miller (1837).*
Mountain men found the Dakotas teeming with elk in the 1830s and hunted the animals
for their delicious meat. This is one of the many paintings of western life Miller made
during his trip with W.D. Stewart.

Early travelers left numerous reports of elk that had not yet learned to fear people. In 1863 an explorer in the Yellowstone wilderness wrote, "We encountered many bands of elk today, who like the bear, were not accustomed to the sight of men, and would stand within thirty yards of us without fear."

The elk's name comes from the German word for the European moose. The best known Indian name for the animal, and perhaps a more fitting one than elk, was *wapiti*. But elk it is to nearly everyone today, Indians included.

In the deer family, the elk is second in size only to the moose. There the comparison ends. While the moose is a mixture of animal parts that seem not quite to fit together, the elk is a graceful and sleek creature. "It seems impossible," wrote Professor William Graf of the giant Roosevelt elk which can weigh up to fourteen hundred pounds, "that an animal which carries itself so elegantly and lightly can weigh so much."

In recent times elk have become a tourist attraction, especially in autumn when the rutting bulls send their shrill bugling calls across the slopes. On these crisp, frosty evenings little caravans of cars wind along narrow roads in Wind Cave National Park in South Dakota, Rocky Mountain National Park in Colorado, Yellowstone, and elsewhere, and people stop to hear this eerie high-pitched wilderness music echoing from the high places.

This is a trying season for the old herd bulls. For weeks they have fed heavily and built their stamina for the coming rut. Through the summer their new set of antlers has grown until they tower above them and weigh perhaps forty or fifty pounds. The antlers, which are bone, may gain weight at the rate of ten pounds a month. This growth levies a tremendous tax on the elk's body. As they grow, the antlers are covered with a soft velvet through which blood flows. By August they reach their maximum size. The bull scratches his antlers on bushes and saplings, leaving strips of velvet dangling around his face.

Then, with hormones flowing, the bull begins collecting females into his harem, sometimes rounding up twenty-five or more, over which he must stand guard or risk losing them to other males. He becomes a tyrant. No female leaves his flock if he can prevent it. He will fight to keep her and watch that she doesn't slip away to join another bull. For a month or more the rut continues, and the old bull may have little time to eat, and no interest in anything but his duties as herd sire.

This duty ends just as winter is coming on, and food is increasingly difficult to find. But if he is strong, he will survive the winter to sire more calves the following year. There is a species survival value in all this. The bull elk is retested every year by the elements, and the prize goes to the strongest. The calves are the offspring of the most powerful bulls, the ones most capable of passing on those genes that promise survival in a harsh and competitive world.

How did the magnificent elk, which once numbered in the millions, fall to a level that threatened its extinction early in this century? Some elements of the story are familiar. The story is repeated in capsule form in a government report written by W. Ludlow following his inspection trip through Yellowstone in 1876, four years after the area became our first national park. Poaching for elk skins, which brought $2.50 to $3.00 apiece, was rampant. Ludlow was convinced that this illegal shooting had reduced elk to dangerously low levels within the park.

Furthermore, by the time the hide hunters were shifting from bison to elk, they had repeating rifles, as well as access to railroads for shipping their product. In addition to the animals taken by white hunters, the Indians were killing large numbers of elk and trading their hides for the white man's guns, powder, knives, cloth, and whiskey. The elk could not stand this mounting pressure and soon vanished from the western plains and mountains just as they had from the eastern states.

The strangest of all reasons for hunting elk was to sell their teeth. Unfortunately for the elk, its special teeth held strong appeal to prehistoric people and, eventually, to a segment of the white population. The teeth in demand were the vestigial canines, believed to be relics of tusks once worn by the elk's ancient ancestors. Each one is a flat, thumb-sized piece of ivory. At times these teeth had high value among some Indian tribes.

In the first half-dozen years of this century members of the Benevolent and Protective Order of Elks began purchasing elks' teeth to wear as jewelry. Demand and prices soared and the elk were in greater danger than ever before. Most of the remaining elk were then found primarily in northwestern Wyoming, and that was where the illegal killing of elk for their teeth was heaviest.

The bulls had the grandest teeth. A pair of fine upper canines from a full-grown male elk upward of four years old brought from twenty-five to fifty dollars. The tusks of the cow were worth perhaps a dollar each.

Those prices were enough to send the professional poachers sneaking through the hills far from any settlement or ranch house. One by one, they dropped the huge bulls, pried out their canines and left behind them hundreds of rotting carcasses.

One gang of outlaw hunters was led by a crusty renegade named Charles Isabel, who felt that he was being unfairly hounded by the state game warden and his deputies. When the wardens threatened Isabel's clandestine operation, he boldly announced that, unless the law officers quit harassing him, the ranchers thereabouts would soon be finding dead cattle in the fields.

The ranchers didn't cotton to this kind of threat. Isabel had gone too far when he threatened an honest man's cattle. The ranchers spread the word: The first time they found a cow dead of gunshot—no matter who shot it—they were going to tie Charlie Isabel's hands behind his back, fit him with a hemp collar, and suspend him from the limb of a cottonwood tree.

Isabel may have been an outlaw, but he wasn't dumb. He gave up on his threat to kill cattle. But he did not give up his elk-poaching business. Every time a rancher came across another carcass, his sense of frustration intensified. In one small valley the lawmen found the decaying carcasses of thirty fine bull elk, all with the canines pulled out.

There came a day when the lawmen surprised and overwhelmed Isabel's poachers. They had not caught them in the act, and consequently had no case against them, but they must have talked to them very plainly, because Charles Isabel and his gang left Jackson Hole. Probably they left none too soon. Wyoming's law-abiding citizens, especially its hunters, had come to detest these elk killers, and the ranchers' elk protection work became a deadly serious business. One of the ranchers even organized the local, normally law-abiding citizens into a vigilante force that was determined to accomplish, by direct action, what a weak state law was failing to do.

The vigilantes became especially eager to catch a gang of outlaws led by Bill Binkley and Charles Purdy. This gang was boldly hunting on the recently dedicated state preserve that had been established to protect the elk. Binkley and Purdy humiliated and con-

WHERE TRACKS SPELL MEAT by Charles M. Russell (1916). The artist suggests that the hunter tracked the elk from a timbered slope to this mountain meadow. Now he proudly signals his partner that they'll have meat for their camp dinner.

founded the trackers by such stunts as wearing their snowshoes backward or nailing elk hooves to the soles of their boots.

The hard-riding vigilantes increased their pressure on the poachers and finally sent them one last warning: they had but twenty-four hours to leave the country. As Isabel's gang had done, Binkley and Purdy decided to light out. "Hell, a few ole elks teeth ain't worth gettin' strung up fer." They scooped their store of elk teeth into a sugar sack, jumped into a buckboard behind a swift team of horses, and raced off into the sunset.

They eventually reached Los Angeles, but they were still in trouble. When they arrived, detectives were waiting for them, and the poachers were soon on their way back to Wyoming under guard. There, a federal judge found them guilty of poaching elk in Yellowstone National Park. One of the pair escaped. The other served a few months in the guardhouse at Fort Yellowstone, the headquarters of the United States Army unit which was then responsible for protecting the new national park. By now the Order of Elks had formally proclaimed its disapproval of elk poaching, and the demand for elk teeth died down.

Once there were new laws to protect the elk, they began to build up respectable herds again where the country was wild enough and the competition from people light enough. Today half a dozen western states have elk herds approaching a hundred thousand animals each, with Colorado's herd being perhaps the largest of all. There are also small herds in a few other states, including Michigan, where they have been reintroduced.

Nobody knows just how close elk had come to extinction in North America. For that matter, nobody knows how many there had been when the white man arrived here. The total was likely in the millions.

Even at their low point a fair percentage of the remaining elk still drifted down from the mountains each autumn to winter in the flat fields north of Jackson, Wyoming. They had followed these ancestral trails long before the earliest white ranchers arrived. In those prehistoric days, the elk passed on through Jackson Hole to winter on the rich wild hay in the valleys beyond. The ranches in Jackson Hole began to shortstop the migrating elk until they simply stayed in that area for the winter. The wild hay that ranchers cut and stacked with much hard labor had to be protected from the elk with high board fences. The ranchers also sent their boys out to sleep in the haystacks and chase the hungry elk away from the cattle feed. Said

Almer Nelson, former manager of the National Elk Refuge, "They yelled at the elk and rattled tin cans with bolts in them and the elk would run off a little ways. But they were starving and they wouldn't stay away from the hay for long."

In severe winters the elk continued to starve until local ranchers began hauling hay to feed them through the worst months. The winter feeding precedent had been set. Soon the people of Jackson Hole asked the state to send emergency rations for the elk. The state raised money for hay. But the elk needed still more feed. The story of the starving elk spread across the country. The federal government began contributing to the elk rations. Then, in 1912 the government established the National Elk Refuge on the broad meadows where the elk have traditionally wintered on the north edge of Jackson.

This parade of elk, seven or eight thousand strong, wandering in from the high country, still occurs regularly each autumn. In the alpine meadows and sparse timberlands the elk live out the summer as elusive, easily spooked wilderness spirits. But when they arrive in Jackson Hole, they temporarily loose some of their fear of man. The bulls arrive first. Then come the cows and young animals, some of them walking eighty miles to get to their wintering area. Suddenly, the valley floor is dotted with elk, wintering on the twenty-five-thousand-acre refuge, and local townsfolk can watch them from their kitchen windows.

This world-famous concentration of elk draws thousands of visitors every winter. Heavily clothed tourists ride out on the range in horse-drawn wagons for a close-up look at the elk. While the elk are on the refuge, the bulls drop their antlers. Jackson has decorated its city square with columns of these antlers.

But the antler worship does not stop there. On a special day in April, Boy Scouts assemble on the refuge to gather antlers and haul them into a central location to be sold at auction. Buyers from the Orient come to Wyoming and bid on the antlers, which are shipped off to distant points for "medicinal" use. The Boy Scouts and the refuge share thousands of dollars annually from this source.

The elk is now secure once more in North America's wildest places. They are wild, free-spirited symbols of the ancient wilderness. We protect them with a determination we have never extended to the wild predators that once shared their world, especially the wolves.

13

No Room for Wolves

One April morning early in this century, the legendary government trapper Bill Caywood arrived in a northwestern Colorado ranch community to try his skills at taking Old Rags, the wolf no man could trap. Back in Denver, Stanley Young, who was in charge of the government trapping program, had said that, if he had any man on his staff capable of taking this famous wolf, it was Caywood. He told people, "Bill thinks like a wolf—only he thinks faster."

Caywood had come to the West at the age of three, riding across the plains and into the mountains in his parents' ox-drawn prairie schooner. He rode and hunted at an early age and came to understand the ways of the deer, prairie grouse, coyotes, and the big gray wolves that still roamed that western land.

In due time Caywood married and staked out a homestead of his own. His resources included good health, energy, and abundant knowledge of the outdoors. But, in addition, he now needed cash for such essentials as salt, powder, and lead. Cash was rare with a homesteader, but Caywood thought he knew how to earn some money.

He heard ranchers complaining that the wolves were eating them out of business. All around him was the age-old conflict between man and his most hated wild enemy. There can be little question that some wolves were taking advantage of the influx of domestic animals, because calves and sheep provided easy prey. But many a

GRAY WOLF by John J. Audubon. Also known as the timber wolf, the gray wolf varies in coloration from white (in the Arctic) to gray to black. Audubon painted the black phase of the gray wolf with buffalo in the background when both were abundant on the plains.

rancher laid practically all of his troubles at the wolf's door. He could shrug off losses of stock to disease, drought, or winter's blizzards as risks that came with the territory, but the loss of a single animal to the wolves infuriated him and sent him out seeking revenge. The most obvious method of striking back at the wolves was to put bounties on the heads of "them murderin', thievin' killers." Rewards were posted; stockmen's associations raised funds to pay wolf bounties. Local and state governments as well as individual ranchers enriched the pot.

Eastern states had set the pattern early in the country's settlement. In 1815, New York State established a bounty payment of twenty dollars for every adult wolf turned in. Franklin County, New York, sweetened the kitty with an added twenty dollars on the head of each wolf. Then the town of Chateaugay added another twenty dollars, making each wolf taken worth enough to buy a horse. In northwestern Ohio, at least one pioneer hunted wolves successfully enough to pay for his land with the bounty money.

Sometimes the bounty for an adult wolf climbed to a hundred and twenty-five dollars. Locally notorious wolves brought much higher rewards. Even pups, sometimes the unborn ones, brought twenty dollars each, and bounty hunters carried shovels to dig them out of their dens.

Caywood always said, in his quiet way, according to Arthur H. Carhart writing in *Outdoor Life*, that wolves paid for setting him up in ranching. "I'd find out what the stock association had put up in cash," he said, "hit the trail, trap like the devil until I had enough animals to clean up the bounty money, then wait until they got more funds raised." During 1912 and 1913, before he became a government trapper, Caywood, killing wolves at fifty dollars a head, collected seven thousand dollars in bounties. He sometimes took his young son to drag the pups out of the dens, one at a time, where he could promptly dispatch them.

This noted wolfer, slightly stooped but powerfully built, wore a broad-brimmed hat, leather chaps, and glasses and carried a .25–.35 rifle with which he was a deadly shot.

After the federal government set up its tax-supported predator killing program in 1915, Caywood gave up bounty hunting for the regular income of a government hunter. Consequently, he no longer had much use for those opportunistic bounty hunters roaming the countryside and killing the dumbest wolves. These amateurs alerted the sly, old, experienced wolves, making the government trapper's job more difficult. Furthermore, the free-lance bounty hunters customarily took the young wolves, leaving the old breeding stock to produce a new crop of pups in time for next year's bounties. The system was also an invitation to fraud. The wolf bounty was collected on various parts of the same wolf—or dog—in adjoining county seats.

The wolfers operating under the bounty system, plus the government hunters, cut down the wolf populations significantly and in some communities eliminated them. In one five-year period Wyoming wolfer Duncan P. Grant, with the help of his brother, killed two hundred and fifty wolves and some five hundred coyotes. He killed his last wolf in 1914.

Once Caywood set off on the trail of Rags it was old-timer against old-timer. Ranchers knew that Old Rags had operated in that area for at least fourteen years. One rancher, Bob Coats, told Caywood that this wolf had taken twenty-five of his steers in a single season. He also told him that, although he had personally caught forty-five wolves, he had given up on Old Rags. "That's no normal wolf," he said.

In the first place, few wolves were as large as Old Rags. It was said that his feet were so large that his prints could easily be set apart from all other wolves in the area. Those who had caught a glimpse of the old renegade said he wore the most ragged coat of fur they had ever seen, which accounted for his name. He also seemed to make a game of teasing men who pursued him. Any cowboy for fifty miles around would have given his favorite pinto to be known as the man who finally outsmarted Old Rags.

This old wolf made a specialty of locating buried traps, then digging them up and flipping them onto the open ground without getting caught. The trap, which the wolf had set off by reaching beneath the jaws and touching the pan, would be there waiting when the trapper returned. This was said to have inspired some of the most creative cussing ever heard west of the Missouri River. The renegade's habit of digging out traps accounted for the fact that the wolf was sometimes known as Old Rags the Digger.

After some tracking, Caywood was finally able to ride off into the evening sun feeling right proud of himself. He had discovered where the old boy operated and left for him perhaps the most skillfully contrived set he had ever created. But the next morning he found the trap on top of the ground waiting for him.

Weeks passed. The brooding Caywood continued to set traps only to suffer the ignominy of having them exhumed one by one and put on public display. As the old wolfer rode the trails between his sets, he thought increasingly about the special talent Old Rags possessed for locating traps and dealing with them. Finally, he had an inspiration.

Caywood began making one more set for the intelligent old wolf. He chose a spot beside the trail that he knew Old Rags traveled.

But the trapper purposely took fewer precautions than he usually did to hide his work. Nearly any reasonably alert wolf could have discovered this set. The ground was left looking disturbed, and Caywood made little effort to mask the man odor. But then he set two more traps, and for those he called into play every trick of camouflage he had ever learned.

He boiled his traps. Then he buried them in the ranch manure pile for several days. He gave the same treatment to every tool he used in making his sets, including his trowel. He carried freshly boiled moccasins and changed to them as well as changing to clean wool socks before he began working on the set.

Then he spread a three-foot square of freshly washed canvas on the ground where he was going to work and placed on it any removed earth he didn't need so it could be carried away. Next he carefully scooped out enough earth to make a bed for the trap. When it was in place, he laid a small square of light cloth over the pan to keep dirt from sifting down beneath it and holding it up. Then he sifted very fine soil carefully over the trap's pan. He brushed away every bit of loose earth and sometimes used a wolf tail to brush the grass as if the wind had blown it. These traps were placed nearby so that any wolf trying to lift the carelessly set trap would surely step on the pan of at least one of the well-hidden traps.

Caywood knew that a strong old wolf caught in a trap might twist and fight until it escaped by sacrificing a set of toes or a foot, so, instead of staking the trap down, he attached it to a drag. On the end of the chain was an iron hook that would quickly hang up in the bushes.

Nobody knows what the old wolf thought when he detected the man odor around the new set, but he began digging carefully beneath it as he had so many times before. When, in the process, he put his heavy foot on the pan of one of Caywood's well-hidden traps, he leaped back too late and felt the steel vise clamp onto his leg. In his panic, he began dragging the hook and chain through the sagebrush. He came to a cliff and tumbled over. Caywood found him at the foot of the cliff taking refuge in a narrow streambed.

The wolfer later said that Old Rags, unable to escape, turned on him, bared his teeth, and began advancing. Caywood confidently raised his rifle, took careful aim, and found that the hammer wouldn't hold. According to Caywood's story, and it makes a good one, the old wolf was a scant eight feet from him and coming rapidly, drag and all, when the hammer finally set and he was able

Old Rags, unable to escape, turned on Caywood, bared his teeth, and began advancing. Caywood confidently raised his rifle, took careful aim, but the hammer wouldn't hold.

to finish his job. As he stood over his dead adversary, a remorseful Caywood stooped impulsively. "You poor old devil," cried Bill huskily, "You poor, lonely old murdering devil."

Other wolves that ranchers condemned as outlaws bore such names as Old Whitey, The Traveler, Three Toes, Two Toes, No Toes, and Mountain Billy. People marveled at their escapes and displays of cunning and learning. They told and retold stories of these wolves' exploits. In building up the reputation of the wolf, the man who killed the wolf embellished his own as well. It took a real hunter to outsmart and take a renegade wolf. Israel Putnam learned this the hard way.

In 1739, Putnam bought a sizable farm in eastern Connecticut, where he set about raising sheep and goats. After losing seventy-five sheep and goats to wolves in a single night, Putnam and some of his neighbors declared war on the old she-wolf that was credited with most of the killing. They could recognize her tracks by the missing toes she had left in a steel trap. That experience had been part of her education, and by now she had become as elusive as the wind.

Eventually, her pursuers and their hounds brought her to bay in a deep cave some three miles from Putnam's home. Word went out. The crowd assembled. By one account, people brought along "dogs, guns, straw, fire, and sulfur to attack the common enemy."

Soon it became evident that fire and sulfur would not bring the old wolf out to face the clamoring dogs and people. Israel Putnam then suggested to various smaller people that they enter the cavern to confront the old wolf on a one-to-one basis. He found no takers. Even the dogs, having tried once and emerged from the cave crippled and bleeding, stayed well back from the entrance.

Putnam could stand it no longer. He said he would go in there himself and take care of the wolf. His neighbors argued with him—perhaps half-heartedly—for the excitement was now running high. Putnam stripped off his waistcoat, tied a long rope around his ankles, grasped a bundle of burning birch bark, and wriggled head-first into the blackness.

He crawled fifteen feet, turned a corner, crawled down another ten feet, and then started down a sixteen-foot gradual decline to where the old wolf awaited him at the end of the cave. At last the burning torch reflected the "glaring eyeballs" of the wolf, which sat there in the blackness, growling and gnashing her teeth. Putnam jerked the rope, and his neighbors, believing him to be in serious jeopardy, hauled him out hand-over-hand so swiftly that the rocks pulled his shirt over his head and severely cut and scratched his torso.

Now, the bleeding Putnam had his dander up. He straightened his clothes, poured a measure of buckshot down the muzzle of his long gun, tightened the rope around his ankles, squared his shoulders, and turned back to the cave.

This time he approached the wolf even closer, leveled his gun and touched the trigger. A cloud of black smoke choked him, and the reverberating roar of the explosion deafened him as his anxious friends dragged him topside once more into the fresh air and sunlight.

Again the determined Putnam crawled into the subterranean darkness. There he touched fire to the nose of the wolf and she did not move. Taking a firm grip on her, he jerked the rope, whereupon both wolf and man were pulled from the bowels of the earth to the joyous shouts of the excited crowd.

Israel Putnam's conquest over the old wolf soon became the stuff of legend. Years later, when General Putnam was a hero in the American Revolution, storytellers were still repeating the tale of the general's encounter with the outlaw wolf, giving it equal rank with accounts of his exploits against the Redcoats.

In time, some would admit that the worst of the wolves were uncommon individuals that had learned to specialize in stock killing and that not all wolves were troublemakers. But all were seen to have the potential to become killers, so people fought back by condemning all wolves. Genocide became the common answer to the wolf problem.

Change comes grudgingly. No animal in the history of our association with wildlife has been more feared, detested, and persecuted than these large wild canines. For generations fathers, mothers, and grandparents in many countries told children stories of the big bad wolf. The wolf was once native to nearly every environment, except the deserts and the highest mountains tops, of the northern hemisphere. Settlers coming to this country brought with them their Old World prejudices against the wolf.

Remembering these stories from childhood, pioneers traveling in the deep dark woods of Pennsylvania, Ohio, or Kentucky lived with their wolf fantasies and phobias. That old Maryland hunter Meshach Browning told of having a pack of wolves split up and threaten to attack him from two sides. He credited the odor of gunpowder with discouraging them.

I n the late fall of 1807, Mary Robinson, the attractive teenage daughter of a southern Ohio settler, was riding home through a snowstorm when darkness closed in. Mary, thinking herself lost, dismounted to investigate the trail. It was then that she heard the howling of an approaching wolf pack.

When she tried to remount, her skittish horse would not let her near. According to the *History of Clermont County, Ohio*, Mary spent the entire night trying to keep close enough to the horse to keep the wolves from dragging her down but far enough away to keep from being kicked by the frantic animal. "So she walked backwards and forwards the entire night, the wolves keeping up their fiendish howls, and the horse his stamping and kicking," says the account. "If . . . she had wandered away she would have exposed herself to the mercy of the wild beasts thirsting for her blood."

The wolves departed around dawn, giving Mary and her horse the opportunity to make their way to neighbor John Mitchel's house. " 'Why, Mary,' said John, 'have you been in the wilderness all night?' She had," concludes the account, "hardly been assisted from her horse before her strength gave way, and she fell into a swoon."

One scarcely knows what to think of some of those early wolf stories. Perhaps there really were cases of wolves attacking people in pioneering times. What does one say for example of the unnerving experience in the early days of Ohio's settlement of George Ely, who said that he was chased by a pack of wolves on the East Fork of the Little Miami River. According to the account duly recorded in a county history, Ely shot a deer and was in the process of dressing it when the wolf pack arrived. The "ravenous" wolves drove him into a creek, where ice was forming along the edges, and kept him there. Ely had never heard of hypothermia, but he could sure tell that he was getting pretty danged cold. He also knew that his chances of

"So she walked backwards and forwards the entire night, the wolves keeping up their fiendish howls, and the horse his stamping and kicking."

being rescued were slender, so he waded the creek upstream for a mile. There his cries, "mingled with the howls of the wolves," summoned help. The wolves were finally driven away with firebrands. Says the account, Ely waded ashore and "always thereafter had a spite against wolves."

An Iowa hunter reported in *Forest and Stream* in 1877 on what he considered an attack by a wolf. He was hunting wolves when he heard a noise in the bush ahead of him. Having never been through a hunter safety course, he leveled off a blind shot at the noise, figuring this might be one way to find out what was in there. He was overjoyed to see a giant buck whitetail leap up and fall back dead. Like Ely, he was dressing the deer when a big wolf arrived. He gave the wolf the contents of the second barrel, injured it, and was chasing it across a beaver dam when the wolf turned on him "with open mouth."

The man fell into the shallow water and managed to stumble to shore, followed closely by the wolf. The affair terminated only when he broke the stock of his gun over the wolf's head. Broken gun or not, this became a banner day for him. He had collected a splendid buck plus the hide of a large wolf. Furthermore, he found that the wolf was a female carrying nine unborn, but fully developed, young. He scalped them all and carried the evidence off to the courthouse, where he collected a one dollar bounty on each of them.

Whether such frontier accounts establish that American wolves were once less fearful of man than their modern descendants are or whether they show that grandpa was one hell of a storyteller, or both, must be left to conjecture. Perhaps as wolves became increasingly rare, those that survived were the ones that learned to adapt to the presence of man. A person who goes through life convinced that wolves eat people is likely to attribute blood lust to any wolf encountered. But if wolves once attacked people, they seem long since to have changed their ways. There is no account in modern times of a wild North American wolf staging an unprovoked attack on a human being.

One of the few places on the continent where wolves are still relatively numerous is Algonquin Park in Ontario, Canada. Naturalists point out that thousands of people, including groups of children, canoe and camp in this wilderness every year, but attacks or threats from wolves are unknown. In *The World of the Wolf*, Dr. Douglas H. Pimlott expressed his conviction that nine hundred and ninety-nine of every one thousand lurid stories of wolves threatening people are either imagined or exaggerated.

Our characterization of the wolf down through history as a bloodthirsty beast and mortal enemy of man may be largely our rationalization for what we have done to the animal. Throughout most of America the wolf is a beast of the past. As settlers moved from the eastern seaboard to each new section of the continent, the wolf was condemned and its execution begun. Wolf bounties were in force in Massachusetts by 1630, in Virginia two years later, and in New York by 1683.

Our thinking has evolved. As the wolf's numbers fell, and the age-old conflicts were forgotten, attitudes toward the creature softened. The fewer the wolves, the more likely we were to see them as desirable. We are more inclined today to view the wolf as an interesting element in the natural fauna, a top-level predator that has its role in a healthy environment. Surely it is an interesting social animal.

Without pressure from people, the wolf is well equipped for life in a variety of habitats. Its heavy underfur and long guard hairs insulate it against heat and cold. In the Arctic it withstands temperatures of forty degrees below zero, while a small subspecies, the red wolf, was once at home in the warm lowlands of Texas and Louisiana.

The wolf is a traveler. It can trot along hour after hour at four or five miles an hour and increase its speed to nearly forty miles an hour for short bursts. When the wind is favorable, a wolf can smell prey a mile and half away.

Wolves have a gestation period of some sixty-three days. They are born blind and helpless, and for some days the female stays with the tiny pups, while the male or other members of the pack bring back food. A pack of five to eight wolves is typical. The leader is normally, but not always, a male, the alpha male. Like the domestic dog, which descended from him, the wolf marks his hunting area with scent posts. Wolfers spread scent around the scent posts to agitate males and make them careless about traps.

On the great open grasslands of this continent the wolves lived with the buffalo herds. They drew from the herds for their food, while the ravens and other scavengers cleaned up the leavings. When the buffalo vanished, it took with it not only the ravens and the prairie dogs that needed the buffalo-cropped grass for survival, but also many of the wolves.

Once domestic livestock was introduced to the wolves' range, cowboys were expected to carry a handful of strychnine tablets and lace every fallen animal they found. Wolves ate the poisoned meat and died. So did ravens, eagles, and coyotes, along with hosts of lesser creatures that fed on the bodies of the poisoned victims.

As the last of the wolves disappeared from the rangelands, the professional trappers who knew them best sometimes regretted the loss of this largest of North America's native wild canids. Stanley Young, who had worked so assiduously in eliminating wolves, wrote, "There remain in America large areas in which wolves can live—where their presence may be tolerated." He may have been wrong about that. Recent efforts to reintroduce wolves to the wild areas of Yellowstone have been met with powerful resistance not only from ranchers but also some sportsmen who see the wolves as competitors for deer.

These attitudes may be robbing the American outdoors of an enriching element. Aldo Leopold, known as the father of modern game management, and in his earlier years also a wolf killer, regretted deeply the passing of the wolves from the American scene. He believed that we may sense not only the presence of wolves in the land but their absence as well. In this modern land, many people are convinced that the world would be more interesting and exciting if at least token populations of the wild free-spirited wolves were still among us.

Today substantial numbers of wolves live on only in Alaska and Canada. Alaska engages in ongoing, noisy debates between the forces wanting to protect the wolves and those wanting freedom to kill them. In Alaska wolf hunters have used single-engine aircraft to spot wolves crossing a frozen lake. The hunters then either land on the lake and shoot them or dive and kill them from the air with shotguns. Wolves have been known to leap and drag down a low-flying plane, making it crash on the ice.

There is something unnerving in the way we have attacked wolves, in the level of gut hatred the animal has stirred in the breast of man. We have tortured these wild dogs, often for reasons not entirely clear, killed them, not mercifully, but with fire, knives, and wire chokes. Some who captured wolves cut off the lower jaw and turned the animal free to starve. Sometimes wolves were set afire. As late as 1928, the woods of Arkansas were still being burned to cleanse them of wolves.

But we may have moved into a more enlightened age. Now that the wolf is gone from most of its original range, we begin to understand that this animal is part of a larger picture that should be preserved, wolf and all.

Respect for Bears

O ne youthful greenhorn traveling west in 1832 had his most
unforgettable adventure the day he found himself in direct eye contact with a massive grizzly bear. He discovered the
grizzly as it lay in the depths of a willow thicket. The records do not
tell us the man's name, but a scientist traveling with the party leads
us to believe that the youngster's confidence exceeded both his
wilderness experience and his common sense. The young man had
permitted his horse to lag well behind the main group, perhaps, the
scientist speculated, due either to the "indolence of his horse or his
own carelessness."

When he saw the bear crouching in the willows, the traveler
viewed it only as a golden opportunity. There had been much campfire talk of bears, and those few who had killed a grizzly were in a
special class by themselves.

The smart decision would have been to slip away quietly and not
disturb the bear's peaceful day. However, the young adventurer rode
instead to within twenty paces of the watchful bear and brought his
nervous horse to a halt. He leveled his long gun and pointed it at the
bear, whose eyes were fixed on him. The puff of black smoke from
the muzzleloader fogged the scene momentarily. But the shooter
soon realized that although the ball had hit the grizzly, it was more
an insult than an instrument of death. The huge bear erupted from
his bed with a deep-throated growl and parted the willows as easily
as if they had been buffalo grass.

The rider urged his horse to full speed. But every creature has its limits, and this steed happened to come from a long line of sluggish ancestors. For half a mile, the grizzly snapped at the horse's heels, while the frantic rider applied quirt and spur. As man, horse, and bear caught up with the main party, the would-be bear hunter screamed "Shoot him, shoot him, shoot him," and a dozen riflemen raced back to join the fun. They surrounded the bear, drew his attention away from his intended victim, and began weighing him down with lead balls.

This, more often than not, was the outcome of any contest between a bear and armed men. The writer who recorded the details of this chase speculated that the greenhorn was, on that day, probably cured "of a propensity for meddling with grizzly bears." But quite possibly the cure lasted only until he met his next bear because man's compulsion to kill bears does not abate easily.

From the earliest days of settlers arriving on this continent, there has been something special about meeting a bear, whether a shy black bear on an eastern mountain or a grizzly in the Rockies. The occasion causes spirits to soar and trigger fingers to itch. Common sense has no place in the equation. The man who killed a bear could wear a big grin and ride tall in the saddle. So, given the opportunity, there was only one answer—meet a bear, kill a bear.

General Thomas James, who was in a party of trappers going into the Rocky Mountains in 1809–1810, wrote of what happened one day when his party encountered a big grizzly and wounded it. The bear gave chase, and the first person it overtook was a French-speaking Indian, who stumbled over some brush and fell to the ground. The grizzly grabbed the man's thick coat collar and stood over his victim, while half a dozen trappers rushed up and emptied their muzzleloaders into the animal. The bear fell dead right on top of his captive who continued yelling at the top of his voice until the bear was pulled off him.

Also in the party was Archibald Pelton who had come out from Connecticut and joined the trappers. Pelton was a cut-up, a kind of stand-up comic who, whenever the party made camp, set up his own mock court and tried various of his traveling companions for assorted sins. He was less jovial, however, the day a grizzly bear surprised him, brought him to the ground, and stood over him staring into his eyes as if considering his next step. Pelton screamed with such earsplitting volume that the bear departed and never looked back. The event may have had a lasting effect on poor

Pelton. It was later reported that he was roaming about the country-side deranged, and he ultimately dropped from sight without a trace.

Many a bear hunter, looking back on youthful adventures, admitted that he would have been wiser to leave the bears alone. Among those who waited too long to adopt this wise course was Hank Winter. In 1879, Hank was out with Bed-Rock Jim, prospecting in the mountains of western Montana. He awakened one night to the commotion of a bear raiding their grub and spooking the horses. Come the morning, he said he'd just go out and take care of that bear. Bed-Rock speculated that Hank might be a heap smarter not to go messin' with a bear that left tracks that big. Hank told Bed-Rock he had a bit of a yellow streak and started out alone. In due time he picked up the tracks and soon took the bear by surprise at close range. He was so rattled that he shot and missed, and before he could chamber another shell the grizzly was all over him.

The bear ripped his arm to the bone. "I try to use my knife," Hank said in a story in the *Judith Basin County Press*, "but my hand is that slick with blood it slips my hold an' falls to the ground."

Just when Hank was certain that he was about to die. Bed-Rock Jim catches up with him and shoots the bear. As the grizzly dies, it takes a death clamp on Hank's leg. Somewhat to his own surprise, Hank comes to. Bed-Rock is prying the dead bear's jaws off his leg. Hank recalled that he didn't have "rags enough on me to pad a crutch."

In later years if anybody asked Hank why his leg was crooked and he limped so badly when he walked, he gave them his standard reply. "It ain't no birthmark. The way I got this game leg is looking for a bear and findin' him."

There simply was no animal in the land that inspired storytellers more than the grizzly bear did, and it is sometimes difficult to sift truth from fiction. Early in this century *Denver Field and Farm* related

OVERLEAF →

THE CONTESTED GAME by William de la Montagne Cary (1879). Cary went west in 1861 in search of adventure—and found it hunting with the mountain men and Indians in northern Montana. These Indian hunters, two of whom are equipped with rifles, have downed a buffalo on a snow-swept plain, only to be challenged by a huge grizzly for the precious meat.

the run-in that Joe Showers had one day when he was out trying to catch a mess of trout in the headwaters of the Rio Grande. He was sitting on a boulder above a beautiful pool of clear water, catching a fish every now and then. He pulled out the biggest trout he had caught all day. Just as he was about to unhook it, he took a blow on the side of the head that knocked him clear down into the water.

When he surfaced, sputtering and wiping water from his eyes, he found a giant grizzly sitting on the rock munching trout. About this time the bear finished its first trout and picked up the one that Showers still hadn't unhooked. As it chewed on the fish, it set the hook firmly in its mouth.

The more Showers retold the story, the better it began to sound. He said that if things hadn't been happening so fast maybe he could have thought straighter, climbed out, taken up his rod and reel, and played "that 'ar tarnal varmint right up to my cabin." Instead he climbed out of the pool, picked up a rock, and bounced it off the bear's nose. In the process both bear and man lost their balance and tumbled into the stream.

The story of a bear being attracted by a trout rings true enough, but now it begins to sound as if Joe Showers, knowing the appeal of a good bear story, was playing to the audience. But who can say? Perhaps, as he claimed, he and the bear really did roll and tumble and fight through three sets of cataracts until they tumbled over a waterfall and the bear broke its neck on a projecting rock, saving Showers by giving him a soft bear on which to land.

The bear hunters who explored the West more often than not had their earliest bear-hunting experiences with the black bears of the East. Some of these eastern hunters killed bears in numbers that today seem unbelievable. Ebenezer Brewster, who died in 1850, claimed to have killed twelve hundred bears around his southwest Virginia home. About the same period, Squire Thomas Peery, affectionately known throughout the Virginian countryside as "Squire Tommie," was credited with an even one thousand bears, along with uncounted wolves and deer. Squire Tommie's score might well have been higher if he had not often neglected his hunting to pursue the building of his sizable fortune—a choice that made him an oddity among early hunters. The famous hunter Meshach Browning, who started hunting in Maryland in 1795, told of killing seventeen bears in one autumn season. Of the hundreds of bears he had seen in his lifetime, he killed all except three.

He gave credit for some of his success to the good dogs that

When Showers surfaced, sputtering and wiping water from his eyes, he found a giant grizzly sitting on the rock munching trout.

always accompanied him. He trained the dogs to travel one in front of him and the other behind. The lead dog's job was to scent the bear, then lead the hunter around to the downwind side to take the bear by surprise. The second hound was an attack dog.

By the time the dogs brought the bear to a fighting stop, Browning was rapidly approaching the scene, and, as he put it, "a shot was certain death." However, at times the dogs and bear were so entangled that he was afraid to shoot. "I never in my life shot a dog in a fight," he said, "for I always took the knife in a close contest."

Settlers claiming more and more of the frontier and setting the land to cultivation soon reduced the numbers of bears. The longing to kill a bear, however, remained as strong as ever, and any bear that came into view was almost certain to bring on an attack by man, dog, and gun. A Florida settler once wrote the editor of *Forest and Stream* telling of his experiences. While clearing his land and building a home in 1869, two of his helpers so inspired him with accounts of their conquests over bears that he could hardly wait until he met his first one.

His chance came one day when he spotted a large black animal swimming the river. When his helpers identified the beast as a bear, all other work ceased abruptly. The settler grabbed up his old Springfield musket as well as his Smith and Wesson, and all three men scrambled into a boat and set off in pursuit of the bear.

As they pulled alongside, the hunter gave the bear the contents of his musket. "I thought I had my bear," he said, "as he was quiet." He fashioned a slip noose at the end of the boat's rope and dropped the loop over the bear's head. What he did not know was that his lead ball had only grazed the animal's skull and glanced off.

As the hunter snubbed the rope down tight, the bear began to revive. It saw the nearby boat as a refuge and, despite the boat being already crowded, lunged for it. A second shot, this time from the Smith and Wesson, seemed not to slow the bear down at all. The situation was getting serious. The bear, intent on coming aboard, now had his forepaws on the gunwale.

The hunter began beating the bear about the head with a boat hook, causing it to release its grip on the boat. Since none of the men had a knife, they could not cut the rope and cast free of the bear.

The hunter grabbed a short pole from the bottom of the boat, hit the bear on the head, then, in one inspired motion, ran the pole down the bear's throat as far as possible. Next, he held the animal beneath the water's surface to drown him—a feat that did not come easily. The fight continued for nearly an hour before the strangling bear finally succumbed and the hunter could, as he wrote, "then tow him home in triumph." Reflecting on his experience, the settler said, "I learned one thing in this struggle, and that is, that a bear will never do to tie to."

As bears became less abundant, the log-cabin settlers turned their attention to smaller game. But even then an unexpected encounter could merit a story in the paper. In 1818, *The Louisville Courier Journal* told of the Kentucky woodsmen who decided to take their hounds into the nearby forest to tree raccoons.

Within minutes, Old Driver, a yellow cur said to be among the finest 'coon dogs in Kentucky, opened on the hot trail of an animal that had taken refuge in a large hollow tree with a high cavity. One of the hunters stood back, eyed the tree knowledgeably, studied the claw marks, and speculated, "Maybe that there animal ain't no 'coon a'tall."

"Ain't nothin' else," declared the dog's owner. "Old Driver never follows naught but a 'coon's trail cause that's the way I trained him. Besides before we started, I rubbed his nose again in that 'coon skin I got nailed to the side of the house."

The doubtful hunter shinnied up a sapling to where he could peer down into the darkness of the hollow tree. He figured the eyes he saw reflected there were a might far apart to be a 'coon, but what the hell, let 'em find out fer 'emselves!

Next, one of the 'coon hunters climbed the sapling and began punching the animal with a long sharpened stick. At that, a massive black bear poked his broad head out of the cavity and looked down upon his tormentors. This sudden apparition caused the bear poker to tip backward out of the sapling. He was saved a nasty fall when his belt caught in a fork of the tree, but now he hung, bear bait, and not much he could do about it.

However, the bear ignored him, lunged from the tree, tumbled to the ground, gained his feet, shook the cobwebs from his head, and charged the nearest 'coon hunter. Although this man held an ax, he discovered that he was too scared to use it.

By this time, Old Driver had recovered from his initial surprise. He sprang forward and took a firm grip on the bear's rump. The bear turned to deal with Driver. By then, the dog's owner had recovered his senses sufficiently to get in a lick with the ax. Old Driver, deciding that this was no game for a 'coon dog, set off for home and never looked back.

The bear attempted to regain his refuge in the hollow tree, but as he clawed his way up that giant trunk, he had to pass the hunter who was still suspended in the sapling and who now jabbed at the bear with his butcher knife. The bear again tumbled to the ground, where it was finally shot dead.

The "bear tree" became locally famous. Uncounted people from miles around rode out on Sunday afternoons just to see it, sometimes taking a picnic along. Once in a while a visitor would ask Old Driver's owner, "Do you still rub yer dog's nose in a 'coon skin afore you go fer bears?" Old Driver, it seems, lost some of his natural enthusiasm for hunting raccoons or any other game. It was said that he even gave up sleeping on the bearskin rug in front of the fireplace.

The threat of serious injury seldom stopped the frontier bear hunter in his pursuit. An early hunter in western Virginia, where bears were said to be thick as butterflies in a thistle patch, hacked off three of his fingers in a bloody encounter with one bear. His accident occurred the day he found a half-grown bear in a live trap that he had set up in a laurel thicket. When he went to check his trap, he took along a few friends, thinking they might have some fun if he caught a bear. He had "the boys" stay back at the edge of the thicket and left his rifle with them. He slipped up close to his trap, but, instead of calling his friends, he lifted up the gate of the trap, let the bear rush out, and set his dogs on the animal. The bear squeezed under a log. One of the dogs took a firm grip on one of the bear's hind legs and hung on as if he had lockjaw. The dog's owner climbed up onto the log, drew his knife, and prepared to deliver the *coup de grace*. But his knife struck a branch, throwing him off-balance. He fell off the log heavily, so it is written, and in the process hacked off three of his fingers. That feat seems possible only if (a) he was carrying the typical large butcher knife that hunters of those times used, (b) his knife had a keen edge sharp enough to merit bragging, and (c) he was unfortunate enough to fall with his body weight on the knife. At any rate, he figured his companions would laugh at him if he allowed a bear to escape simply because he lost a few fingers. So, as he saw it, he did the only thing he could do, shifted the knife to his left hand and killed the bear. Then he called "the boys" to help him bind up his bleeding stumps.

There have been many hunters who met bears in ways that made the excitement of the moment overwhelm common sense. Colonel William D. Picket, an Alabama-born veteran of the Mexican War

A Tennessee bear hunter, circa 1895. Although by this time breechloaders were common, this mountaineer probably couldn't afford one and still shot a Kentucky flintlock.

went west in 1876 to hunt along the Upper Missouri. He and a companion were out one day searching for bears. Pickett, who told the story in the Boone and Crockett Club book *Hunting At High Altitude*, shot a couple of bull buffalo for bear bait, along with assorted other game, including deer and pronghorns.

In due time the hunters spotted a large grizzly, which escaped into a thicket so dense they could no longer see the animal. Not to worry. They would bring him out. They separated and from two angles began shooting blindly into the thicket where they believed the grizzly to be lurking. They were shooting four-hundred-and-fifty-grain solid ball with ninety grains of powder, which "penetrated the willow admirably." Under this pressure the bear erupted from the heavy cover and began running off.

Both gunners hit him with running shots, and the bear wheeled and rushed back into the thicket. Now they could hear heavy breathing. They shot at the sound. Again the bear rushed from the thicket, but this time he had a definite mission in mind: take Pickett out of the picture. Pickett overshot him. After a short charge at Pickett's horse, the grizzly again returned to the thicket. The hunt continued for a couple of hours until finally a heavy snow started falling. The shooting, which Pickett described as "wholly by guess," eventually took its toll. The next day they found the bear dead of multiple wounds.

Rare indeed among these early hunters was the one who allowed a bear to go its way unmolested. Isaac Rose, who in the early 1800s departed his quiet Pennsylvania farm community for the excitement of beaver trapping in the land of the Blackfeet, never forgot the close call he and Mark Head had one day along the Bitterroot.

Rose, riding ahead as they worked their way down into a ravine, stopped suddenly. Mark came up with him, and Rose pointed to a huge grizzly bear moving off through the brush. Not only was the grizzly a welcome diversion but its hide was also worth four dollars from the fur company.

Rose slipped from his saddle, worked his way into the cover, and was in place waiting when the bear's progress brought him into an open spot a short distance opposite the hunter. At the sound of Rose's muzzleloader, the old bear rolled over on its side and began snapping at the spot where the bullet had penetrated. By now Rose was reloading. "Caleb's a gonner," he told Head.

But the bear stopped biting himself, rolled to his feet, and loped into the thicket. Rose figured that the bear had simply gone into dense cover, lain down, and died. The hunters tied their horses and worked their way into the brush. Head was relieved to find the giant grizzly motionless before him. "Dead as a mackerel," he announced as he slipped the knife from his belt and took a firm hold on the bear. He was making his initial cut when he suddenly realized that the bear was gripping his head in its broad paws and pulling him toward its open mouth.

The bear was chewing vigorously on Mark's head when Rose shot the beast in the lungs. This distracted it enough that Rose could grab Mark's legs and pull him away. "Are you dead, Mark?" Rose

Bear attacks were the stuff of legend on the western frontier. Every bunkhouse raconteur had a stock of bear stories, which he constantly embroidered in the retelling.

DISPUTED TRAIL by Olaf Selzter (1913). Selzter and Charles Russell made many pack trips together in the Rockies, sketching and studying wildlife, and this painting may depict an actual episode. Although one horseman is levering a round into the chamber, he wouldn't shoot at such close quarters and risk a head-on charge.

asked his blood-splattered companion.

"Putty near, I tell ye now," Mark whispered. "My head's all chawed up, and my skull's cracked all to flinders."

Rose got his companion back to camp, bound him up as best he could, and a few days later both of them were back on the trail, ready for whatever happened.

As a people, we were slow to develop a sense of respect for bears. Ranchers and farmers saw the bears as varmints that should be eradicated. Hunters viewed them as the ultimate challenge. The bear, regardless of species, color, size, or sex, was seen as deserving death, and there were no controls on how death might be administered. It was easy to convince oneself that bears were disposable animals and that the bear killer was performing a public service. Men devised all manner of ways to kill bears with their knives and hatchets. But bears were also roped, stretched out between horses, and stabbed. They were trapped in deadfalls and live traps. They were killed with set guns. They were poisoned.

The old frontier bear-hunting ethic is not entirely dead even today. Not long ago a planeful of southern sport fishermen arrived at the sleepy Eskimo village of Whale Cove on the Arctic coast of Canada's Northwest Territory. The notes kept by one of these fisherman tell how the whole village came to life late one morning. "There was pandemonium. People ran toward the bay. We followed and saw a polar bear come over the rocky hills from the south to the edge of the settlement. Great excitement. Guns started to fire—about fifty shots—and only three hit the bear."

The pilot was shaken by the experience, not because he feared the old male bear that had wandered into the village, but because the wild shooting was endangering his aircraft. One bullet through an aluminum float could strand him beside the Arctic Ocean. The last shot hit the bear after he had leaped into the bay trying to escape. It struck him in the head, killed him instantly, and made the Eskimo rifleman the hero of the day. The jubilant throng of men, women, and children waded into the shallows to tow the carcass to shore and skin it out.

One wonders what the frontier bear hunter might think of some modern bear hunts if he could return to the hills where he once carried his muzzleloader. Where Meshach Browning slipped silently through the forest so long ago, the modern bear hunter still goes searching for black bears. But today's hunter is a new breed. He probably belongs to a bear-hunting club that on opening day of

CROSSED TRAILS by John Clymer (1968). As the grizzly population has declined, bear encounters have diminished. When they do occur, as portrayed here, the outcome is never certain. These modern hunters, returning from a hunting trip with a bighorn trophy, have come face to face with a grizzly and her cubs—always a bad situation.

the annual season joins other clubs, searching for bears with various modern aids. One Virginia wildlife biologist described the scene: "I've seen what is called a mobile base station set up. They have about twenty mobile units, and I would guess about half of them have dog packs operating out of this one base station. They just fan out over a large area, and, as soon as somebody finds a trail or any sign of bear whatsoever, they establish radio contact with everybody else, converge on the spot and release a pack of dogs. Tired dogs are replaced with fresh packs. You can count on a dead bear."

Another indication that we still look upon the bear as deserving less than a sporting chance comes from the poachers. Late in 1988, United States Attorneys in Georgia, North Carolina, and Tennessee issued indictments charging forty-three people with the illegal killing of black bears in the Great Smoky Mountains. A primary source of these stolen bears is the Great Smoky Mountains National Park, where there are now said to be fewer than six hundred bears. Biologists in the three states believe that poachers take at least as many bears as law-abiding hunters kill.

Poachers sold undercover agents two hundred and sixty-six bear gallbladders, three hundred and eighty-five claws, seventy-seven feet, four heads, and nine hides, plus a gallon of moonshine and three stolen cars. Disassembled and sold in parts, a bear can bring poachers as much as a thousand dollars. Claws and teeth are converted to jewelry, and the gallbladders and feet are sold in the Orient—the gallbladders for folk medicines and the pads for making soup. Heads and hides go for trophies.

Obviously, a segment of the human population still shows too little respect for the wild bears that lived here long before we came into the picture.

15

Tracking the Big Cat

From the earliest days, settlers viewed the native mountain lion, or cougar, as man's mortal enemy. They hated it because it sometimes killed domestic animals. They feared it, often unreasonably, because it is large enough and strong enough to kill a human being.

Prehistoric natives of both North and South America held the cougar in high, sometimes mystical, regard. Parts of the animal were prescribed for treatment of serious human ailments. The cougar gall was a tonic, helping a sick person to ward off disease. The dried paws of a mountain lion, dangled above the head of an ailing person, were believed to be strong medicine and a sure cure for many ailments.

Early Inca societies worshipped the cougar. The animal was also used to punish people who broke the rules. In their book *The Puma*, Stanley P. Young and Edward A. Goldman tell how ancient Inca rulers in Peru utilized the giant cats as agents of punishment. Traitors and assorted miscreants were thrown to the lions, and these early South Americans included a few refinements the Romans may never have thought of. The Inca dungeons housed not only hungry pumas but also jaguars and contained blind corridors populated with vipers and vermin crawling about a floor studded with sharp flint points. The victim was pushed into this chamber to live out whatever hours, or minutes, might remain of his life.

From the earliest days, European settlers waged a campaign to

191

COUGAR by John J. Audubon. When this picture was painted, the cougar ranged from coast to coast. A feared predator, the big cat is shown here over a calf it has just killed.

rid the land of the cougar. In California the early Jesuit priests offered anyone killing a mountain lion a reward of one bull. Later, beginning in 1907, the state of California set a twenty dollar bounty on the big cats. Because the cougars continued to thrive, in 1913 the state started sending official lion hunters to search out and kill the cats. This continued until 1963. Then, for several more years, California, like many states, classed its cougars as varmints and anyone was free to kill them any time. Even then, California's cougars did not disappear. The state still has a substantial population of them. Eastern states offered bounties on cougars as early acts of government. In 1764, Massachusetts was paying bounties on these giant cats. Meanwhile, everyone who could get a shot at a cougar helped eliminate them as rapidly as possible.

Phin Temple, a hunter in Wayne County, Pennsylvania, who claimed to have killed thirty-five hundred deer and four hundred bears, reported how he once brought a cougar into range. He was walking one day near Preston when a "large catamount" stopped him right in the middle of the road. At the moment Temple didn't have his gun along, but that's the way the dice roll. He was, however, accompanied by his hound, which soon put the cougar to flight.

The whole affair set Temple to thinking. This cat had not acted normally, being right out in plain view. "I figgered sure as anything she had some kittens around there somewheres." Such an opportunity was not to be passed up lightly. Temple began searching through the brush and beside fallen logs. He soon discovered a pair of little spotted cats with sparkling eyes and long tails. When he reached home he had them with him, one in each coat pocket.

The following morning he was back where he had found the kittens, and this time he had his gun along. He also carried one of the little cats in his coat. "I tied the little critter to a bush, then backed off some distance and hid myself, figgerin' this would bring her if anything would."

Temple had it figured out about right. Before long the mewing kitten coaxed the female out of the dense cover whereupon, as Phin Temple reported, "I shot her plumb dead."

Anywhere on the frontier this was considered an act of good citizenship. But given this kind of dedicated pursuit, plus a complete lack of legal restrictions, the cougar began to vanish from one eastern state after the other. None was seen in Pennsylvania after 1891, and the animal was believed to be gone from Ohio by 1850. Today the cougar is gone from practically all of the East. In Florida, which probably has the last of the eastern cougars, they are highly endangered. The cougar, however, still prospers in several western states and in southwestern Canada.

This is far from what it once was, because no mammal in the Western Hemisphere had a wider distribution. Cougars were once found, not only from coast to coast in North America, but also from northern Canada through Central and South America to Patagonia.

There can be no question that the cougar is strong enough to kill a person, and knowledge of this feeds our fear of the big cats. Scientists have not yet found a way to measure the strength of the cougar's powerful jaws. Experience tells us, however, that the cat

This drawing appeared in a book entitled "In the Wilds of Florida," published in 1888 when the cougar evidently posed a threat to young ladies out for a pleasant canter. Luckily, this one was accompanied by a rifleman.

can, with a single bite, punch through the skull of a deer or other large animal, and that it can break the neck of a victim as it brings it down.

We also know that one of these cats, weighing perhaps a hundred pounds, can drag off an elk or calf weighing several times its own weight. The story is told of a Texas rancher who went for a team to drag away a dead six-hundred-pound steer, only to return and find tracks proving that a mountain lion had already dragged it off.

The adult mountain lion normally weighs from eighty to two hundred pounds. There have been heavier ones recorded. Perhaps the largest one known was a two-hundred-and-seventy-six-pound male taken some years ago in Arizona. A fully grown male measures around nine feet in length including the ropelike thirty-inch tail. On the average, an adult male weighs about a hundred and twenty-five pounds, the female about a hundred pounds.

The cougar's short fur is commonly colored a tawny yellowish brown, although on occasion the color will vary. Young kittens are spotted and have rings around their tails.

This long, slender cat has short, rounded ears on a head that seems small for an animal of its size. Noticing its plain, unmarked coat and its body size, a careful observer would be unlikely to confuse it with any other native North American wild animal. People have been known, however, to confuse other animals, including yellow Labrador retrievers, with cougars and also to report "black panthers" where, almost surely, no panthers of any shade lived.

The feet of the cougar are rather small for its size, about four inches long. The toes, five on the front feet and four on the rear feet, carry retractable claws which are of no help in locomotion but instead are extended and used for holding prey. In a close-up fight with man, dog, or other beasts the claws can become highly destructive. They are the claws of the common tabby cat multiplied innumerable times. In 1909, California physician Dr. J. T. Higgins treated a woman scratched by a mountain lion. The victim was Isola Kennedy, who ran to the rescue of a boy being attacked by a lion only to have the lion drop the boy and turn on her.

Held on the ground by the cougar, she tried to kill it with a hatpin to the heart, but the cat used both front and hind feet to scratch her. This continued until a neighbor rushed up and shot the animal in the head. By the time the doctor reached her, she had some fifteen deep gashes reaching from her shoulder to her wrist.

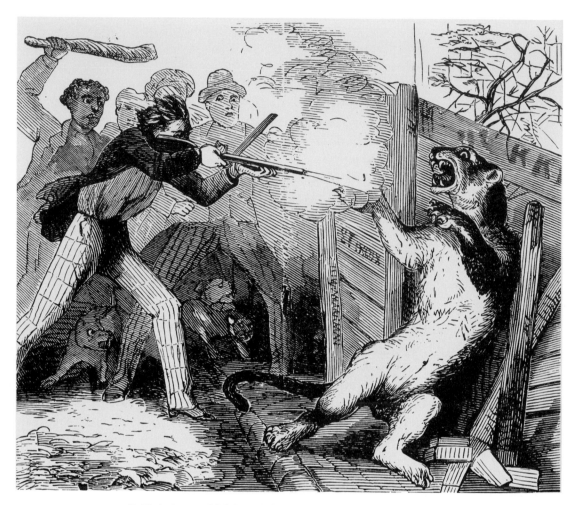

Published in a Mobile, Alabama, newspaper in 1890, this drawing suggests that the cougar terrorized people even in populated areas. All the hatred and violence vented against the cat are captured in this one picture.

The doctor announced at the time that he believed Miss Kennedy would survive unless her wounds became infected. He was wrong. All seemed to be going well, until about seven weeks after the attack the victim began feeling ill. She then died of hydrophobia. The lion that attacked her had apparently been one of those rare known cases of a cougar with rabies. The boy involved in that attack also died of hydrophobia. Eighty years later this remains the only recorded instance of a human death caused by a rabid cougar.

Perhaps the first person killed by a cougar in this country was a Pennsylvanian named Philip Tanner. He met the cat one day in Chester County along the edge of a woods. They found Tanner, gathered up his remains, and buried them in the local cemetery. They erected a headstone, and after the fashion of the times, the engraver cut on the stone a picture depicting the cause of Tanner's death, in this case the image of a cougar. Beneath the rough likeness of the big cat he chiseled the words, "Here lye the body of Philip Tanner who departed this life May 6 1751 aged 58 years."

Such events have been rarities in this country's modern history. Cougars normally do not seek human prey. They are timid animals intent on staying out of sight and avoiding people. It may be that cougars on the frontier quickly adapted to the presence of men with guns and learned to slip quietly into the underbrush instead of attacking the beast that walks upright. One of the rare exceptions occurred one December day in 1924, in Okanogan County, Washington.

That day a thirteen-year-old boy was sent on an errand to the neighbors. As he normally did on this trip, he took a shortcut leading through a coulee. Ordinarily he was perfectly safe on this trail. After all, he carried in his pocket his good luck charm, an empty cartridge marked "U.S. C. Co., 38-S.W.—center fire."

Later that day, when the boy had not returned, two members of his family went searching for him. They found his remains beside the trail, covered them with his bloody coat and ran for help.

Within an hour, a search party of neighbors assembled at the scene. The story was easy to read in the fresh snow. The boy had run to the base of a small tree, started to climb and been dragged down by a cougar.

When the search party returned, the boy's coat had disappeared. The following morning it was discovered on a ledge a couple of hundred feet from the kill. Now the search was on in earnest. Hunters, carrying guns of considerable variety and leading packs of hounds, came from throughout the region, determined to track down this mountain lion that had dared take a human life. It was not, however, to be a simple matter. The lion eluded man and dog.

Eventually, a rancher checking his coyote traps some miles from the scene found a female cougar in one of his traps. He promptly killed her. Authorities sent her stomach to the laboratory of the U.S. Biological Survey for analysis. Among the items recovered from the lion's stomach were scraps of blue denim and a ball of human hair.

There was also an empty cartridge marked "U.S. C. Co., 38-S.W.—center fire."

Another instance occurred early in 1974, at Arroyo Seco, New Mexico. Two boys were playing that morning while, screened from them by vegetation, a young cougar stalked them for several hundred yards. The cat's explosive attack killed one of the boys, eight-year-old Kenneth Nolan. Kenneth's father and a neighbor were soon on the trail. They tracked the cat and killed it. Investigators declared the cat to be healthy although it was scrawny and underweight.

This might indicate that the cat had been a captive animal that never had parental guidance in learning to hunt deer and other wild game on which cougars normally subsist. Nobody knows how many cougars have been taken home as kittens and kept as "pets." Such experiments, now generally illegal, most often end in frustration as the growing cat gains strength and begins to follow its natural predatory tendencies. The owners, not wanting to kill the cute little fellow, take it off some distance and drop it beside a country road. Chances are that it starves to death. But if it survives, conditioned as it is to people, it might hang out around farms or villages. Then, driven by hunger, it could become a threat to people, especially children.

No state has had more problems with cougar scares, and actual attacks, in recent times than has California. This heavily populated state still has wilderness enough to harbor healthy populations of the great cat. In recent years cougars have been emerging from the wild places and appearing increasingly around settlements and subdivisions. They have been especially prominent in and around the Ronald W. Caspers Wilderness Park south of Los Angeles. This wilderness park covers seventy-six-hundred acres in the foothills of the Santa Ana Mountains. Adjacent to it are the wild mountain lands of the Cleveland National Forest as well as other privately owned wild lands, giving the cougars and other wild animals a broad expanse of heavy cover over which to roam.

SHOOTING A COUGAR by Alfred Jacob Miller (1837). Although he traveled widely in the West, Miller probably never saw the elusive cougar at close range. This cat, with its pointed ears, looks more like a lynx. He did get the trapper's pistol right—a flintlock.

One dramatic encounter with a cougar in Caspers Wilderness Park began, according to *Audubon* magazine, during a family outing in October 1986. A local couple and their two small children went to the park to hike and picnic. During the afternoon the father took a picture of his family standing on the trail. Says *Audubon*, "The developed picture caused a sensation." It revealed what the father had not seen previously, the head of an adult cougar staring at the family from the nearby bushes.

People in the area were already jumpy about the actions of the local cats. Some months earlier a five-year-old girl had been dragged down and seriously mauled by a lion in the same park. The day after the man unknowingly photographed the cougar, the six-year-old son of another couple was attacked. The boy had run ahead of his parents in the park and stopped to tie his shoe, putting him in a vulnerable position. A cougar pounced on the boy and had him by the head when children's screams brought the father to the scene wielding his knife. The cougar dropped the kid and departed. The boy's injuries healed. Officials promptly closed the park to visitors and kept it closed for many weeks.

Out of the controversy following these attacks came a refreshing defense of the cougar. The old frontier insistence that all large predators should be killed for the good of man was no longer a universal belief. There was broad public support for cougars and for the wilderness they inhabit. Increasingly, people were insisting that there is room in this world for both people and cougars.

The truth is that cougar attacks on people are rare. At the University of California, Davis, wildlife specialists began collecting information on such attacks as far back as 1750. The list includes all recorded attacks on people within the Americas. Some of the records are questionable. Over a span of two hundred and thirty years there are listed sixty-six such attacks in the Western Hemisphere, only thirty-three of them in the United States and, of these, fewer than a dozen proved fatal. The cougar's defenders assert that this is far fewer than the number of deaths from bee stings or snake bite.

Any wild animal, however, should be treated with respect. Campers, hikers, and hunters in cougar country should at least be aware of the presence of the cats, and small children should be kept in view. This awareness need not dampen the outing. The known presence of the big cats adds spice to the time afield. There is an element of pure wilderness excitement in knowing that a wild, free-roaming cougar may be watching you.

Outdoorsmen might wisely consider that they are invading a cougar's home territory. For example, a New Mexico geology student might have slept better one October night in 1977 had he looked around his chosen campsite in the Magdalena Mountains before pitching his tent. While he was bending over, lighting his Coleman camp stove that evening, he heard a heavy animal thump against the ground nearby. When he wheeled about, there was an adult cougar within three feet of him. The student yelled at the lion and threw more wood on his campfire, thinking this would scare off the cat. The cougar stayed, however, and as the camper moved about his camp he occasionally caught reflections from the eyes of the big cat in a nearby thicket. The camper may have dozed off. He wasn't certain. About five o'clock in the morning there was no longer any sound or other indication that the lion was still around. Very quietly, the student broke camp, packed up, slipped away and went down the canyon to his car.

The student reported his encounter to the New Mexico Game and Fish Department, which sent an agent to investigate. He studied all the signs. One set of tracks established the fact that the cat had been within six feet of the campfire. Slightly farther out, the tracks were abundant. Then the agent studied the rock ledge four feet behind the campfire. "On this ledge," he wrote in his official report, "were the tracks of at least two small mountain lion kittens." The camper, failing to check the area around his chosen spot, had pitched his tent beneath a ledge where the lioness and her family had prior claim. The official report recommended that no action be taken against the mountain lion, and suggested that campers henceforth not camp between mountain lions and their young.

Today, the cougar is finally classed as a game animal in most western states where it is still found. It is no longer a varmint stripped of legal protection. State wildlife agencies now have a responsibility for protecting the cougar and limiting hunting to levels that will not endanger its long-range security.

16

The Wild "Rooshians"

The typical wild hog hunter in the Great Smoky Mountains, decked in camouflage, stops quietly beside a woodland trail on a cool autumn morning. He can hear the hounds coming up the mountain. This is good news because they are coming his way, and they must be moving one of those wild hogs toward him. The guide has said these dogs just won't run anything else but those wild "Rooshians."

His dogs are a mix. There are Plotts hounds, a couple of red-bones, and one that is half-Airedale and half unidentified. They are all fight-to-the-death hawg dogs. Their trainer said he'd seen to that all right. "About every two weeks I mix a dash of old-fashioned black gunpowder in their feed. That makes 'em fiesty. Then, when they're still pups I learn 'em to fight on them half-wild acorn-splitters we got around here, and I only keep the ones that really like to fight. I train 'em so mean they'll tear a hornet's nest apart and eat them hornets, no matter the stingin'."

This is the brand of training, say the mountain hog hunters, that's needed because, "them wild Rooshians don't fight gentle." Furthermore, these hogs that trace their ancestry to the mountains of Europe seem not to care what they attack. In the hills of Appalachia more than one man has been chased up a tree by a tusk-bearing European wild hog. Perched there on a limb, he has time to take a careful look at this creature.

It is not an animal of great beauty. Roly-poly little barnyard pigs

The European wild boar is a vicious-looking animal. Its curved tusks can be used to slash the belly of an enemy or to dig for roots in the earth. Its shoulders are covered with a hide so tough it has been known to turn small-caliber bullets.

may be attractive to some observers, but the European wild boar is cut from different cloth. It stands high in the shoulders and glares at you with squinty little black eyes set in a long knobby face. Its tusks may be eight inches long and curved upward, forming hooks that can slash the belly of an enemy, or in more peaceful moments, dig roots for food. The upper and lower tusks are self-sharpening because they grind against each other. Old males are known to use their tusks to fight to the death over possession of an estrous female, and hunters have been seriously slashed by the tusks when dogs, hogs, and people mix it up. When fighting, the wild boar sweeps his head sideways and upward, bringing his tusks into positions that can cause maximum damage to the enemy. The high shoulders are blanketed with layers of fat and covered with a hide so tough it is said to turn bullets from small-caliber guns.

One observer who studied European boars in Germany was astounded at the speed with which they can disappear in the woods. They leap nimbly over mountain streams, cross downfallen logs, and negotiate the roughest terrain at speeds up to thirty miles an hour. "The fact that they never stood still for more than a second or two," he said, "showed that they had the wild animal's appreciation for the fact that the price of liberty is constant vigilance." These wild hogs are extremely watchful and alert and, although their eyesight may be poor, their wariness is supported by superior senses of hearing and smell. They are primarily nocturnal in their feeding and movements.

The hunter waiting for the hounds was one of the more fortunate on the mountain that morning. An old boar had run half a dozen miles or more and now decided that he had run far enough. Deep in a tangled laurel thicket he stopped and turned on the pack of dogs and was fighting the hounds when the hunter reached the scene.

Although one cannot speak for the hog or the dogs, the hunter was happy and so was the state wildlife agency. Hunting the wild European boar has become a sizable business in eastern Tennessee and western North Carolina, and those who first brought these ill-tempered creatures to the Great Smokies are still praised by those who think the introduction was a good idea.

The presence of these wild hogs in the Great Smokies tells something about us. There seem always to be individuals who are not content with native wildlife. They look to other parts of the world for fish, birds, and game mammals that they think would enrich America's waters, forests, and fields. As one author expressed it, "Man, the supreme meddler, has never been quite satisfied with the world as he found it, and as he dabbled in rearranging it to his own design, he frequently created surprising and frightening situations for himself."

Although some wildlife introductions are unintentional, many have been purposely made. We have the carp because somebody considered it a good idea to give it a fresh start on this continent. The house sparrow and starling were brought here purposely and set free. There are dozens of others, and in almost every instance the release was made with inadequate knowledge of what damage these imported animals might cause. The exotics compete with native wildlife for space, food, and nest cavities. They can bring their own diseases and parasites. Some pollute the gene pools of related animals.

But most of all they may bring unpredictable surprises because we do not know how an animal introduced to a new environment may change its habits to adapt and survive. When the eastern gray squirrel was taken from New Jersey to the British Isles, it developed an entirely new eating habit: it began girdling and killing valuable trees, although in its native land it was not a bark eater. The European wild boar was imported at a time when little thought was given to what harm it might cause to native ecosystems.

Credit for the arrival of these animals in the southern Appalachian Mountains is most often traced to the fact that, in 1908, two English brothers, Frank and W. S. Whiting, purchased vast acreages of wilderness forest from the Great Smoky Mountain Land and Timber Company. Much of that mountain country was company owned. It simply wasn't true, as some have believed, that those hills and hollows were owned only by folks who hunted squirrels, or specialized in making and consuming home-made whiskey, or amused themselves on the front porch by picking plaintive ballads on their banjos.

In due time, the Whiting brothers had, as we call it today, a cash-flow problem. They needed a couple of million dollars, and for this they turned to George Gordon Moore, an American who worked as a professional adviser to English investors.

Moore soon arranged a loan and guided the Whitings through the closing of the negotiations so skillfully that they felt obliged to reward him. They granted him permission to build a private hunting preserve on sixteen hundred acres of fine timber around Hooper Bald, a beautiful mile-high mountain property in the Snowbird Mountains of western North Carolina.

Moore was thinking big. According to a North Carolina Wildlife Resources Commission report written by Perry Jones, Moore began, in 1909, to bring his dream to reality. First, he needed a road up the mountain. Local folks, looking up at Hooper's Bald, allowed that was going to be a right smart job. But in due time, hiring local help, Moore completed the narrow winding trail. Then, Moore and his workmen began hauling building materials up the mountain and constructing cabins and a lodge. They also built long fences, enclosing areas for the animals he was about to import. The job called for twenty-five tons of wire, which was hauled up the mountain by oxen. According to Perry Jones, Moore used the fencing to close in a fifteen-hundred-acre "buffalo lot," as he called it. Then he built a smaller one of five hundred acres, and this was called the "boar lot." It was enclosed with a split-rail fence nine rails high.

Moore's mountaintop dream was rapidly becoming a reality. All it needed now was the animals, and by the spring of 1912 the beasts were arriving, and citizens of the little town of Murphy, North Carolina, saw some strange sights.

The railroad ran through Murphy, and this made the town the shipping center nearest to Hooper's Bald. One day the train brought in four huge, shaggy buffaloes. By now, however, the people were waiting especially for the wild Russian hogs, and when the crates arrived, they held fourteen of the cantankerous swine, some of them displaying long curved tusks and snorting and complaining in a fearful manner.

Their crates were soon loaded onto wagons, and the oxen leaned into their yolks. The trip up the mountain took three days. One of the sows died of stress en route, but finally the procession dragged into Hooper's Bald.

Neighbors climbed the mountains to witness the release of the wild hogs into the big pen. As one observer recalled, "as the beady-eyed tuskers whooshed from their crates, some of the mountaineers went shinnying up trees like scared squirrels. They had been used to wild mountain razorbacks and acorn-splitter hogs all their lives but these wild pigs from abroad were something different."

There was more: up the mountain road came eight buffalo, fourteen elk, six mule deer shipped in from Colorado, and thirty-four bears. Nine of these were Russian brown bears, the same species as our grizzly. In addition, Moore brought in two hundred wild turkeys and ten thousand ring-neck pheasant eggs. All except the European wild boars were turned out in the big buffalo lot. In with them went a hundred and fifty of the turkeys plus an equal number of sheep on which the imported bears were expected to feed themselves.

To oversee all this, Moore needed a game keeper. His choice was Garland McGuire a towheaded youth known in those parts as "Cotton." Cotton McGuire must have liked the work or the location because he was there on Hooper's Bald for the next thirty-one years. During those years he became famous as an authority on the European wild boar. While it would be pleasant to report that he learned to love the wild boars, he is instead quoted as saying, "They're just plain hateful. They take food that bears better deserve."

"As the beady-eyed tuskers whooshed from their crates, some of the mountaineers went shinnying up trees like scared squirrels . . . these wild pigs were something different."

There were days when he must not have been very fond of his bears either. Probably because some of them had come from zoos, they were adept at fence climbing. They would leave the buffalo lot more or less at will. Then, McGuire and his crew would have to lasso the bear's front feet and stretch him around a tree long enough to fit him with a collar and long chains by which they would lead him back into the pen while trying to stay away from his claws and jaws.

The years took their course and the size of the menagerie dwindled. Local poachers took the turkeys. The European boars stuck around where the food was and multiplied.

For George Moore, the project had been like a kid's tree house; the fun was in the building of it. Once the shooting preserve was complete, he came a few times and sometimes brought guests. Gradually, support money, then even Cotton McGuire's salary, stopped coming. McGuire was hard pressed. He finally tramped down the mountain to the county seat and chatted with an attorney who henceforth wrote to Moore in behalf of his game keeper.

As a result, Moore asked McGuire to come to New York to talk over what they should do about the Hooper's Bald property. In New York, McGuire was pleasantly surprised. Moore wrote him a check for a thousand dollars and, in addition, handed him a newly signed title to the Hooper's Bald property and all its imported critters.

As Cotton McGuire bumped along on the train that carried him back to the mountains, he began to wonder what he was going to do with all these new possessions. By the time he reached home he must have already settled on the fate of his hateful wild hogs. He couldn't rightly tell how many there were living in the big pen but figured there must be somewhere between sixty and a hundred of them. "I'll shoo them critters outa there and let 'em root for 'emselves."

But in the process he intended to have some fun. McGuire set a date for his friends and neighbors to come up the mountain and participate in a grand hunt, the first authorized hunt for genuine European wild boars in the Great Smokies.

On the appointed day his friends were on hand with their rangy hounds and old shotguns. The hunt was even wilder than McGuire anticipated. He opened the gate to the big pen and the hunters and their dogs crowded through. Then the hounds, suddenly realizing that they had gone to heaven where game trails were so thick a dog didn't even have to search for them, raced off howling joyfully after the hogs.

At this point all hell broke loose. Hogs and dogs began chasing each other in every direction amid barking, growling, grunting, and bodily contact, leaving eviscerated hounds upon the ground. Meanwhile, the mountain hunters who had come up the hill figuring on shooting one of them wild Rooshian pigs had all scrambled into nearby trees where they perched on limbs like big-eyed gargoyles looking down on the damndest scene they had ever witnessed.

It was a one-act drama and it ended quickly. Every one of the hogs, from old boars to little spotted piglets, headed for the deep woods, scattering dogs and chunks of rail fence in their wake. That was the day the European boar truly went wild in the Great Smokies. To the delight of some people and the despair of others, they have lived there in relative prosperity ever since.

Once peace and quiet returned to Hooper's Bald, McGuire began selling off the remaining elk and buffalo. The Whiting Manufacturing Company then sold its property to a major paper company, which hired Cotton McGuire for fire warden duty. He continued to work on the mountain until he died in 1957, at the age of sixty-two. Remnants of the old buildings and fences could be seen there on Hooper's Bald for many years. Today the site of the shooting preserve is within the boundaries of the Nantahala National Forest.

Descendants of the European wild hogs that escaped from Hooper's Bald roam widely through the forested mountains of that region. Without question they crossed with some of the half-wild razorbacks roaming those hills. But whatever the blood lines, today's wild hogs ranging the southern Appalachian Mountains retain the rugged features and mean disposition of the genuine European wild boar. It is a hog with a reputation that draws hunters to the mountains year after year. The North Carolina Wildlife Resources Commission and the Tennessee Wildlife Resources Agency view their European wild hogs as a valuable resource, manage them to maintain a huntable population and collect special fees from all who come to hunt them. The wild mountain swine are also considered important by motel operators, restaurant owners, and merchants.

Others, however, especially the staff of the Great Smoky Mountains National Park, see the wild hogs as a scourge and long for a way to exclude them from the park. The Park Service lists several reasons for its uncharitable attitude toward wild hogs. Its general policy favors preservation of native ecosystems. Introduced species do not belong, and the hogs have spread throughout the park, migrating to the higher elevations for the spring and summer months. Wherever they go they tear up the forest understory, especially in beech woods. The hog's choice of foods, as well as its foraging habits, keep it high on the rangers' hate list.

They have seen the transplanted hogs kill and eat fawns of the whitetail deer. They are also concerned for the rare plants of the Great Smokies. As the hogs root about for food, they dig up as much as eighty percent of the forest floor. In the process they dig up the tubers of the rare turk's cap lily, and may have been the prime villain in the disappearance of Gray's lily, which has not been found since the 1950s. Other foods, both plant and animal, taken by these wild hogs number in the dozens. Berries, tubers, acorns, nuts, carrion, salamanders, and the eggs and young of ground-nesting birds are all choice to a wild hog. They consider copperheads and timber rattlers delicacies. They compete for food with deer, bears, squirrels, and turkeys.

The Park Service people fight back by trying to trap the hogs and move them far enough out of the park that they will not return. This is difficult, but the rangers set their special traps wherever they find that the hogs have rooted, or wallowed and rubbed their muddy hides against nearby trees. They bait the traps with an irresistible mixture of fermented corn, molasses, and yeast.

When they find a wild hog in one of their traps, they call the state wildlife workers in Tennessee or North Carolina, who are glad to have the animals. They come in pickup trucks with hauling crates in which they transport the animals to either the Cherokee National Forest in Tennessee or the Nantahala National Forest in North Carolina. Sportsmen help with the transplanting. In North Carolina, the Graham County Sportsman's Club has helped move hundreds of hogs from the park to areas where they can be hunted during the open season. One year they moved three hundred and twenty-five.

Perhaps the largest and meanest was a boar weighing two hundred and fifty pounds. He carried long ivory tusks and made it plain that if he could get out of the crate in which he was imprisoned he would do damage to the people on hand. One of the biologists

Wild hogs compete for food with other animals. They consider copperheads and timber rattlers delicacies and kill and eat the fawns of whitetail deer.

moving the old boar said, "It was a hot day in mid-August and we wanted to cool him off as soon as possible following the ride, so we backed the pickup down to a little creek. We thought that there, where he could hear and smell the water, he would rush right into the stream." But they underrated the level of the boar's anger. Instead of seeking the relief of the stream and the safety of the forest, he ran around the truck in pursuit of the man who had hauled him across the mountain, sending him scrambling onto the roof of the truck, where he remained until the hog gave up and departed.

Farther north, wildlife biologists with the West Virginia Department of Natural Resources looked out across their part of this ancient mountain range and began thinking about wild hogs. They reasoned that the European wild boar should prosper as well in the hills of West Virginia as it does in nearby states, and that they could share the license and permit fees.

This led them to Tennessee, where in 1971 they purchased basic stock, which they then released on the forested mountainsides of southern West Virginia. The "Boone County Boar," as West Virginia likes to call its European hog, has since spread across more than one hundred square miles and is still going.

Eight years after their release the wild boars of West Virginia were hunted in that state's first legal hog season and three animals were taken. Now, in the annual fall hunt, there are usually four or five hunters per hundred who take home a wild hog.

Nearby in the mountains of eastern Kentucky these imported hogs are classed as varmints. Kentuckians feel much the same about the European boars as Cotton McGuire felt toward them. "We have them," says a Kentucky wildlife biologist, "but we don't want them."

This was also the attitude of wildlife biologists in Washington state in the early 1980s, when they discovered that a group of hound owners had imported and released, without approval, seed stock of wild hogs to run before their dogs. The hogs prospered until the Washington Department of Game, to its horror, learned of the importation and rushed to correct the mistake while there might still be time. Said one biologist, after inspecting the hog damage, "Wherever those hogs went, it looked like a flock of rototillers came through." Washington got out of the hog business quickly by encouraging everyone to shoot them.

But if any arguments against exotics were known to George Moore when he planned his grand experiment atop Hooper's Bald early in this century, he did not allow them to deter him. That's why Tennessee, North Carolina, and West Virginia have their "wild Rooshian" boars today, and why Kentucky has them too whether she wants them or not.

17

The G-Men
Go Hunting

For more than three-quarters of a century the federal government has been in the hunting business in a big way. This began at the request of ranchers who ran their cattle and sheep on public land at pitifully low returns to the government, as they still do, but felt that the government owed them protection from wild predators. They eventually applied sufficient pressure on Congress to get their way.

By the late 1890s, a major subject discussed at any gathering of two or more stockmen was the bounty payments handed out for killing predators. The bounty system was widely believed to be efficient, but stockmen and officials alike wanted to see it standardized. In other words, they wanted to institute a broadside plan that would attack wild predators throughout the West.

The Forest Service was the earliest agency to view predator control as a public duty. It requested help from the Bureau of Biological Survey, which in time would become the U.S. Fish and Wildlife Service. In 1907, using mostly poisons, and trapping and killing the young in dens, bounty hunters in the national forests had a record year. They killed more than eighteen hundred wolves and twenty-three thousand coyotes, plus assorted other creatures. The Forest

Service calculated that this meant a two-million-dollar saving for stockmen.

This kind of talk fueled the effort to bring the government into the predator business, full-scale, across the West. As a result, in 1915, Congress made its first substantial appropriation for hiring government hunters to combat what was commonly called "the menace." This initial expenditure was $125,000, intended primarily for killing wolves. Once the plan was set in motion, it just kept growing.

Soon the Bureau of Biological Survey's new Branch of Predator and Rodent Control subdivided the western range country into predator control districts. Each had its trappers and supervisors.

These "gopher chokers," as the government trappers came to be known, were all business. This was no job for a lazy man. Every trapper was expected to get out there and kill his share. In a 1923 letter, Predatory Animal Inspector M. E. Musgrave of Phoenix,

A hunter employed by the Bureau of Biological Survey in Montana displays his February (1917) catch of wolf and coyote skins. Hunters received points for every predator killed, and were fired if they didn't make their monthly quota.

Arizona, told his trappers, "Remember our slogan: 'Bring them in regardless of how.'" In the same letter he explained the point system. A trapper was given a half point for killing a fox, one point for a coyote or bobcat, ten points for a bear, and fifteen points for a lion or wolf. If the trapper killed dogs that were doing damage to livestock he was given points for that as well. The trapper earning fifteen points in a month, half a point per working day, made the Honor Roll. The trapper failing to kill a reasonable number of animals could expect to be fired. Said Musgrave, "If the animals are in your district to be gotten, we feel that you should get them and I do not feel that it is necessary for any man to work any length of time without catching some predatory animals."

Killing predators was not limited to the West. In the East, state after state and county after county had offered rewards for killing animals. The idea is still alive. Nor was the bounty system limited to large meat eaters. Pennsylvania, in 1885, passed a law offering payments for killing hawks and owls of all kinds. This led to the deaths of more than 125,000 birds of prey and took the pressure off the rodents that ate the farmer's crops.

Once the federal government had set itself up in this wildlife-killing business, it began hiring the most skilled trappers and trackers in the West and turned them into professional wildlife eliminators. Over the years their work has had a tremendous effect on the native wildlife populations, especially the large predators.

The government trappers began taking staggering numbers of wolves, coyotes, bobcats, badgers, foxes, bears, and mountain lions, along with prairie dogs and other smaller animals. Old government records show that there were numerous years in which more than a hundred thousand coyotes were killed. In its first three decades this federal program would kill 1,792,915 coyotes. In a later thirty-two-year period, beginning in 1937, they also took some fifty thousand red wolves, a species that was, in time, completely wiped out throughout its range.

Figures of known kills by government agents for 1972, a typical year, show that these workers killed 190,763 larger mammals, or about five hundred and twenty-two daily. Coyotes made up two hundred and forty-five of this daily score, while bears and mountain lions were also killed by the government almost every day somewhere in the West. In 1971, when the government trappers killed a total of 121,135 mammals, the roster of dead included coyotes, bobcats, bears, mountain lions, badgers, foxes, opossums, porcupines, raccoon, skunks, nutria, mountain beaver, beaver, woodchucks, muskrats, weasels, gray wolves, rabbits, and mink. Their targets have also included mice, gophers, bob-o-links, and blackbirds. The government trappers have proved to be relentless, rugged, skilled, and experienced. But they have rarely destroyed enough of America's wild animals to satisfy their sponsors.

Government agencies, once established, find all manner of justifications for continuing and enlarging their work. After three quarters of a century, government hunters, supported by western congressmen, are still in business. Their control work has spread eastward to the Atlantic seacoast.

Furthermore, the annual budget for this wildlife "control" continues to grow. In the fiscal year 1981, Congress allotted the "animal damage control" program, which is the official name for the government trapping, shooting, and poisoning of wildlife, $15,900,000. By fiscal year 1988, federal taxpayers were kicking in $24,000,000 to support this program, and to this was added another $12,000,000 in state and local funds. No matter how much a debt-conscious administration tries to cut this figure, Congress invariably responds to western stockmen's demands, and the subsidy we pay for wildlife killing grows.

The government is reluctant now to give out figures showing how proficient it is at killing the native wild animals. As public pressure has risen against the use of public funds to kill publicly owned wildlife, agencies responsible for this work have quietly stopped publishing figures on what they kill. To learn the total loss we would have to know the federal trappers' kill, plus figures for animals killed by state hunters, ranchers, and the free-lance agents hired by ranchers and stockmens associations.

With the wolf gone, the coyote was elevated to the very top of the government trapper's list of public enemies. Stockmen have been fighting coyotes since the country was settled, and although the coyote chasers kill enough animals to win a battle here and there, the coyote is that rare wild animal that seems to be winning the

war. This wild dog is a survivor. In the face of all the money and
effort spent to kill it, the little song dog of the night, adapting to
man-made changes in the landscape, has steadily extended its
range until it lives in all forty-nine mainland states.

The coyote, measuring twenty-one inches high at the shoulders
and weighing perhaps twenty-five pounds (a little less for the female), specializes in adapting to new conditions. Left to its own
devices, it is a superb catcher of mice and other rodents. But its list
of natural foods has expanded to include cantaloupes, garbage, and
an occasional sheep or turkey.

The coyote arouses an unreasoning hatred in some sheepmen.
Instead of concentrating on the individuals that have learned to kill
sheep or turkeys, ranchers have historically condemned all coyotes.
The hatred for coyotes has prompted people to burn them to death,
starve them by cutting off the lower jaw or wiring their jaws shut,
then releasing them, and sometimes hanging them in trees as targets for handgun practice. One of the prime weekend activities in
some areas is running coyotes down with off-road vehicles.

One newspaperman told his readers about the cooperative coyote
hunts in Kansas when he grew up there during the late 1930s and
early 1940s. "It was common," he said, "to see 2,000 men and boys,
armed with shotguns, form a circle that would encompass several
hundred acres and close the circle." The grandest such hunt he
recalled occurred in 1941. Eight thousand coyote hunters partici-
pated. They surrounded two counties, and as they closed in, small
airplanes flew back and forth over the crowd, keeping the people in
formation. The hunt reduced the local predator population by an
estimated two hundred coyotes.

Perhaps the most unusual outdoorsman ever to serve as government trapper was Ben Lilly, a gangly, bewhiskered character who
was either eccentric or mad, depending on your definition, and not
at all typical of the breed of outdoorsman the government normally
hired for this work. Lilly worked awhile for the U.S. Biological
Survey.

There is nothing surprising in the fact that the government would
seek Lilly out and offer him employment as one of its professional
predator hunters. Lilly may have been the most effective tracker and
hunter of his time. He was surely the most tenacious. Once he took
up the trail of a bear or cougar—and these were his specialties—he
planned to stay on that trail until the animal was dead. By some
accounts he killed six hundred cougars in his career and perhaps

Gene Payson, an Arizona government hunter who specialized in mountain lions, with his famous pack of hounds (1930). Wildlife "control" still continues today.

four hundred bears. His favorite meat on the trail was cougar. He claimed that it kept him agile.

Lilly was born in Alabama in 1856 and began hunting at an early age. He followed the game westward into the Big Thicket country of eastern Texas and eventually hunted in New Mexico and Arizona. His hunting was so mixed with Bible reading that both appeared to be elements of his religion. He pursued predators as though tracking Satan, and there is some evidence that this is what he actually thought he was doing. He might stay on the trail of a cougar or bear for weeks or even months. Or he might simply stay away from home for no explained reason. Folklorist and historian J. Frank Dobie, who wrote *The Legend of Ben Lilly*, told of the time Lilly's wife handed him his gun and told him to go shoot the neighborhood "chicken hawk." Lilly returned three years later saying, "That hawk just kept going."

His hunting for the government was in Arizona and New Mexico.

Precisely how successful he was as a government employee is somewhat fuzzy. By this time, however, Lilly was in his late middle-age and already a considerable legend.

He wore what Dobie called a "Santa Claus beard" and had clear blue eyes. He was lanky and was said to be so athletic that he could jump out of a barrel without using his hands. He was always accompanied by two or three long-legged hounds which were usually tied to his belt by a rope. He used one of his dogs as a pillow at night. Even when there was a bed available, Lilly slept on the ground or the floor. If the ground was too wet, he climbed into a tree and spent the night perched in its branches. He said he couldn't sleep properly if he was too comfortable.

Among his possessions was a small tattered Bible which he read regularly and from which he could quote at length. He never worked on Sunday. If his dogs treed a lion or bear late on Saturday, they just had to stay there with it until Monday morning.

The wildest hunt Ben Lilly ever conducted was probably his pursuit of a grizzly bear beginning in the summer of 1921. Dobie, who was personally acquainted with the old hunter, recorded the story of this remarkable hunt. Lilly was then sixty-five years old and spent much of the time as far from people as he could manage. But the hunt planned by Oklahoma oilman W. H. McFadden was enough to bring him out of the wilderness.

McFadden had a grandiose idea for a free-wheeling hunt that would take him and his friends, first class, on a plush outing all the way from the Mexican border to the wilds of Alaska in pursuit of whatever game they encountered. This was to be another of those grand hunts staged in the style established by European noblemen in the previous century. Lilly's job was to find a large grizzly for McFadden, then point McFadden toward it.

He first came upon the track of a bear he considered worthy in the mountains above Taos late in June. The chase was on. He trailed the grizzly through the mountains of northern New Mexico and into Colorado. He saw where it fed, slept and left its tooth and claw marks on the bark of trees. Lilly thought little of trailing an animal for days without eating, and he slept wherever night overcame him. "It hurts me to let a bear rest," he once admitted.

The memory of this bear hurt him for the remainder of his life. Even though he trailed the bear for six months, McFadden's unpredictable schedule never permitted Lilly to bring hunter and hunted close enough to complete his mission.

Ben Lilly, perhaps the most skilled tracker of his time, worked as a government hunter during the 1920s. Known for his tenacity on the trail, Lilly slept on the ground with one of his dogs as a pillow. His favorite meat in the field was cougar.

He later took occasional employment hunting cougars for ranchers, but as time passed he withdrew deeper and deeper into the hills and into himself. Those who met him remembered his penetrating blue eyes and how he talked about animals he had known in a kind of chant that made him seem to ignore the people around him. Some folks said, plain out, that Old Lilly was nutty as a fruitcake.

But nobody ever doubted that he possessed an uncanny knowledge of the ways of bears, lions, and the other creatures he pursued throughout his life. It would be fitting to learn that Ben Lilly died on the trail of his last victim, the cow horn call he used for his dogs slung from his shoulder, his hound dragging him along by its leash, while his blue eyes recorded the clues that led him inexorably into position for a telling shot from his straight-shooting old gun. But this was not to be. He died in 1936, a ward of the county, in Silver City, New Mexico.

More typical of government trappers were western outdoorsmen like Bill Pullins, solid citizens and reliable workers, performing what they saw as a valuable public service. Pullins was a coyote-trapping specialist. Some years ago a reporter for *Audubon* magazine drove into the village of White River, South Dakota, looking for Pullins. He found him at home in a little white house on a quiet back street, and through much of that summer afternoon the reporter sat and talked with the old trapper in his kitchen.

Speaking quietly, Pullins, a barrel chested man with a ruddy complexion, recalled various coyotes he had trapped over the years prior to his retirement. He said that he really liked coyotes and considered them highly intelligent and appealing animals. He explained how he had kept coyotes to collect the urine needed for making scent baits for use around his trap sets, and how he became attached to these individuals as a person might to any pet. Finally, he began talking about the animal he considered the most intelligent coyote he ever encountered.

The rancher who called Pullins in to take this coyote claimed that it had been killing sheep. Pullins found the trail it normally followed on its hunts and proceeded to make his set. This called for extreme care. The trapper spread a square of canvas on which to kneel. He dug a place for the trap and set it slightly below ground level. Then, he used a square of clean cloth, free of the odor of soap or any other foreign substance, to keep dirt from sifting beneath the pan and blocking its action. Finally, he sprinkled loose dirt over the trap, camouflaging it completely. He carried the excess soil away from the set. Then he carefully dusted the area free of any impressions and sprinkled a dash of coyote urine on a nearby bush to take the animal's mind off traps and set him to thinking about the competition from his own kind.

Pullins soon learned that he was dealing with an experienced old coyote. The next morning the trap was empty, but it had been carefully dug out, set off, and left in plain view on the trail. Pullins grinned as he recalled the morning. "I knew I had a problem," he said. "It was going to be a game with him."

This game went on, morning after morning, until Pullins invented a new trick for the old coyote to solve. He half buried a dead prairie dog beneath the edge of a rock, then surrounded it with four carefully set traps. He stood back, admired his work, and slipped away, figuring that this time the coyote was as good as caught.

Not quite. The next morning he found all four traps set off and the prairie dog gone.

After six months of the most concentrated effort he had ever expended in pursuit of a single animal, Pullins managed to catch the coyote. But he never forgot him. Professional trappers often develop an understanding and deep affection for the animals they pursue. "I have a lot of admiration for the coyote," Pullins told his visitor quietly, as he looked out the kitchen window into the distance, his mind a long way off.

To this day some government hunters prefer traps to all other weapons in their pursuit of coyotes. Often their trapping began when they were still kids, and the challenge of outwitting their prey stayed with them until it became the backbone of their profession. But poisons were also used early in the war against wildlife. Strychnine was a common poison for more than a century. Egg or meat baits laced with strychnine accounted for long lists of hawks, owls, foxes, coyotes, rodents, and other animals. Coyotes soon learned to recognize the bitter taste and avoid strychnine baits.

According to Jenks Cameron, writing in a 1929 government publication, "Placing of poison for animals of the truly satanic cunning of wolves and coyotes has in fact become a fine art." Cameron noted that in a single season, 1923, "Over two hundred thousand square miles were covered with one million seven hundred and three thousand placed baits." In 1920, the federal government established a new laboratory in Albuquerque to study and produce poisons that would be more effective in killing wild animals.

The most efficient poisons were still to come. One of these can be traced to the earliest days of World War II. When Germany invaded Poland in 1939, two Polish scientists hurried out of their native country and made their way to England. They carried with them information about a new poison chemical—sodium fluoroacetate.

In this country the government was confronted by a need for

effective ways to combat rodents, especially rats, and replace poisons it could no longer obtain abroad. When the details on sodium fluoroacetate reached America, under wartime secrecy precautions, it was assigned to the U.S. Fish and Wildlife Service laboratories for study. The Fish and Wildlife Service gave it a code number: they called it 1080.

Government workers began testing the new poison. The Fish and Wildlife Service was intrigued by the fact that 1080 was more deadly for some species than for others. While at various concentrations it killed mammals and birds of all kinds, it was most toxic to members of the dog family. This meant that it was especially suited to killing coyotes. Tests showed that one pound of 1080 could be mixed with twenty-eight hundred pounds of meat to make a bait that would kill a coyote after it ate only one or two ounces of the treated bait.

This colorless, odorless, and nearly tasteless poison caused death in chain reactions. Many kinds of animals that ate from the carcasses of 1080 victims, or picked up the poisoned vomitus of a coyote, died. Eagles, bears, and pet dogs fell victim. But the substance became a standard weapon in the arsenal of the Fish and Wildlife Service's war on predators. It is known among the trained government agents that concentrations of 1080 capable of killing canines might not kill eagles or other predators that feed on the bait. This was explained in 1958 to a group of sportsmen by Weldon B. Robinson of the U.S. Fish and Wildlife Service Research Laboratory in Denver, Colorado. As Robinson explained, "If 1 unit of 1080 is needed to kill a given weight of coyote, then the number of units needed to kill equal weights of other mammals and birds . . . would be magpies 6, bobcats 6, martens and badgers 10, raccoons above 20, golden eagles 50, most hawks and owls 100, and opossum 600."

These findings convinced the predator-control specialists that they had found the perfect coyote poison. All they had to do was control the dosages and they could expect to kill coyotes while sparing most other wild animals.

Before long, however, 1080 was also being bootlegged outside official circles. Ranchers and their workers were moving on their own to establish bait stations in remote areas, and the ranchers and their crews were far less careful and knowledgeable about the dosages used than the professionals were. Any animal gorging itself on the poisoned bait might ingest enough to kill it.

Some sheepmen, in their conviction that all coyotes should be killed, did not limit their 1080 bait stations to sheep range. The chemical showed up on public lands, even in national parks. It was also found in watersheds flowing into recreation areas and reservoirs used by the public.

Conservationists began working to get information on the hazards of 1080 across to the public. Gradually word spread. Concern mounted, especially because 1080 was killing entirely too many nontargeted animals. Finally, in 1972, the Environmental Protection Agency banned the use of 1080. Sheepmen never let up in their efforts to regain use of the wartime poison, and the government now permits its use in a few western states where it is placed in collars worn by sheep to poison coyotes that attack these animals. Nobody will ever know how many wild animals have been killed by this wartime poison. Added to the count of known bodies must be the uncounted thousands of animals that slipped away to die in hidden places. This is only one of the poisons still being used to kill predators.

Cyanide has been widely used, especially in a device known as the "coyote-getter." This creation allows its victims to execute themselves by pulling on a bait. When an animal pulls at the bait, sodium cyanide, propelled by .38 Special cartridge, is shot into its mouth. A similar device, but spring operated, is the M-44. Death from these devices comes in seconds, sometimes to coyotes and sometimes to household pets.

But there is hope that we may be outgrowing our love affair with poisons that kill wildlife. The government's animal damage control people are sensitive to mounting public opposition to broad-scale killing of any wild animal.

Besides, some ranchers no longer harbor the deep prejudices that led us into a government sponsored war on predators. Wildlife is part of their world, and perhaps increasingly, they see room on the land for the occasional wild predator, even a coyote. There is a growing understanding that we should at least restrict our predator killing to those individuals known to be causing losses and allow the rest to live on the wild foods around them. Enlightened stockmen are beginning to substitute guard dogs, frightening devices, and electric fencing for poisons. But old prejudices die hard. The coyote, and often the legally protected eagles, bears, and mountain lions, must move with extreme caution through a heavily peopled world.

18

Bare Hands and Wolf Fangs

There have always been unorthodox hunters with their own peculiar ideas, but perhaps no man ever developed a stranger, or riskier, system for taking wolves and coyotes than John R. Abernathy did. His specialty was catching wolves with his bare hands. In his jaunty manner, he would come riding into camp with his victims hogtied and helpless across his saddle, still very much alive.

That anyone should possess such a talent was uncanny. Hunters who understood the ways of the wolf usually had trouble believing the story until they saw it done. How could this runty cowpuncher actually have taught himself to capture full-sized wolves with his bare hands? In the early days of his wolf catching career, Jack Abernathy weighed in at a hundred and thirty pounds, spurs and all, but he was rawhide tough. Like many lightweight men, Jack possessed lightning-fast reactions.

He kept his face clean shaven, had bushy eyebrows and a shock of straight, dark hair that fell over his forehead. Jack's self-confidence bordered on cockiness. While most westerners wore their broad-brimmed hats planted squarely on their heads, Jack Abernathy usually tilted his hat to one side. He was always ready for a scrap, and despite his size, possessed the strength and agility that gave him a decided edge over most adversaries, man or beast. Whether he was catching wild animals, dangerous men, or breaking wild horses, he stuck to his job until it was finished. If born with any capacity for fear, he either lost it early in life or learned how to hide it. He often said, "There's nothing I'll back away from," and he couldn't recall ever having felt any different. In a tight situation, the straight line of his mouth clamped shut, accentuating the square-ness of his jaw. Even so, folks told him that he was risking his life every time he tackled a wolf without a weapon. But Jack allowed as "'twarn't much," and went right out and did it again.

He always lumped wolves and coyotes together. To him they were big and little versions of the same critter. Either one had canines sharp enough to tear out a man's throat. Most of the thousand or so wild canines that he claimed to have taken barehanded were coy-otes. In a good day, with the aid of his quick-witted horse and faithful hounds, he could catch two coyotes in the morning and a couple more in the afternoon. But he also subdued full-sized gray wolves that sometimes weighed about as much as he did. It was one of these beasts that first awakened him to the revelation that he could catch a wolf barehanded.

At the age of fifteen he had hired on as a full-time cowboy with the J-A, a sprawling cattle spread in central Texas. From the first, his lack of fear around animals, especially horses, made him a favorite with his boss. There was rugged work to do, and here was a kid who didn't back away from the toughest job.

Jack had been on the J-A about three months when he learned that the bronc buster who rode first saddle was leaving. There was more money in bronc busting than in ordinary cow punching, and Jack said to himself, "That's my job."

When he walked up to the leathery-skinned foreman and an-nounced boldly that he was applying for a job of first saddle, the foreman glanced at the other cowboys. "All right, Jack," he said, with a sly wink at those gathered around the corral, "you can have the job if you can sit Haystack long enough to roll and light a smoke."

The others were quite willing to let little Jack have a try at that job. Only one other rider had ever mounted the outlaw horse and what happened to him gave the horse its name. He was thrown all the way out of the corral onto the top of a haystack.

But the teen-age kid rode Haystack long enough to qualify for the job and the foreman was true to his word. The little bronc buster went on to break three hundred and eight horses on the ranch, often riding two wild horses in the morning and two more in the afternoon.

The whole crew, including the little bronc buster who rode first saddle, was out on the range working the round-up one day when Jack's horse slipped and rolled down a cliff. The next day Jack was too sore to wear his six-guns comfortably so he left them back at the ranch. Otherwise he might never have learned of his strange power over wolves.

He had been out about an hour, in the first light of day, when he worked his way down a long draw and rode right up to two large gray wolves who were tearing their breakfast from a beef carcass. Jack automatically reached for his six-guns before remembering that they were back in camp. Instead of running, the wolves lowered their heads, growled once at Jack and returned to their breakfast.

Jack's duty was clear. Wolves were enemies of cattle. He had no choice but to chase off the wolves even without his guns. He spoke to his dogs and they leaped at the wolves. One wolf departed. The other one promptly killed one of the dogs, then tackled the second one. Their snarling filled the canyon, and the dust storm they raised helped obscure the action.

Almost without thinking, Jack leaped from his horse to go to the aid of his dog. As he recalled the story later, he landed within a few feet of the wolf, which now left the dog and with lips curled over gleaming white canines turned on Jack.

The little cowboy could have mounted his horse and made his escape, and nobody would have faulted him for it. But the thought never crossed Abernathy's mind. Instead of trying to escape, he stuck out his right hand for the wolf to grab—and that's what the wolf did. Jack intended to wrap his other arm around the beast's neck and give himself enough leverage to break its neck. To his surprise, he never felt the wolf's teeth cut into his hand. He had made a great discovery: he had reacted with such vigor that he grabbed the wolf's jaw *behind* the canines. Now he clamped down with an iron grip and simply wrestled the animal to the ground, then landed on top of it. Man and wolf thrashed around in the dust, but Jack did not relax his grip.

He was already subduing the wolf when another rider's horse slid to a stop a few feet away. The rider drew his gun. Jack yelled "don't shoot." He had the animal under control. He tied the wolf's mouth

Abernathy had reacted with such vigor that he grabbed the wolf's jaw behind the canines.
He clamped down with an iron grip and wrestled the animal to the ground.

shut with a piece of baling wire, trussed it up and slung it over his saddle for the ride back to camp. Jack became the camp hero. His wolf was said to weigh about a hundred pounds.

Jack followed this initial act with more bare-handed catches. He never had any competition in this strange business. More than once he offered to teach other hunters how to take live wolves with their bare hands. Occasionally one of them took him up on the offer. "But they'd all get scared at the last minute." Jack complained. "Just as they were supposed to grab the wolf's jaw, they would pull their hand back. They couldn't seem to help it. Then's when the wolf would grab them." The lesson would end with yelling and swearing and Jack wading in to rescue his student and teach the wolf some respect. "I never succeeded in teaching one person how to catch wolves by hand," he admitted.

Wolf catching became a spare-time business for Abernathy. He found that circuses and sideshows would pay fifty dollars each for big wolves in good condition—which his invariably were.

What were the special qualities enabling him to capture wolves bare-handed? Jack Abernathy always claimed that, in addition to his quick hands, sure eye, physical strength, and determination, it was a wolf's natural habit of leaping at its victim that gives a man just the right chance to get an iron grip on its lower jaw. Wolves had never had to adapt to an enemy like Jack Abernathy.

Jack standardized his wolf-catching system. He rode a horse well-trained to the sport, and kept a pack of greyhounds to help bring the wolf or coyote to bay. He would normally ride off with a pair of his dogs trotting beside him. Sooner or later, he would spot a coyote or wolf slipping away in the distance. The chase was on. It might lead over rough country and through prairie dog towns for miles. But eventually his dogs would gain and dash in for a close-quarter fight with their wild cousin. At this point, Jack would vault from his horse and order his dogs back. From here on the fight belonged to the master.

Reporters sometimes insisted that Jack wore heavy canvas gloves. This was not so. "A heavy glove," he explained patiently, "won't let you get the grip you need on a wolf's mouth, and you may take a good slashing for your trouble."

Jack, the wolf catcher, was born in Bosque County, Texas, in 1876, when the West was still wild. His parents, hard-working, serious-minded people of Scotch origin, had pushed westward across the country with the earliest settlers. Buffalo, bear, and mountain lions were still common. The nearest neighbors lived ten miles away, and Indian raids remained the number one hazard of the times.

In those pioneering days, schooling was a luxury. Jack's total classroom experience was limited to a couple of weeks, but he learned to read by studying the labels on tobacco sacks.

His lack of formal education, however, was no major barrier in his life as a western range rider and hunter. By the age of five he was an accomplished horseman, and when he reached ten he was already working on the range with the men, sleeping out at night with his saddle for a pillow and his six-guns close at hand.

Both Jack and his brother had a streak of musical talent. Jack was capable of playing sweet tunes on the violin, could make a piano do his bidding, and was passing fair as a vocalist. This musical ability brought him one of his first paying jobs. He and his brother began singing and playing on the first floor of a local business establishment whose second floor was divided into bedrooms. They worked until their parents learned where the money was coming from and put a sudden stop to their musical career. After all, Jack Abernathy was only six years old.

As Jack's wolf-catching exploits continued, his fame grew. Before long, his feats were known throughout the West. Stories of his wolf catching eventually reached the White House. "Bully," said the President. In the spring of 1905, Teddy Roosevelt was planning another of his hunting trips into the rugged western big-game country. "I'd like to stop off," he said, "and see the man Abernathy catch a wolf."

The president's hunting camp in the Big Pastures section of Oklahoma presented a strange picture that spring. There were twenty tents, lines of horses, and a pack of coyote-chasing greyhounds brought in by Abernathy. Around the whole compound, soldiers stood security guard over the president of the United States.

April's warm, pleasant winds swept across the prairie that first morning when Abernathy and the president rode off at an easy gait. They sighted the first coyote of the day and broke into a gallop. Jack's greyhounds stretched their long legs. The coyote gained on them for the first couple of miles, as Jack knew it would. After that, it was only a matter of time before the hounds overtook their quarry. When they finally brought the coyote to bay, the president saw the dogs fall back precisely as Jack's feet hit the ground. The coyote, too winded to break and run, grabbed for Abernathy. Almost faster than the eye could follow the action, Jack's hand shot out and grabbed the animal's lower jaw in a viselike grip. He turned, grinning, and held the animal up at arm's length for the president to see. For a moment Roosevelt was silent. He shook his head. "This beats anything I've seen in my whole life," he said, "and I've seen a good deal."

For six crowded days Jack Abernathy and the president continued to run and capture coyotes. That week Jack caught seventeen coyotes. It was a fine outing for the president, and for Jack Abernathy a high point in a strange career.

A few weeks later, after the president returned to his office in the White House, Jack received a telegram. The president wanted him to come visit him in Washington.

Abernathy marched down to call on the manager of the local bank. "I need to borrow enough money to travel to Washington, D.C. and back," Jack said, "because the president wants to see me." He displayed the wire from Washington.

"That's the first time anybody ever brought that story in here, Jack," said the banker as he counted out the bills.

Washington was a strange and confusing place to this man of the western prairies. He knew nothing about protocol, or waiting for appointments, so he simply asked directions to the White House. Then he marched right up to the White House and told the man at the door that he had come to see the president of the United States.

After they had recalled every coyote that ever ran before them, the President looked Jack squarely in the eye. "Jack," he said, "how would you like to be United States marshal for the State of Oklahoma?"

For once, Jack Abernathy was speechless. Such jobs were generally considered political plums for party workers of long standing. Senators and representatives pushed their favorite contributors for such jobs, bringing all available political pressure to bear. Here, with a few simple words, Jack had been handed the job.

He became one of the youngest U.S. marshals in history and discovered that catching wolves was similar in some ways to catching outlaws. He soon became one of the most respected marshals in all the West. He arrested hundreds of outlaws, and according to his

Jack Abernathy with his sons Louis (left) and Temple. The boys gained nationwide fame for riding horseback, alone, from Oklahoma to Washington, D.C.

own recollections, placed seven hundred and eighty-three of them in the penitentiary. His favorite gun was a Luger automatic, which "shot daylight through many a bad man." In later years, when he visited New York to see the sights, in the company of O. Henry, he still carried his Luger.

Abernathy passed along to his two sons his zest for life. They too gained a degree of fame and became known nationwide as "those amazing Abernathy kids." If they had a hare-brained idea, Jack was more than likely to go along with it. Their first claim to attention came when they traveled from their home in Oklahoma to Washington, D.C.—by horseback. One of them was ten years old, the other six. When they set off, Jack's only instructions were to limit themselves to fifty miles a day, don't ride through water too deep to see the bottom, and don't travel on Sundays. When they arrived in Cincinnati, that spring of 1910, the mayor told the *Cincinnati Enquirer*, "Why, they're hardly bigger than seventeen cents."

When they told their father that they intended to buy a $485 Bush Motorcar and drive it back to Oklahoma, Jack quickly granted permission. The one-cylinder vehicle, which was manufactured for half a dozen years, was described as, "Wooden body, wooden axles, wooden wheels, and wooden run." But it ran all right for the Abernathy kids. Three weeks after leaving the East Coast, the ten-year-old, now an expert driver, tooled the car into the drive at Abernathy's Oklahoma ranch.

Catching a wolf always worried Jack far less than some of the things he was later called on to do. As his fame spread, he found himself giving occasional public talks. But he never liked it. "I'd rather catch a wolf than make a talk any time," he insisted. "I'm more at ease with a wolf."

Show promoters and movie makers began offering Jack appealing sums to catch wolves before the cameras. In addition to his fling at show business, he made and lost a couple of fortunes in Texas oil booms.

He caught his last coyote in 1928, when he was fifty-two years old. Friends talked him into staging the chase. That was as strange a hunt as he ever conducted. He rode, this time, on the running board of an automobile, out across the prairie where he had ridden so often before. Soon, so the story goes, the car was bearing down on his victim.

How did it feel to catch the animal bare-handed after so many years away from the sport? Jack flexed the fingers of his right hand.

"Well," he told the reporter, "they pinch a little tighter than they did thirty-five years ago."

In August 1930, Jack suffered an oil field accident that took him to the edge of death. A steel cable snapped, snaked around his body in a massive coil, cut into his flesh, broke several ribs and made his eyes bulge. Nearby workers immediately figured he was a dead man. But they had failed to reckon with the tenacity of Jack Abernathy. He recovered. Then, the more he thought about his miraculous recovery, the more firmly he was convinced that he had been spared by the praying of a San Antonio preacher who advocated the doctrine of divine healing.

With characteristic directness, Jack Abernathy became an evangelist. He attacked Satan with the same fervor and determination that he had always applied to wolves.

But time was running out for the little wolf catcher turned preacher. He died of a heart attack at the age of sixty-five while making a movie in Long Beach, California, figuring that he could still subdue a wolf bare-handed if he set his mind to it.

19

With the Help of Hounds

The story of Daddy Steward's close call while training a young bear dog was repeated for years. This event occurred shortly after the first settlers came to the deep mountain wilderness of western Virginia. In those days Steward's dogs could pick up a bear trail almost any time their master took them to the woods. But bears had killed so many of Steward's hounds that he was down to a single old dog, called "Runner." Then he acquired a fine looking pup. The only problem was that the pup probably had never seen a bear.

Steward, planning to give the youngster some idea of what a bear looks like, brought out a bear skin he had acquired on an earlier hunt. He called in his son, James. As Steward wrapped the bear skin around his lanky form and laced it shut in several places, he carefully explained his plan to James. "You tie old Runner to the porch," he ordered, "and tie him real good, hear?"

Steward instructed James to hold the young dog until he had a head start, then he loped off in his bear skin through the meadow and into the apple orchard. "Let the pup go," He yelled to James, as he dropped down on all fours and began growling and running about in bear fashion.

The young dog rushed the "bear" but drew back whenever Steward scratched the ground, snarled and counterattacked. After several minutes of this, old Runner could stand no more. As he lunged and strained at the rope that held him, the rope weakened. The seasoned old hound lunged some more, and the rope snapped. Now, Runner was off in full cry and with a bear in plain view.

Steward, fully aware of the peril of his position, stood upright and ran as hard as he could for the nearest apple tree. He had not quite climbed beyond Runner's reach when the old dog arrived. Now the young dog got the idea. He could see from example what a bear hound was supposed to do, so he joined old Runner, trying for a firm grip on the bear skin. Meanwhile Steward was yelling at James, "Beat them off, James. Beat them off me."

By this time James was convulsed with laughter. "Just a little longer, Daddy," he yelled back. "Just a little longer. This will sure be the makin' of the pup."

Mrs. Steward arrived in time to help rescue her husband. Around the neighborhood it was common knowledge that Steward had to spend several days in bed, recovering from his dog training experiment. And, although it had seemed like a good idea at the time, Meshach Browning, who told the story, said this was the last time Steward ever volunteered to play the bear's role for his dogs.

This was just one more example of man and dog sharing their skills in a common interest. The association of man and dog in the hunting of wild game began so long ago that nobody can be certain when they first teamed up. The oldest firm evidence goes back some twelve thousand years, but early hunters probably kept dogs to help them capture wild animals long before that.

They had sound reasons. As one scholar wrote, "It would appear that man was able to fight his way up from a state of nature to civilization only with the aid of the dog." Early man had to become a hunter to survive. He had certain advantages fitting him for a life of pursuing and taking the wild animals around him. He possessed a brain large enough to give him the reasoning powers to devise tools and weapons. In addition, early man could study the habits of his prey and invent ways to ambush or trap the animals he needed.

But, compared with the animals he pursued, this early hunter was not very fast on his feet. Besides, he had an inadequate olfactory sense. While his weapons and his cunning helped him compensate for his slow speed, he simply could not depend on his nose to protect him against danger or detect game. Dogs were not only fast

Since primitive times, hunters have depended on dogs to compensate for their own inferior sense of smell and slowness afoot. As the huntsman in the 16th century print above sounds his horn, his companion releases the last two dogs of their pack. In the early 19th century print at right, a hunter leaves his village with seven dogs, each of a different breed.

runners but also had an uncanny ability to pick up odors at long distances. The late George M. Sutton, a noted scientist and specialist on the Arctic, wrote of one day telling his dogs to "find animal." They set off in a straight line, crossed a frozen lake and stopped where a dead lemming lay on a rock. The distance was three miles.

Because of its sharp sense of smell, primitive spear carriers in all parts of the world learned to appreciate the dog and use it for hunting. It has been said that without the help of dogs, man would never have become the hunter that he did. This partnership could have started in various ways. Hunters doubtless found litters of helpless pups whose mothers were dead, or off hunting, and perhaps brought the pups home for their children. These dogs knew only the hunter's camp. Other early dogs may have come to the edge of the

hunter's camps to feed on bones and scraps and gradually viewed these camps as their homes too.

The most common belief is that wolves are the ancestors of today's dogs. Gradually, as they were used for different kinds of hunting, and in various climates, they developed different characteristics. Some became specialists. Short-legged dogs were selected for going into burrows to kill badgers. Long-legged dogs became swift runners after deer, while dogs with powerful jaws specialized in fighting wild boars. Early settlers coming to these shores brought their dogs along, but the native people, all the way from the Arctic to the tropics, had kept dogs for thousands of years.

The importance of a dog to its owners continued as civilization advanced. As people found that they had freedom from the demands of food gathering to pursue other activities, some continued to hunt simply for the fun of it and took their dogs with them to the fields and woods. Kings and noblemen became famous dog fanciers. Some kept kennels with hundreds of dogs and large crews of specialists to care for them. In the Middle Ages wolf hounds wore heavy collars with protruding nails or even curved, razor-sharp blades to aid them in close-up fights.

One of the pleasures of dog ownership is telling others about the remarkable ability of your animal. This may have gone on as long as dogs and people have been associated. Artist John J. Audubon joined the ranks of the dog braggers with a favorite story about his bird dog, Juno. Audubon had hand raised a turkey gobbler that he found in the forest when it was perhaps two days old. Everyone around Henderson, Kentucky, came to know the bird. It would follow anyone who called it. But, regardless of the special status and easy life around the village, the turkey, at the age of two, began spending more and more time in the forest until at last it disappeared and did not return.

One morning much later Audubon "was going toward some lakes near Green River to shoot, when, having walked about five miles, I saw a fine large gobbler cross the path before me, moving leisurely along." Audubon ordered Juno to chase the gobbler. The dog was off like a flash.

The turkey did not try to escape, and the dog slid to a halt in front of it, then looked back at its master. The dog and turkey recognized each other. Audubon took the turkey home and tied a red ribbon around its neck for easy identification, but the following spring a neighbor shot it by mistake. Speaking of the actions of dog and turkey that day, Audubon asked, "Was it the result of instinct or reason . . . the act of an intelligent mind?"

Today's dog owners can be just as boastful as their ancestors, and perhaps as immodest as well. Some years ago a young reporter traveled into the hills of eastern Kentucky to find Hughes Atkinson. He went to talk with Atkinson about his foxhounds.

Atkinson did not kill foxes but considered it treat enough to sit the night away beside a hilltop campfire, listening to his hounds as they tracked the fox over ridges and through ravines. "Listen! Hear that? Old Chaser's leadin' again. Out front like always. No mistakin' that deep choppin' mouth."

Among the hounds that specialize in running foxes are the Walkers, Triggs, Julys, and some with ancestry not easily identifiable. But for Hughes Atkinson none of these could measure up to his breed, the Goodman. "Lot of people don't realize," said Atkinson, "that Goodman's the best foxhounds of all. But they could tell soon enough if they was to put them all together in one chase. That's all you gotta do to tell 'em apart. The one that comes out ahead is the Goodman. When it comes to runnin', the Goodman's got other hounds chained to a post."

Another Goodman owner was quick to agree. "A Goodman hound on the trail of a fox," he explained, "doesn't stay in one place long enough to shine light on."

Some dog stories, even though known to be true, smack of the unbelievable. After talking with Hughes Atkinson in Kentucky, the young reporter traveled to Illinois where, one evening in an old farmhouse, he heard the remarkable story of Hightail.

Hightail was a foxhound. She was one of those notable animals that possessed an uncanny homing ability. She was famous among fox hunters for her ability to stay on the trail through all kinds of terrain in all manner of weather. Her fame created a steady demand for her pups.

Her owner always farmed the dog out with a friend who was a professional trainer and boarder of dogs. To Hightail, this trainer became the world's most important human being. Eventually, Hightail's real owner died. The hound was getting old by this time, but the new owner arranged for Hightail to be shipped off to Virginia to the kennel of a friend who wanted to try to raise another litter of her pups. Sadly, the trainer crated the old hound up, took her to the train station and sent her off, certain that he would never see the faithful old dog again.

In Virginia, Hightail birthed and raised two more litters of pups with great fox-running capabilities. Hightail's senses were no longer as alert as they once had been. One day she ran in front of an automobile that she apparently neither saw nor heard. Although she survived, she was thereafter in bad shape. She was now totally deaf in both ears and blind in one eye. Furthermore, she limped badly. Fox chasers, hearing about this stroke of ill fortune, figured this was the end for the famous Hightail, and those who owned her descendants felt especially blessed.

One of these men lived back in Illinois about a hundred and twenty miles from where Hightail was born. He wondered if the old girl might yet give the dog world one last litter of her pups and began negotiating. As a result, Hightail was once more crated and hauled to the depot.

When the time came for the train's arrival, her new master was on hand watching for her crate. He opened the box and the grizzled old dog that limped onto the station platform brought sadness to the man's heart. Here was a hound that would surely not run away for the simple reason that she was unable to travel on her own. Convinced of this, the man took Hightail home and gave her the run of the farm. "You can run free here in whatever time you have left," he said quietly.

By the end of the day, however, Hightail had vanished. No amount of neighborhood searching turned up a trace of the ailing old dog. She was driven by a nagging compulsion that would not let her rest. Some strange longing urged her on along country roads and across fields, mile on mile, always in the same direction. For two weeks she alternately traveled and rested.

One night her original trainer was in the woods fox hunting. He was sitting in the darkness beside his fire, listening to his hounds run a fox, when he became aware that a ragged old dog stood looking at him from the edge of the night shadows. He stared in disbelief. In all his experience he had known only one dog with these markings. He had heard that Hightail was back in the state, and knew that the man who brought her back lived a hundred and twenty miles distant on the other side of Illinois. Scarcely believing his eyes, the trainer asked, "Hightail?" The old dog limped over to him and placed her chin on his knee.

When he reached home that night, the fox hunter promptly called his friend across the state. It was the middle of the night. He had to let the phone ring for some time. "You lose old Hightail?"

"Yeah, she's gone. Why?"

"I got her here. She came up to me in the woods when I was out

THE DISPUTED SHOT by John Mix Stanley (undated). This painting would not be complete without the hunting dog. It is believed that wolves are the ancestors of today's dogs. Depending upon climate and hunting situations, they developed specialized characteristics and evolved into different breeds.

hunting tonight." They talked for a long time about the mystery. Hightail had been in Virginia for several years. She had suffered a crippling accident. But she had somehow sensed that, in her last months, she was within traveling distance of her Illinois birthplace again, and set off. "I'll crate her up and send her back," the trainer said. "If that's what you want."

There was a slight pause. "Why don't you just keep her," the man said. "If she wants that much to come home, that's where she belongs."

Some years later another Illinois dog, an Irish setter named "Jessie," became lost. She belonged to a young man who always wanted to see the Rocky Mountains. One day he started out for the Rockies, taking Jessie along in his car. She was a good companion, intelligent, and eager to travel.

They rode along smoothly on their grand adventure for several hundred miles. Then, in Nebraska, on a sweltering June day in 1977, the driver blacked out and his car ran off the road. He was unconscious when the ambulance arrived and carried him away. Apparently nobody linked the injured man with the Irish setter lingering around the edge of the crowd.

The patient didn't recall anything else until he awakened in the hospital. One of his first concerns was Jessie. Had anybody seen a beautiful big Irish setter? Nobody had a clue.

Out of the hospital some days later and back at the scene of the accident, he could still find no trace of his dog. He searched for her all that day, then sadly gave up his trip to the mountains and returned to Illinois.

Sometimes in the months that followed he would say to friends, "I have this strange feeling that I still haven't seen the last of Jessie."

After four months, however, there was still no news of the dog. The young man moved from the farm where he lived and returned to Elgin, twenty miles down the road, to live with his parents. The old doghouse where Jessie had stayed when she and her owner visited her owner's parents was still there although it had been moved across the yard.

In early December, six months after his accident, the man went off to his job, as usual. Later that day his brother went to the backyard. There was a big Irish setter sniffing around the spot where the doghouse had originally stood. "Jessie," he yelled, and the setter bounded up to him. Jessie had apparently first gone to the farm, and not finding anyone there, had come on into town, the other place she associated with her owner. She soon regained her strength. Her coat became shiny once more and her sore pads healed.

Although not everyone becomes emotionally attached to his canine hunting companion, the loss of a favorite dog can pitch an owner into deep depression. The story of an Alabama coonhound named Troop demonstrates the depths of this feeling.

For years, coon hunter Key Underwood of Tuscumbia had heard about Troop's skills chasing raccoons through the nightwoods of

Bird hunters are nearly helpless without a dog. Here a hunter fires at a brace of woodcock flushed by his dogs, which hold their stance in readiness for the retrieve.

This early waterfowler knows that when his ducks fall far out on the marsh, his trusty spaniel retriever will dash to the rescue.

northern Alabama's Freedom Hills, a region noted, at least in part, for the fierce resistance of its native people to ax-wielding federal officers seeking whiskey stills to destroy. Those who followed the bootlegger's profession sometimes had their life work interrupted temporarily while they served a couple of years in the state penitentiary. This happened to Troop's first owner, and with no prospect of her man returning for a couple of years, the man's wife decided to give old Troop away to another hunter.

"That's where Troop was when I heard the news," said Key Underwood. "I knew right off that I wanted that dog." He drove down and agreed to pay seventy-five dollars for Troop. He figured that was a lot of money for an eleven-year-old cross between Redbone and Birdsong, but was willing to risk it for whatever years Troop had left. Troop was, after all, widely known as a bragging-quality dog.

From the first, Troop was a pure joy to hunt with. Underwood ranked him as the best coonhound he ever owned. "Lots of dogs," Underwood explained, "can chase a raccoon up a tree, but that doesn't make 'em good coonhounds. Say it this way: he was just a special smart coon dog." Troop went on chasing the raccoons of northern Alabama into the treetops until he was fifteen years old.

The evening the old dog died, Underwood and a couple of suitably respectful friends were sitting up late and talking about how they might best honor this deserving hound. Before the evening was over they agreed to take him up to the edge of the Freedom Hills where he had run so true.

The next morning, which was Labor Day, 1937, while they stood around the fresh grave, they agreed that Troop deserved a headstone. Underwood chose a fieldstone about two feet high. He took a hammer and chisel from his car and carved on the stone the date he thought Troop was born and the date he died. He also carved the dog's name. Then, searching for some fitting special tribute, he chiseled into the stone the likeness of the boar raccoon's peculiar penis bone, the "toothpick," which serves as a symbol of the chase among coon hunters in the southern hills.

Underwood never suspected that they would ever bury another dog out there. "We'd just done this for Troop because it seemed the right thing to do."

But there was also a house dog in the Underwood family, a little rat terrier called Trixie, the favorite pet of Mrs. Underwood. One night Trixie jumped into the car when Key was headed out hunting. It was a bitterly cold night and Trixie caught pneumonia and soon died. "We'll take her out and bury her beside Troop," Mrs. Underwood announced. Underwood didn't think it fitting that he should object and, at the time, wouldn't have known on what grounds to object.

One burial makes a gravesite, two a graveyard. Before long one of Underwood's friends wanted to bury a coonhound beside Troop. Others followed. Underwood had created a special cemetery for coonhounds, the only one he knew about anywhere. He painted a sign, "Coon Dog Grave Yard," and nailed it to a white oak tree. Other bereaved hunters continued to come, asking permission to add their hounds to the burial grounds, and Underwood's only stipulation was that they be respected coonhounds and properly interred.

Once or twice, as Underwood admitted, he gently suggested that Trixie doesn't really belong out there in that hallowed ground among all them coonhounds. But any suggestion that they move her remains never went over well at home so, to this day, Trixie is the only non-coonhound in Key Underwood's Coon Dog Memorial Park. There are more than a hundred coonhounds there with her, and still they continue to arrive.

One group of mourners even flew over from Mississippi in a small private aircraft. They carried a little polished box in which rode the ashes of a locally famous coonhound called "Old Red." The escort included, in addition to several raccoon hunters, a parson, a couple of game wardens, and the high sheriff who had come for the wake. They spent most of the day on the mountaintop swapping dog stories and consuming the supplies they'd brought along.

The pulpwood company that owns the ground deeded the graveyard over to the local raccoon hunters. There is a picnic shelter plus restrooms and picnic tables, for the convenience of the four thousand or so visitors who come each year from many parts of the country. They come to honor hunting dogs, and especially the one responsible for it all—old Troop. To Key Underwood, Troop remains the finest of the lot. He says he has never heard of a better one, and that includes all those buried here as well as those that might be eventually.

20

From Wild Lands to High Places

One late August day when white puffy clouds scudded across the deep blue Montana sky, two hunters stepped down from a grimy train in the mountain hamlet of Divide. One of them was a master of all frontier skills named John Willis. His companion was also highly skilled in riding, shooting, hunting, and other outdoor pursuits, but he was of a different cut. A young man, he was slender in build, wore steel-rimmed glasses and spoke as if he were the product of eastern universities. His name was Theodore Roosevelt and he would some day become the country's best-known big-game hunter, claiming honestly that "it was my good luck to kill all the various kinds of large game that can properly be considered to belong to temperate North America." He had come to climb the high rocky crags of western Montana with a specific trophy in mind: he wanted a mountain goat.

Willis and Roosevelt rented a creaking old wagon and a couple of skinny horses draped in half-rotten harness. They loaded their camp goods and headed out into the valley of the Big Hole. The snow-fed Big Hole River, still a famous trout stream, flows through one of the more beautiful valleys in all the American West. High mountain ranges flank the valley where broad fields of bountiful

249

grass and countless stacks of wild hay nourish large herds of sleek white-faced beef cattle.

When Roosevelt and Willis went there, settlers were already scattered sparsely through the Big Hole, tending their stock and living in small houses made of pine logs dragged down from the hills. The two hunters followed the mail road up the valley for a couple of days, shooting grouse for their meat and sleeping at night beneath their wagon.

After a few days they had worked their way up into the mountains as far as the wagon could go. No longer were there even faint trails,

These drawings by Frederic Remington are from Roosevelt's book "Ranch Life and the Hunting Trail." Above, the young easterner and his guide inspect the mountain goat shot on a Montana hunting trip. At right, a typical ranchman of the 1880s returns from a hunt with a spike buck across his saddle. All are carrying Winchester lever-action rifles, probably the Model 73, the most popular hunting rifle of the period.

so they set up their camp, hobbled their horses, erected their tent beside a swift-flowing brook and made scaffolds for storing the elk and deer they would shoot for camp meat. They gathered pine boughs for their mattresses, and wood for the big cheerful fire they built each evening in front of the tent. Theirs was a classic western hunting camp. Later, Roosevelt wrote in one of his books that he "cherished with wistful pleasure" the memory of those magic days in the mountains above the Big Hole.

His eyes saw more than the big game living in that wild land. He had time to notice the chickadees, sparrows and "nervous little chipmunks," as well as the flying squirrels that glided from tree to tree in the twilight. To him, each of these creatures was a member of its wild community. He saw the field mouse as surely as the elk, the songbird as clearly as the eagle. When he went hunting, he was in the field for more than killing game. He sometimes paused in writing about a big-game hunt to spend several pages telling about the smaller creatures encountered.

One morning Roosevelt and Willis hiked upward toward the rocky crags. Although they expected to be gone from camp for three days, the food they carried consisted of a loaf of bread and some salt. Their main food was grouse, roasted by the evening fire. The second day of climbing was long and difficult. "Mountaineering," wrote Roosevelt in his book *The Wilderness Hunter*, "is very hard work; and when we got high among the peaks, where snow filled the rifts, the thinness of the air forced me to stop for breath every few hundred yards of the ascent."

By early afternoon they had climbed to a bare rocky ridge and started down the other side of the mountain. They had seen sign, but still no mountain goats. Then, easing down from ledge to ledge until they came to a more level spot, they saw their first goat of the trip. It was feeding along a terrace below them. Roosevelt figured the distance at a hundred and twenty-five yards. He overshot, but he killed the goat on his second shot. It had hardly come to rest when they spotted four more goats even closer and Roosevelt killed the largest of these with a running shot.

They packed up the skins and heads of the goats and started back to camp, but later realized that they were confused in their directions. This happens easily in the wilderness. "Were we in this watershed before? That peak is unfamiliar." But they arrived back in camp only one day late, and Roosevelt had with him the trophy he had come to western Montana to claim.

John Willis was of the breed of pioneers who saw the wildlife around him as a resource put there for man's profit. But by the end of this trip he had begun to see wild game and the outdoors in a broader view. Day after day, and into the evenings, he listened to the enthusiastic talk of his hunting companion. Roosevelt spoke of the shame of commercial hunting and the disappearance of the wild animals. He wanted people to see wildlife as a resource deserving better protection than it was getting and he missed few opportunities to spread the word.

He was not the only pioneering conservationist of his day, but he strode across the political stage at a critical period for the American outdoors. The nation was awakening to the fact that market hunting had reduced wildlife populations to all-time lows, and that greater care was needed to protect the land, water, and forests. Roosevelt's interest in hunting had made him a keen observer of the land and its animals. His role in government permitted him to set in motion conservation programs that would help awaken the country to the needs of the land and its creatures.

His lasting interest in the outdoors began when Roosevelt was a young boy. He saw the birds in the trees outside his window in the family's New York home, but they were often blurred in form and dull in color. Not until he began wearing glasses did Roosevelt realize what he had been missing. When he was stricken by recurring attacks of asthma, and by other ailments, he worked hard to overcome his physical problems.

He read whatever he could find about the West and its wildlife. He was still a teenager in school when his brother Elliott returned from Texas. Elliott's wild tales included accounts of stampedes, escapes from wounded buffalo and of the Indians and frontiersmen he had met. Theodore could not get the West out of his mind. He dreamed of a wild land where a man could test himself against the elements and prove that determination, strength, and grit were the qualities of wilderness survival.

A few years later, when he was in his twenties, he headed west to shoot a buffalo of his own. His studies told him that although the great buffalo herds were vanishing, the animal could still be found in the plains and badlands of North Dakota. These buffalo too would soon fall victim to the hide hunters.

On a dark September night he stepped off the train in a settlement of dingy, rundown buildings called Little Missouri, and known locally as "Little Misery." The place had a bad reputation. Even across the border in Montana, the *Glendive Times* had said, "Little Missouri is fast gaining a very unenviable reputation. It seems as though what little law does exist in the place cannot be enforced, and the better class of citizens being in the minority, a committee of safety [vigilantes] is out of the question."

But the railroad promoters were working hard to attract new business to the area. With the Indians moved to reservations, cattle were beginning to thrive on the nutritious prairie grasses. Furthermore, the railroad was promoting the hunting opportunities and urging sportsmen from the East to take advantage of the abundance of wild game. The same month Roosevelt arrived in town the newspaper bragged, "This town, situated on the banks of the Little Missouri River, and surrounded by the Badlands with their fine scenery, is one of the most prosperous and rapidly growing towns along the line of Northern Pacific . . . Game of all kinds is plentiful in the surrounding country and it is becoming quite a resort for pleasure seekers and those who love the chase."

Roosevelt had no local contacts and had no idea of how he would find a guide willing to take him to the buffalo. The next day, however, he was directed to Joe Ferris, part owner of a little ranch some miles out of town on the Little Missouri River. Ferris must have wondered how he was going to cope with this easterner. Roosevelt was pale, thin, and weak looking from his recent illness. Besides, he wore glasses, and spectacles were for sissies.

But on the other hand, Roosevelt was willing and able to pay his way. Ferris suggested that they go out to his ranch where Roosevelt became one of four men bunking in the ranchhouse, a log cabin with a dirt floor. Roosevelt, although to the manor born, could quickly adjust to new situations. He genuinely liked people and was interested in learning from them.

Ferris said, yep, he'd take this easterner out looking for buff, but it was sure to be a considerable ride. The best chance of finding any of the animals, he explained, was off toward Chimney Butte some forty miles by horseback. Ferris said they best wait for better weather, but his client said he was ready to get started at once. Ferris shrugged and began saddling up, and soon they were riding

Young Teddy Roosevelt in 1885 dressed in buckskins, wore a big skinning knife in his belt and cradled a Winchester rifle across his knees—every inch the western big-game hunter. From his experiences out West, Roosevelt evolved the ideas that would one day lead to the passage of important conservation laws.

off across the plains beneath banks of dark, threatening clouds. Each morning of the hunt Roosevelt rode out into the rain cheerfully, resting his rifle across his saddle and peering from beneath his broad-brimmed hat as he scanned the prairies for sign of buffalo.

At night the weary Ferris was ready to wrap himself in his buffalo robe and sleep, but Roosevelt seemed as fresh as ever and was ready to talk. He wanted to know more about the West, the wildlife and the people. The longer he rode over the open country, the stronger he became.

One day they finally came upon fresh buffalo tracks. A solitary large animal had walked here before them. They stalked and surprised the huge bull, but it gave them the slip in that gullied and wrinkled country.

Late that day they spotted three buffalo far off across the plains. By this time, darkness was settling over the plains. Ferris understood by now that it was futile to suggest that they wait until morning. The horses were bone weary, but Roosevelt set off in full pursuit. He cut across to head the buffalo off, but the bull, deciding that his turf had been invaded, now turned and charged.

Roosevelt's pony sensed the danger of its position, wheeled, and threw its head sideways so violently that it struck Roosevelt's rifle, slamming it against the rider's forehead and bringing blood flowing down across his eyes.

Ferris then dismounted and took a couple of ineffective shots at the enraged bull, which finally gave up and dashed off into the gathering darkness. The disappointed eastern hunter quit, but only for that day. He still had not taken his buffalo.

The hunt continued with one bad break after the other until Ferris wondered when this easterner would give up and admit defeat. The thought of quitting, however, never occurred to Roosevelt. Instead he continued with bulldog tenacity and seemed to thrive on the hard knocks. Then one day he followed a set of large tracks to the crest of a ridge. He eased himself up where he could scan the other side and found that he had a clear shot at a magnificent bull. At last he took his trophy.

Roosevelt felt so healthy and vigorous out in this wide-open country that, with characteristic directness, he decided to go into the ranching business. He joined with a partner some miles out of Medora, and purchased the registered Maltese Cross brand for his stock.

He later returned to New York, but after both his wife and his mother died on the same night, he felt a strong desire to take refuge once more in the West. The following summer he was back in the Badlands. Before the end of the summer he selected a spot some forty miles from his ranch and there began establishing a new ranch. He found a set of locked elk antlers marking the spot where two huge bulls perished as a result of their combat; he called his ranch Elkhorn.

During those years as a North Dakota rancher, Roosevelt hunted mostly when his crew needed meat. The remainder of the time he was busy working with the cattle. He rode alongside his hired hands and learned to use the lariat and handle cattle during the annual roundups.

His western neighbors, who had at first questioned his fitness for this life, changed their views about the easterner in the steel-rimmed spectacles. His reputation was enhanced by a couple of early encounters with unsavory types.

The first of these occurred one evening in a ratty little hotel in the wicked town of Mingusville, now Wibaux, Montana, on I-94 just west of the Montana-North Dakota state line. Mingusville had its resident bully who terrified the locals whenever it pleased him. He noticed Roosevelt as soon as the stranger walked in.

Roosevelt didn't like the man's attitude. Neither did he appreciate his foul language. But he especially did not like the fact that the man was waving a pair of cocked pistols around freely. "Four-eyes," he yelled, "is going to set up drinks for the crowd."

Thinking that he might escape a nasty encounter, Roosevelt sat down beside the stove and tried to ignore the problem maker. Then, the man walked over, waved his cocked guns around Roosevelt's head and told him in unfriendly obscenities that it was time to set up drinks for the crowd.

Saying, "If I must, I must," Roosevelt stood up, measured the distance with a boxer's eye, and let the rowdy have a hard right straight to one side of the point of the jaw, followed with a left, then another right. As the man slid toward the floor, he fired both guns, but missed. Roosevelt tensed himself ready to drop on the man's chest with both knees but this was rendered unnecessary when the

falling man cracked his head on the corner of a table. Others carried the rowdy out to the shed for the night, and before daylight he caught the train out of town.

Such stories spread fast. "You hear about ole Teddy Roosevelt cold cockin' that guy over in Mingusville?" Roosevelt's stock rose in the eyes of the local people.

He had another opportunity to deal with lawbreakers one spring day when the hired hands on his Elkhorn Ranch reported that the boat he kept on the ranch had been stolen. Roosevelt did not take this affront lightly. With two of his crew, he set off downstream in another boat in pursuit of the thieves.

They found them camped at the mouth of Cherry Fork, slipped up on them and took them captive. Roosevelt, however, was a thorough man. He did not consider the job completed until the thieves were delivered to the law. There was so much ice in the river that several days passed before the three men and their prisoners could set off for the sheriff's office. Roosevelt passed the time reading. He finally borrowed a wagon and hauled his prisoners to Dickenson where he turned them over to the sheriff. Two of them were given terms in the penitentiary.

When he finally sold his ranch business, he had lost more than fifty thousand dollars. But out on those western plains he had perhaps gained more than he ever lost, and almost certainly his country benefitted because it was there that Theodore Roosevelt's thinking about conservation and man's use of the land matured. These ideas would eventually surface in sweeping new developments that put the federal government into the conservation effort in a permanent fashion.

Again in New York, he was getting deeper into politics. Before going to North Dakota he had served in the New York legislature. After his ranching days he ran for, but did not win, the office of mayor of New York. He became Governor of New York in 1899, and was elected vice president in 1900. When President McKinley was assassinated in 1901, Theodore Roosevelt moved into the oval office. "That cowboy in the White House," as his enemies called him, was

Teddy Roosevelt never lost his love for the rugged outdoor life. In 1905, after being elected president, he left the White House to ride on a Colorado bear hunt.

*With naturalist John Muir in 1906, Roosevelt posed on a peak in Yosemite National Park.
Both men fought for the establishment of wilderness areas to conserve our resources.*

reelected, enabling him to continue taking giant steps toward conservation of American resources.

Roosevelt's interest in saving American wildlife was already well known from his books, including the volumes dealing with his hunting trips. He had also, in 1887, organized an influential conservation club which still promotes conservation and sportsmanship. The idea took shape during a dinner given by Roosevelt in New York for a select group of big-game hunting friends. Led by Roosevelt, and fired up by his enthusiasm, these outdoorsmen were concerned about the commercial hunting that was out of control on public lands, especially in the West. This was the beginning of the Boone and Crocket Club, and Roosevelt became its first president.

Today's sometimes strident animal protectionists, concerned as they are about the individual animal, might insist that Roosevelt was no conservationist because he hunted. But who among them has accomplished more for North American wildlife? Roosevelt understood that what is really important is the welfare of the species. As President of the United States, he was in a strong position to begin turning things around for American wildlife. This was a time of awakening, not alone on his part, but in the minds of other leaders as well. The slaughter of buffalo, elk, antelope, and other animals had become a national disgrace. We had come to a land of plenty and laid waste to it. Now Roosevelt and others were doing what they could to improve the situation, and they made giant strides.

In 1905, while Roosevelt was president, the National Forest Service became a reality. Two years earlier he had declared a three-acre pelican nesting island off the east coast of Florida to be a wildlife sanctuary, and this was the beginning of our internationally famous system of national wildlife refuges. There are now more than four hundred of these refuges. They are found in nearly every state, providing habitat for all species of animals, game and nongame.

Among the areas set aside during Roosevelt's tenure was a block of wild country on the north side of the Grand Canyon, and this became the setting for one of the strangest wildlife management efforts in the history of the country.

21

Unbelievable Deer Drive

One summer day in 1924 George McCormick arrived in Phoenix, Arizona, to outline for officials what he believed would become the largest, and most successful, deer drive ever conducted anywhere. Everyone, including the deer, would be happy with the results. He saw no reason why his plan would fail. But McCormick had much to learn about deer, people, and what the combination of foul weather and the rugged canyon country of northwestern Arizona could do to the well-laid plans of men.

Most people agreed that his aims were laudable. His planned deer drive was designed to solve a major problem that could be traced back to 1906. That was the year that President Theodore Roosevelt declared that a million acres of canyons and forests on the north side of the Colorado River would henceforth be known as The Grand Canyon National Game Preserve for "the protection of game animals and their breeding places."

This new game preserve, created where much of today's Kaibab National Forest stands, included some of the most rugged and beautiful country in the American West—the North Kaibab Plateau on the north side of the Grand Canyon. On three sides, the plateau is bordered by spectacular world-famous canyons. To the north and

Mule deer spend their summers in high country; in winter they move down to feed in protected canyons. When the government banned hunting and tried to exterminate the predators on the Kaibab, the deer population increased—with unforeseen consequences.

northeast lie sage and desert country. Here in the grassy openings among the spruce, fir, and pine live the sprightly little Kaibab squirrels with tassels on their ears, and one of the finest herds of Rocky Mountain mule deer anywhere. The mule deer spend their summers in the high open country and, with winter's approach, move down the slopes to lower country where they survive the cold months nibbling cliff rose, juniper, and sage in the protected canyons. The deer in particular were the animals that everyone hoped would flourish in the new preserve. The general conviction was that there simply couldn't be too many deer.

In those early years of this century any wildlife management efforts might by modern standards be considered primitive. When the Kaibab deer herd came under intense management, people did not yet understand fully the importance of relationships between plants and animals, predators and prey, the relation of animal behavior to food sources, and other factors that might control wildlife populations. Folks reasoned that by simply keeping as many deer from dying as possible these large graceful animals could multiply ad infinitum and flourish on the Kaibab Plateau as never before.

This could be done by instituting some fundamental practices. First, they would close the Kaibab to all hunting. Then they would order the killing of the predators, especially cougars because they normally eat deer. For a quarter of a century the government dispatched hunters to the Kaibab to trap, shoot, and poison predators. They killed seven hundred and eighty-one known cougars, five hundred and fifty-four bobcats, twenty wolves, and nearly five thousand coyotes. Still others, nobody knows how many, were taken by ranchers and their hired hunters.

But perhaps a far more telling step was taken when the government limited the numbers of livestock in the area. Both sheep and cattle were reduced by about two-thirds what they had been on the Kaibab. With abundant food suddenly available and a lid on the more obvious causes of mortality, the mule deer, which probably numbered only three thousand when the Kaibab became a preserve, increased dramatically year after year. Eventually they numbered some sixty thousand, all scrambling, along with the remaining domestic stock, for the native vegetation. The starving deer reached higher and higher into the trees, creating a sharply defined browse line.

The pitiful story of the Kaibab's emaciated deer was soon being heard by sympathizers all the way to the East Coast. Across the country, newspapers and magazines reported on the plight of these deer. Hunters, biologists, foresters, and range specialists all argued that the number of deer must be reduced, and the most direct answer was to open a hunting season in the Kaibab. This did not settle well with anti-hunting groups. Nationwide, they demanded that the Kaibab's mule deer either be left to the mercies of nature or, better yet, be live-trapped and moved to other areas. These same arguments are still advanced by animal protectionists today when wild populations outgrow their food sources and wildlife managers recommend reducing their numbers.

The Forest Service dutifully responded with a campaign to live-trap the deer and offer them for sale at thirty-five dollars a head. This program fizzled for various reasons. Trapping success was limited. Under stress, the deer frequently died in the pens or in transit, and besides, the demand for the trapped deer was limited.

Finally, Arizona, responding to a Forest Service request, opened the Kaibab to deer hunters for the first time in nearly two decades. Rugged country and rough mountain roads limited the number of hunters, and the herd was reduced by only six hundred and seventy-five animals. For the deer the food shortage remained as serious as ever, and this was the state of affairs when George McCormick hit upon what he thought was the perfect answer.

The idea was said to have originated in the fertile mind of Zane Grey, the Zanesville, Ohio, native and one-time dentist turned western fiction writer and big-game fisherman. Grey reasoned that the way to deal with the overabundant deer of the Kaibab was to turn the case over to the Riders of the Purple Sage. He said that America's western cowboys were the world's best at driving ornery, feisty critters, and these men were capable of moving any range animals anywhere they wanted them. Grey believed that professional cowboys could round up deer and drive them off the Kaibab faster than you could say "howdy podner."

Sportsmen around Flagstaff, meanwhile, also backed this budding plan to drive the Kaibab deer to better feeding grounds. The scheme gained momentum. A group of its promoters searched out George McCormick, who knew the rugged Kaibab well. If the deer had understood what was being planned for them they might have departed on their own.

The planners spread out their maps. What they had in mind was pushing those excess mule deer into the broad expanses of open country to the south. The only obstacle standing in their way was the Grand Canyon. But the human spirit thrives on challenge.

Promoters in Flagstaff promised George McCormick two dollars and a half for every deer, up to eight thousand, that he moved to the south rim. According to his contract with the state, he was to drive a minimum of three thousand mule deer down into the bowels of the Grand Canyon, then up the far side.

McCormick had an idea for a supplemental source of cash from the big drive. He lined up a Hollywood filmmaker to photograph the event. The movie people were cautious enough not to commit any up-front money, but they did promise McCormick a dollar a head for all the deer he could push past their cameras. To McCormick, this translated into a bundle; he calculated that he could put ten thousand deer past the lenses.

With his business arrangement completed, and the required permissions acquired from the U.S. Forest Service, McCormick began arranging the practical details. He planned as carefully as a general laying out a military operation. He had no trouble finding riders. Cowboys and ranchers for miles around flocked to his call. When word reached the Navajo Reservation that McCormick was enlisting recruits, Indian braves arrived to enlist. While the cowboys rode horses, the Indians would move through the brush on foot flushing deer from their beds.

McCormick now began baiting deer into an area some ten miles wide. He spread apples, salt, and other delicacies. Soon there were deer almost everywhere he looked. An estimated one-third of the Kaibab deer, some thirty thousand hungry animals, were concentrated right in the area where McCormick wanted them.

Meanwhile, he had a crew out erecting drift fences in strategic locations, especially across any area that looked as if it might become a deer crossing or offer the animals an invitation to slip away from the direction of the drive. Once the deer were in motion McCormick wanted them moving dutifully forward toward the spur canyon leading down to the Colorado River. Modern deer fences are usually eight feet high with a couple of strands of barbed wire along the top. McCormick's drift fences were made from six-foot-high hog wire.

The route chosen for the big drive was down through Saddle Canyon, into Nankoweep Canyon, within the Grand Canyon, and finally across the river, then up the Tanner Trail to the south rim. The route would, as McCormick liked to envision it, lead the milling throng of mule deer, horses, and men along the steep, narrow, twisting trails for thirty miles of the most rugged terrain on earth.

The big drive was originally set for the balmy days of autumn when the aspens would stand yellow on the mountainsides. But there was no precedent for a deer drive like this one. There seemed to be delay after delay for reasons nobody had anticipated. Gradually the autumn days dwindled away and the morning temperatures grew sharper. The final date set for the drive was December 16.

Two days before that date all the participants met at McCormick's base camp to make final preparations. The Navajos arrived from their reservation. McCormick, who did not speak their language, hired Indian trader Buck Lowery from down Marble Canyon way to supervise the Navajo force. The cowboys were there too, all on their finest horses. The movie people arrived.

As the drivers made their final plans everyone scanned the darkening skies with growing concern. This late in the year the weather could turn nasty any time.

December 16 dawned gray and gusty. The troops drew their coats tighter about their bodies and, all morning, hunkered down about their campfires. McCormick had delayed his departure too long. Snow began falling so heavily in the mountains that the men had trouble seeing each other. The wind whipped through the trees. The temperature plummeted. One journalist reported that it fell to twenty degrees below zero.

The Indians were unprepared for the fierceness of this mountain weather. They built lean-to shelters from brush and huddled miserably around smoking little fires grumbling about going back to the reservation. The shivering camera crew didn't fare much better.

But by early afternoon all was ready. The drivers spread out through the forest. The camera crews were stationed at a strategic location ready to record the passing of ten thousand mule deer. The Indians, carrying cowbells and buckets of stones, were instructed to beat their way through the bush making an unholy racket, which they now proceeded to do. Mingled with the whine of the winter wind and the Navajo chants were the curses of the yelling cowboys. Thousands of deer lifted their heads in wonder at the first strange sound then bolted from their beds, and began moving off ahead of the line.

McCormick wanted everything to move in calm and orderly fashion. The drivers were to watch out for deer that might turn back and gently but firmly point them once more in the proper southerly direction.

Any experienced deer hunter could have predicted the results. Deer have familiar home territories where they feel comfortable and which they are reluctant to leave for strange and unknown places. They do not like to be crowded into new country.

Cowboys began seeing the ghostly forms of deer slipping back toward them through the curtains of snow. Deer spotted the drivers at the last moment and changed directions. Before long thousands of confused and frightened mule deer were running in all directions. Somewhere out front, the shivering and cursing camera crews

One cowboy reported seeing two giant bucks and four does bound out of the woods and clear one of McCormick's drift fences with altitude to spare.

watched in vain for deer to dash past them in the swirling snow.

Mounted drivers fought the brush and snow-laden limbs. They had trouble keeping up with the Indians, who were slipping through the brush like shadows, banging on their noise makers. The milling deer, now thoroughly alarmed, were constantly breaking back through the line of Indians, who could neither stop them nor slow them down. When the escapees came to the cowboys, they broke through that line too, if indeed it was still a line, until cowboys, Indians, and deer were all chasing in every imaginable direction. The fences were of little help. One cowboy reported seeing two giant bucks and four does bound out of the woods together and clear one of McCormick's drift fences in formation with altitude to spare.

The Indians reached Saddle Canyon well ahead of the cowboys and quickly built fires to thaw their frozen digits. The cowboys drifted in with tales of seeing more deer than they ever saw before in their lives. One observer summed it up best: "At Saddle Canyon there were no deer in front of the men but thousands of deer behind them." McCormick had stationed deer counters in strategic locations to tally the number of animals moved out of the North Kaibab so he could keep tabs on his profits. Now the counters shook their heads; they had recorded zero deer.

The camera crews had an identical number. Photographic equipment was packed and hauled back to civilization. Cowboys returned to their ranches, Indians to their reservation, mule deer to all that broad area across the Plateau where they would spend the winter gradually forgetting the deer drivers and all the stress they had brought to the Kaibab.

Officials finally had to face the facts; there was no simple solution to the problem of too many deer on the Kaibab Plateau. There was no quick fix to keep anti-hunters happy while salvaging the habitat. Instead they now sent in detachments of paid government hunters to shoot excess deer, but these professional hunters could not even keep up with the new crops of fawns dropped each spring.

Eventually the solution was worked out in the state capitol in Phoenix. The state legislature created the Arizona Game and Fish Commission. This put game management into the hands of the professionals. They promptly set up sport hunting seasons for the North Kaibab. In the fall of 1929, hunters removed four thousand deer from the herd and the following year they took another five thousand.

In the following years hunting, plus starvation, continued to whittle the herd down. Modern biologists believe that the role of predator control in building the population may have been exaggerated. The food base was the main key to the vigor and health of the mule deer herd. With the food suddenly available, the deer population exploded beyond the carrying capacity of the land. The gaunt and restless deer went into the harsh winters already weakened by hunger.

Today the Arizona Game and Fish Commission and the U.S. Forest Service have a cooperative deer management arrangement on the Kaibab. Arizona keeps a full-time deer biologist working with this herd. The aim is to match the annual hunting pressure with the size of the herd, and the herd with the carrying capacity of the range. A herd of some sixteen thousand mule deer seems about right most years.

This is the lesson of the Kaibab Plateau: Nature shapes its animal populations to what the land can support. Surplus animals cannot simply be driven off to better places. That's what George McCormick learned.

22

The Changing Hunter

There is a bewhiskered joke that has an old-timer saying, "Things sure aren't what they used to be," and his buddy answering, "No, and they never were."

In the world of North America's wildlife the clouds of ducks and pigeons that once obscured the sun are gone, and the herds of bison roaming the plains are history. In their places are people and their works, their crops and domestic animals.

But the picture still has its bright spots. There are happy stories of some unendangered species. Consider the case of the wild turkey, that giant spooky bird once known only to the deep forests, then eliminated from much of its original range. Since World War II, wildlife scientists working with sportsmen's money learned how to transplant wild turkeys successfully while the woods recovered enough from decades of slash and burn to support them.

The turkeys, taking full advantage of the opportunity, adapted to life even in small blocks of woodlands. They are seen daily by people who, in their youth, never saw a wild turkey. These giant birds feed on the edges of our fields, roost in trees behind the barn and, in spring, send their gobbling calls rattling across the country-side. Here and there a farmer even complains that the wild turkeys feed too heavily on his crops. Furthermore, turkey hunting promises to improve in the coming years. Every year, thousands of first time turkey hunters call in a gobbler, then serve it to their families as their ancestors did. Meanwhile, bird watchers once more add this spectacular bird to their daily lists because hunters' money brought the wild turkey back.

At the same time, on the rolling western grasslands, the pronghorn antelope, down to perhaps twenty-five thousand early in this century, has returned to sound population levels that not only provide hunting seasons again but also allow tourists to see these big game animals.

The whitetail deer, which half a century ago was completely absent from some Midwestern states, wanders through front yards and even leaves deer tracks in the fresh snow on suburban sidewalks. Although the annual hunting seasons yield thousands of deer for home freezers, the herds still increase.

These are rough times for ducks, but even the world of waterfowl has its exception to the scarcity rule. The giant Canada goose, largest of all the sub-species, flourishes in greater numbers every year. These heavy birds often live within city limits and fly out into the surrounding farm country to feed.

These are animal success stories and hunters have played their role in each one. Even the most strident anti-hunters should admit that sportsmen have been foremost in this country's wildlife conservation efforts. For decades, hunters have invested time and money to help bring American wildlife back to respectable levels. Over more than half a century the federal government, through the Pittman-Robertson Act, has collected tax money willingly paid by sportsmen on arms and ammunition, and returned it to the states for wildlife research and habitat development. Millions of dollars in duck stamp funds have also gone to purchase wetlands for wildlife. Ducks Unlimited and other sportsman groups raise millions more for habitat work. Universities train professional wildlife managers and research specialists. State wildlife agencies invest hunting and fishing license fees in research and habitat, bringing benefits to both game and non-game species.

Furthermore, states have established their own wildlife areas, generally paying for them with funds raised by the sale of licenses to hunters and fishermen. These lands, provided by sportsmen, preserve habitat, not only for ducks and deer but also for warblers, butterflies and salamanders, all a part of their interwoven wildlife communities.

Hunters meanwhile form and join all manner of organizations working to improve conditions for wildlife. In addition to the general sportsman organizations, they have created separate societies for the conservation of prairie chickens, ruffed grouse, desert bighorn sheep, trumpeter swans, wild turkeys, whitetail deer, ducks and geese in general, the canvasback, bears, cranes, birds of prey, wolves, quail, pheasants and others. Typically, in one year, one such organization, the Rocky Mountain Elk Foundation, raised nearly three-quarters of a million dollars for research and habitat improvement.

This is only part of the evidence pointing to the fact that today's outdoorsman has a deep concern for the welfare of the wild animals around us. As our society matured, the attitudes of hunters evolved. The excessive killing, whether of bison, passenger pigeons, or ducks had been born of the frontier mentality. The store of wild creatures seemed endless. There were few if any legal restrictions on killing wildlife. Frontier life demanded that the resources be taken for survival.

All this changed, and sportsmen led the way. They supported formation of state game and fish departments and demanded laws to limit the taking of wild game to numbers the species could replace. Hunters insisted on laws setting bag limits as well as restrictions on hunting methods and seasons. They are often a jump ahead of public officials in wanting seasons and bag limits cut back to protect a species that may be in trouble.

Before game laws evolved, hunting had tremendous impact on North American wildlife. Overshooting helped bring some species to extinction or nearly so. But modern hunting, practiced within the legal framework, is usually no threat to the species hunted.

The measure of our personal outdoor ethics is our behavior when nobody is watching. There are outlaw hunters among us as there will always be, and stopping legal hunting would not change this. Societies have always had to deal with the law breakers. But sportsmen have also joined the fight against these outlaws. Their money pays officers who protect wildlife—both game and non-game. In addition, numerous states now have successful systems encouraging sportsmen and others to tip off the conservation officers and thereby help break up poaching operations.

The largest single cause of diminishing wildlife in the world is the destruction of wildlife habitat that comes with the expanding human population. Eliminate the woodlands, prairies, and wetlands and the wild creatures that live there are sure to go.

Today's sportsman is a conservationist, perhaps more so than the highly vocal anti-hunter. Being an outspoken anti-hunter does not make a person a conservationist. Writing letters to save a wetland or old growth forest could accomplish more of real value. But some people, lacking facts to guide them, are driven by emotionalism rather than by logic. Too often preservationists seem to be so distressed by the death of an individual animal that they overlook the importance of protecting habitat on which whole species depend. There are limits on the number of individuals of any species that the habitat can support. Predators, winter starvation, disease, flooding, intra-specific pressures and more all help establish population limits. Mending one bird's broken wing usually does little to help preserve the species. Neither does the anti-hunter accomplish much for wildlife by insisting that hunting should stop. As long as hunters can go into the field practicing their sport within the law, they continue to pool their license money and provide more protection for wildlife.

Furthermore, non-hunters and anti-hunters must share the guilt when wildlife vanishes. Each of us, hunter, non-hunter, animal protectionist or none of the above, whether vegetarian or practicing omnivore, has an impact on wildlife and wild places simply by virtue of the fact that he or she is here.

Those who would bring an end to all hunting claim to possess a special sensitivity toward animals. But they eat meat from slaughter houses where others are paid to do their killing, and they enjoy vegetables, fruits and grain grown on lands taken away from wildlife.

From the youngest milk-drinking infant to the oldest grandparent, we share responsibility for what happens to wildlife. We all play our roles in changing the face of the earth. The hope is that we can learn to soften our impact on air, water, soil, plants and animals for the good of both ourselves and those other forms of life that share this beautiful and remarkable world.

To tell the whole story of man's impact on American wildlife we must speak of far more than hunting. We have to think of forests cut and burned, prairies plowed, rivers dammed, marshes drained, roads built into wilderness areas, habitats covered with concrete, the invasion of foreign plants and animals, chemical wastes released into the air, water and on the land—and more. These changes are fostered both by private citizens and by government agencies acting in the name of all of us. Wildlife lands are still being transformed into people places and, as a nation, we continue to view the rate of new construction as a measure of our prosperity and economic vigor.

We hear talk of "consumptive" and "non-consumptive" uses of wildlife. Bird watching, wildlife photography, hiking in wild places and sitting by a bird's nest contemplating nature's marvels are said to be non-consumptive uses. All such activities disturb the wild animals involved and consequently have their impacts. University of Alaska ecologist Robert Weedon reminds us that, "There is no such thing as a non-consumptive user of wildlife. There are," he adds, "only consumers who care and consumers who don't care."

The hunter venturing into the outdoors today, with his gun in hand and his dog at his heels, follows an ancient and respected tradition with its roots deep in the very beginning of our evolution. We should all acknowledge with gratitude the hunting skills of our ancestors. Had they not been successful hunters we would not be here. The desire to hunt, even when hunting may no longer be essential to survival, is a natural drive and, ethically pursued, an honorable activity, a segment of a heritage to be preserved.

Index